ANNIE LENNOX

ANNIE LENNOX

Sweet Dreams Are Made of This

LUCY O'BRIEN

St. Martin's Press
New York

For Stuart, my friends and family

Grateful acknowledgment for the photographs in the insert is made to: Todd Kaplan/Star File, Inc.; Bob Scott/Star File, Inc.; Dominick Conde/Star File, Inc.; Joe Roulo/Star File, Inc.; Dominick Conde/Star File, Inc.; Chuck Pulin/Star File, Inc.; Frank Ziths/Star File, Inc.; David Seelig/Star File, Inc.; Gene Shaw/Star File, Inc.; Vinnie Zuffante/Star File, Inc.; Bob Gruen/Star File, Inc.; Bob Gruen/Star File, Inc.; Al Pereira/Star File, Inc.

Library of Congress Cataloging-in-Publication Data

O'Brien, Lucy.
    Annie Lennox : sweet dreams are made of this / Lucy O'Brien.
        p.   cm.
    Discography: p. 208
    Includes bibliographical references.
    ISBN 0-312-09740-9 (pbk.)
        1. Lennox, Annie.   2. Singers—Biography.   I. Title.
    ML420.L386O2   1993
    782.42164'092—dc20
    [B]   93-5177
                                                                                 CIP
                                                                                 MN

First published in Great Britain by Sidgwick & Jackson Limited

First U.S. edition: September 1993

10 9 8 7 6 5 4 3 2 1

Contents

Acknowledgements

Many thanks to Stuart Cosgrove, Ruth Kirk, Gill Paul, Fred Dellar, Jenny and the Turner family in Aberdeen, and Neil Spencer.

Also: Laurence Stevens, Jack Steven, Joe Bangay, Sheila Sedgwick, Lindsay Shapero, Geoff Hannington at Logo, Pete Phipps, Martin Dobson, Lewis Ziolek, Nathan East, Fred Defaye, Jon Roseman, Michael Radford, Maggie Ryder, Vic Martin, Jon Bavin, Diane Mackie, Frances Penny, Irene Burnett, Bill Spittle, Roger Burton at Contemporary Wardrobe, Chrissie Clark, David Daglish, Jana Chantelau, Muriel Vieu, Kristina Heikkinen, Deborah Pierce, Mark McAuley, Jane Garcia, Jane Turner – and the folks at Bhaktivedanta Manor, the Royal Academy and Shelter. Thanks also to Alan Jackson, Dave Hill and Robert Sandall for inspiration.

And thanks to Johnny Waller's Eurythmics book *Sweet Dreams: The Definitive Biography*' (Virgin, 1985).

ANNIE LENNOX

Introduction

'Bit neurotic, bit Scottish, but I like her', that arch pop fiend Malcolm McLaren once said about Annie Lennox. It's proof of her charisma that she could charm the former Sex Pistols manager and professional cynic, an enduring quality that she constantly plays down. It's more significant that she has outlasted his success by years.

'I feel too young to have a biography written about me,' she says. Until the advent of pop music, biographies were written posthumously or at the end of a long, illustrious career. The intrusion and proliferation of pop has injected its own rules into the genre, with the result that more and more artists are being written about long before their fortieth birthdays. With the emphasis on youth and beauty, many a pop life has its Warholian fifteen minutes of fame. Pop stars often peak early, but their impact at the height of their fame is dramatic.

In conventional terms, at thirty-seven years old Annie Lennox is too young for an analysis of her life, but her fifteen-year career has thrown up some of the most challenging images in the business. With Dave Stewart and Eurythmics she has also massively popularized a form of synthesized soul with the barest of equipment and a surfeit of style.

When she sat in a chauffeur-driven car in the 1983 'Love Is A Stranger' video and ripped off her blonde wig to reveal the close carrot crop beneath, it was Annie Lennox the pop star incarnate. She had the ability to stun the audience, to change her identity in an instant, and in mixing up bits of everything from punk to glam, and country and western, an absolute refusal to stay in the same character for too long. Plundering from European art-house cinema to combine soap opera with surrealist pop, Eurythmics transformed the possibilities of pop video. Through careful calculation and a desire to create their own pop mythology, they have attracted an international following and become part of rock's elite.

Pop stars, however, do not happen in a vacuum. There are the complex factors of background, family and social milieu that surround them

1

and make them who they are. This is not a chronological biography, therefore, being as much an exploration of the cultural themes that loom large in Annie's life and an analysis of the personal loves and motivations behind her stardom.

Throughout her life story the narrative of her own voice resounds in bold type. She remains the best commentator on her career; the mischievous cross-dressing she engaged in at the start of her career for instance, an androgynous image that, far from appearing out of nowhere, has a long and rich show-business tradition stretching from music hall veteran Vesta Tilley to clubland heroine Grace Jones. There is her marriage in 1984 to Hare Krishna monk Radha Raman, and her ensuing flirtation with Eastern philosophy. Pop spirituality has always been a strong force and Annie's dalliance with Eastern religion follows a pattern of pop stars – from the Beatles with the Maharashi to Tina Turner's Nichiren Shoshu Buddhism – looking for a new kind of spiritual sustenance once they have found material gain. There is also her political transformation, achieved in the context of post-Live Aid pop, where global campaigning became a respectable if not dynamic force and pop stars became cultural ambassadors, blurring the boundaries between themselves and party politicians.

Annie Lennox's story is as much the tale of modern 1980s pop, refracted through an acutely sensitive, strangely introverted performer. She is a reluctant rock star, often fighting shy of the limelight yet at the same time eager for recognition. Coming from a strict working-class Aberdeen background, she fiercely protects her private life, yet injects into her songwriting a highly personal vision, taking inspiration from rigorous poets like Sylvia Plath or pop individualists such as Joni Mitchell or Debbie Harry.

Wedged firmly at the centre of her career has been the emotional and professional influence of her partner Dave Stewart. A well-known Couple in Pop, they occupy that rare and tricky place of the public relationship – and, like Sonny and Cher, John and Yoko and the Swedish group ABBA before them, they have had to hammer out a notion of pop coupledom that works for them, subordinating Romance for Art.

In the debate about Dave's 'Svengali' influence over Annie lies a central question about women in pop. Although hamstrung by the tabloid 'Tragedy Annie' image, she has still managed to put herself forward as a focal point and a figure of independence rather than pop's floozy. How *do* women keep their credibility within a medium that constantly trivializes their efforts? Since the late 1980s many women have come through as artists in their own right, but when Annie started out, successful female rock role models were thin on the ground. She may carefully qualify what she says, and stress, 'I'm not really that relevant', but the former classical student has carved a unique place for herself as a top vocalist and visual manipulator. Now taking a sabbatical break, the time is right to take stock.

Annie Lennox is still young – too young for a biography – but her story has resonance beyond the music and video industry. After thirty-six years of struggle to become the woman that fifteen per cent of young British women say they'd like to be, Annie can relax. She has created her own pop myth – and in a business where you are only as good as your last hit single, creating a myth is its own kind of lifetime.

Lucy O'Brien

1

I Didn't Ask to be Born

'I took a lot of risks in my personal life. I always lived in a very full way, I can't do anything half-heartedly. I'm not grey, I'm either black or white. I always ran the risk of getting badly hurt through my experiences and destroying myself. I think that's common to a lot of women. It's terrible. They didn't tell me it was going to be like this when I was little.

I look back on my past with misgivings. I know people who are quite rooted in their home town, and they never seem to experience any sense of isolation from the people and circumstances around them. Sometimes I'm envious of that, because I never felt, in my heart of hearts, that I could fit in somehow. I suppose that sounds rather clichéd, but there was always something missing for me up in Aberdeen and I never quite knew what it was.

I was an isolated kid, writing poetry and imagining things a lot. It's always a bit tough being an only child. You tend to be under the illusion the whole world revolves around you. It might have been nice to have had an older brother or sister to take the attention away from me. I was usually labelled a daydreamer because I lacked the ability to concentrate at school.

I used to feel very angry for my father. He built ships and was exploited and abused. He was tired all the time and got old suddenly. I feel very angry about that . . . I suppose singing soul is to do with people who have some knowledge of poverty – the struggle you know, the struggle. I can't say I really know the black experience, but there's something in knowing about the rich and poor and the differences in class, and not being able to get this or that.

I'm Scottish and come from a very working-class family, very earthy. I have no illusions about life. The world is not a place to be passive in. I didn't ask to be born.'

5

SILVER CITY, 1954

At 11.30 p.m. on Christmas Day 1954, Annie Lennox was born in Fonthill Road Hospital, Aberdeen, a squat building that has long since been turned into army barracks. Her entry into the world was regular and inauspicious, but the fact that she was born on Christmas Day seems to have fuelled her spiritual imagination. Time and time again, throughout her music, Annie evokes the image of the angel, a supreme Christ-like being that symbolizes an immovable and inspirational purity.

As Dorothy Farquharson Lennox huddled her bundle home to nearby 109 Gairn Terrace, angels were the last thing on her mind. It was a bitter winter and her main preoccupation was in keeping her first and only child warm, fed and adequately housed. A quiet, crisply neat woman with a sweet smile, Mrs Lennox had given up her taxing job as the school cook when she became pregnant. Her husband Tom Allison Lennox worked long hours as a boilermaker in the local Hall Russell shipyard, planning to earn enough money to move out of their cramped furnished flat. Merely one large room with a sink, a cooker and a loft upstairs for sleeping in, once Annie arrived there was pressure for the Lennox family to move from the small granite grey block.

They lodged with the Middletons, an anxiously respectable couple who had a West Highland terrier called Shaggy and were very protective of their daughter Mhairi, a child of Annie's age who wasn't allowed to play in the road. Frances Penny, an old schoolfriend of Annie's who lived in Gairn Terrace, remembers how they all played hopscotch together.

'We were quite chummy. The Lennox family moved early on, but Ann would come over for afternoons in the holidays when her mother went to visit Mrs Middleton. I remember Mrs Lennox as being a very pleasant woman. She was big-boned – not fat – but a fine figure of a woman, and she had long blondish hair done in a bun. Most mums usually had curly locks and curlers at night, so Ann's mum was a little out of the ordinary.'

This is probably how Annie got a sense of individual style, one that far from the confines of home town and family she would later develop to pop extremes.

Before long the Lennox family had relocated nearer the centre of town to 140 Hutcheon Street, a two-roomed flat that needed some handy renovating. Part of a sturdy three-storey building, the young family shared their new house with five other tenants and a host of children. Even in these crowded conditions, Annie had the ability to play on her own, creating a special childhood fantasy world that included a cast of diverse characters and a musical score.

Annie showed her musical aptitude from an early age, and her father, being an ardent bagpipe player, encouraged her by buying a brightly coloured toy piano. As the television flickered, Annie picked out tunes from the programmes. She accompanied herself singing old Scottish folk songs and was desperate to take up Highland dancing, despite the fact that her parents couldn't afford the lessons.

Tom and Dorothy were proud of their daughter's ability, yet not being particularly musical themselves, they didn't always understand her obsession with music, or her ferocious desire for privacy. Often Annie would creep into bed and draw or read vividly illustrated books, rather than play with conventional toys. 'She was always drawing and I always thought she was musical. I encouraged her, but sometimes it was difficult,' Dorothy said.

Ironically, the nearest equivalent to Annie's strange and special gift exists in football and the career of Denis Law, a child prodigy born and raised near Annie's home in Aberdeen's Torry district. Despite a squint and NHS spectacles, Law became a football star at seventeen, eventually playing for Manchester United and Torino in Italy. His shock of bright blond hair and virtuoso skills was Annie Lennox incarnate. Aberdeen also produced another wayward child in the unconventional talent of Michael Clarke. In the same way that Annie redirected her classical training, Britain's premier male dancer brought punk situationism to the staid world of ballet.

Growing up different in Aberdeen in the 1950s was demanding for any child, let alone someone of Annie's finely honed temperament. There is a resilience, though, about this city on the North-East coast of Scotland that spawns someone of her calibre. Its gifted and garrulous son, the poet Lewis Grassic Gibbon, wrote over sixty years ago that living in Aberdeen 'is comparable to passing one's existence in a refrigerator . . . it has a flinty shine when new – a grey glimmer like a morning North Sea, a cold steeliness that chills the heart. Even with weathering it acquires no gracious softness, it is merely starkly grim and uncompromising.'

The town of utilitarian grey granite has a toughness and self-sufficiency that has as much to do with its hardy history as the stone it was built with. Aberdeen, the granite city, is set right on the North-East coast of Scotland, flanked by the dramatic Cairngorm Mountains and steep Deeside Hills on one side, with the cold North Sea on the other. Aberdeen's economy has been built on fisheries and the off-shore oil industry. Within Scotland it is traditionally stereotyped as a 'mean' and penny-pinching city, but Aberdeen is proud of its virtual independence from the other major Scottish cities Glasgow and Edinburgh, and is protective of its own specific language in which girls are 'queenies' and boys are 'loons'.

The only easy exit from the town is south from Braemar. Straddling the River Dee, Aberdeen developed as a port, but its remoteness meant that until comparatively recently it was the centre of a bleak, unprosperous region, deriving as much influence from Iceland and Scandinavian trawlermen as from the west of Scotland. It was this isolated part of the country that also spawned Denis Nielson, the son of an Aberdeenshire woman and a Scandinavian trawlerman, and Britain's most famous mass-murderer.

Direct communication with the Gaelic-speaking heartlands of the west was difficult and, far from the centres of power to the south, Aberdeen became very self-contained. Its poverty and seclusion meant that a small number of families dominated the area, including the powerful Farquharsons, direct descendants from Annie's mother Dorothy Farquharson Lennox; a family who were assured of a place in Scottish history, but no longer powerful in Dorothy's generation. Aberdeen concerned itself as much with Highland affairs as those in the Lowland, and clan fighting was rife.

'There's something about the Scots people; especially the poetic and the passionate ones – they've a streak of madness in them,' Annie once said, when asked about her Scottish roots. Her summary is acute. Her friend and fellow Scottish musician Billy Mackenzie also feels there is a characteristic streak of eccentricity in the people:

'It's because Scots are so sensitive, they have a high vibration level – like the American Red Indians who were warlike, lived in tents and had clans and tribes. A lot of Celtic music is similar to Indian music in its use of chants, etc. Scots *are* mad, but not in a bad way. It's because they feel things so strongly – that's better than the tight-lipped English going "nothing can faze me". A good Scot is quite warring; one minute very helpful, the next we're all fighting again. We just don't know how to behave.'

In many a Scottish character there is a tension between the

maundering, wayward romantic and a strict structured Presbyterian streak. Aberdeen's history is marked by these extremes, as in 1644 when it was torn by the British Civil War. Victorious monarchist troops led by the fiery Marquis of Montrose devastated the town for three days, killing any Protestant Covenanters they found, and many civilians besides.

Among the warring family factions, it was the Gordons who held sway from the fourteenth century, remaining an influence late into the eighteenth century when George Gordon Byron was born to Catherine Gordon and 'Mad Jack' Byron. Morose, lyrical and eccentric, the poet represented the other side of Aberdeen's austere face. Although from an English aristocratic family, Byron lived his early life in Aberdeen, praised it in his verse, and saw himself reflected in the passionate intensity of the Scottish spirit.

On a fine day the sun shines sharp and direct on the sea, making luminous the golden shore that skirts Aberdeen. Then the light changes a quality in the granite, transforming the grey to silver, the thick sand to a shimmering sheen. The city has an unpredictable flickering softness, a grace, a stability and a reserve that has survived its blustery history. 'One detests Aberdeen with the detestation of a thwarted lover,' wrote Gibbon. 'It is the one haunting and exasperatingly lovable city in Scotland.'

As if she has absorbed those aspects, Annie's psyche is sculpted by the poetry and the pragmatism of her city. Her pain has often been that of dichotomy, caught between two different worlds, with shifting philosophies and changing expectations. Her mother, gentle and warm, came from out of town and spoke with a country dialect. Her father, a strict, authoritarian and committed card-carrying member of the Communist party, came from the city. A man who played bagpipes and fought with the creativity in himself, his life was a frustrating balancing act between hard, dirty, responsible work on the railways and in the shipyard, and a wish to develop his artistic, intellectual self.

The city itself presents two different sides: the cultural and intellectual finerie of the university's Marischal College, the art gallery and elegant nineteenth-century terraces exist alongside robust industrial development. Herring fishing and granite were Aberdeen's staple industries until the economy lurched into an unforeseen overdrive in the 1970s. As the traditional fisheries declined and successive 'cod wars' created a crisis in the trawler industry, oil was discovered offshore.

Despite angry political campaigning by the Scottish National Party (SNP) under the slogan 'It's Scotland's Oil', the rights to mine Aberdeen's black gold were acquired by major multinational corporations led by American oil companies. An unprecedented influx of Americans arrived in the city, sending house prices spiralling and creating an off-shore industry known as 'the rigs'. Perhaps the most famous rig offshore from Aberdeen was Piper Alpha, the oil platform that exploded on 6 July 1988 with the loss of 170 lives.

With the discovery of oil, speculators mounted a Gold Rush and the town was inundated with oil and engineering giants like Brown & Root and UIE falling over themselves to find Scottish sites. The boom-to-bust nature of the industry meant that by the early 1980s, the slump in the price of oil caused many firms to go out of business. Such a recession could break a town, but with characteristic resilience, Aberdeen pulled in its horns and survived. Another incident that illustrates the city's grit and self-sufficiency was during Annie's childhood, when a serious typhoid epidemic broke out and the whole of Aberdeen was sealed off to outsiders. The disease, which originated from some bad Argentinian corn beef sold by William Low's butchery chain, spread so rapidly that children were kept away from school and quarantined at home. Under these severe measures, the epidemic was eventually beaten.

Survival despite the odds is an attractive philosophy to Annie. That straightforward solid analysis in overcoming difficulties is a family trait, making many a Lennox a formidable organizer. The family name is linked to the Dumbartonshire Levenachs, proud and powerful thirteenth-century earls of the soil whose quiet effectiveness was handed down through generations. As Annie was growing up, the Lennox name and socialist family tradition became prominent in the city, when in May 1967, her great uncle Robert Lennox, a left Labour councillor, was elected Lord Provost.

He didn't reach his position without controversy. A painter by trade, and area organizer of the Amalgamated Society of Painters and Decorators, Lennox had been on Aberdeen Town Council for twenty-one years, anxious to 'make Aberdeen a better place'. An outspoken and strategic campaigner, his popularity was tempered by the more panic-stricken of Conservatives on the town council.

'Because of the intrusion of politics into this chamber, we will be forced to accept a man who has sold his freedom of action and violated the principles of democracy to the odious loyalty of his party,' thundered one Councillor Hatch, on the election of Lennox, disapproving of the fact that the Provost should also be a member of the Labour party.

'I don't suppose that birth can come along without pain. To that extent I am grateful to Councillor Hatch for his remarks,' said the new Lord Provost, with stoical self-assurance. Although he had many supporters, there were some in the city who were wary of his outspoken nature. 'I was aware from the way I had been indoctrinated by my parents that Ann had different ideas, and I knew that her great-uncle the Lord Provost was left-wing,' recalls Frances Penny. 'My parents didn't agree with his policies.'

Lord Provost Lennox went on to institute many co-operative initiatives in local government and was well respected, remaining in office till 1970, then becoming re-elected five years later. On his retirement in 1978, Lennox was awarded a CBE by Buckingham Palace for services to local government.

Belief in active citizenship was strong in the Lennox family. With a bustling no-nonsense attitude, Evelyn Lennox, Lady Provost and wife of Robert, worked for the Amalgamated Union of Building Trade Workers and was active in local women's organizations. One of Annie's uncles was a major figure in the Educational Institute of Scotland (EIS), Scotland's biggest teaching union, while another was a staunch Communist party member who saw Russia in the 1930s as a new and exciting place. Annie herself has a strong political commitment, one that didn't confidently and publicly emerge until well into her career. Until then she had quietly sponsored local projects, such as Haddo House, a community arts centre near Aberdeen.

Despite their strong principles, Annie remembers her extended family as 'very quiet people – they would never cause any problems, not provocative, not extreme, very conformist. My parents didn't know what they got when they got me. I was rebelling so hard.' The main focus of Annie's rebellion was in her teenage years, as she struggled to assert her individuality in disagreements with her authoritarian father.

The Lennox family symbolized the respectable working class, manually skilled, hard working, with a thorough intelligence. It was not an environment to breed flamboyance, though Annie's grandfather was a more wayward soul, a gamekeeper and a lover of 'still' whisky and the accordion of Jimmy Shand. He lived in

Aberlour, a village west of Aberdeen on the River Spey in the centre of one of Scotland's malt whisky heartlands. It was here that Annie spent some of the happiest holidays of her life, reading classics in her grandmother's library, writing poetry and walking in the pine glens of the surrounding countryside.

With its small square, main street and compact church, Aberlour is a quiet, pretty place, home of the Aberlour-Glenlivet Distillery which is set back unobtrusively behind the trees. It has played host to the Highland Games, and its cosy village warmth attracts many stray tourists.

Away from the small private world of her grandfather's Aberlour cottage, Annie felt less secure, more detached from those around her. This was accentuated when in 1959, at the age of four-and-a-half she entered Aberdeen's most prestigious High School for Girls. Founded in 1874, it was originally a girls' orphanage in Belmont Street in the town centre, moving up the hill at the turn of the century to 18 Albyn Place. For years this long graceful white building was a private school, later being extended and changed into a selective-intake grammar for over a thousand girls. This meant that many of the pupils were bright children from privileged middle-class families, and coming from a working-class background, Annie felt unconfident and out of place. In later years she would like to think of her childhood self as a lonely musician, a self-tortured soul whom nobody understood.

'I was never one of the gang,' she mused later. 'I felt myself to be a loner. I usually had only one "best friend". I could be gregarious when I felt like it, but generally I was just quiet and thoughtful.'

Annie's friend Frances Penny, who was in the same year as her throughout primary and secondary school, was surprised when Annie said later that she found her schooldays difficult. 'I wasn't aware of her not fitting in. She was averagely popular and mixed well in class, though I don't picture her going round with any particular lassie. I don't remember Ann as being extreme or standing out in any way,' she says now from her home in Motherwell, near Glasgow. Married and working as a pharmacist, Frances recalls her schooldays with warmth.

'The school drew from a broad spectrum of backgrounds right across the city; it wasn't fee-paying so entrance was according to ability. It wasn't a posh school, but it had the reputation of being more desirable to go to than local schools. There were some silly rules and regulations, but they were more irritating than harmful –

I remember once during primary lines were given to the whole class, but lines weren't routinely given, and there was no belt.

'It was actually a kindly, old-fashioned set-up, angled at making you "good citizens" and training you to keep certain standards. Quite a "young ladies" place.'

Another friend of Annie's, Diane Mackie, who was with her from primary one until sixth year, has quite a different view. Born and brought up in the working-class area of Rosehill, Mackie's friendship with Annie flourished because of the similarity of their backgrounds. 'It was a real snobby school,' she says now from her house in Banchory just outside Aberdeen, where she lives with her husband and two children. 'It was very posh and proper, and Ann and I became close partly because we were both working class.'

On her first day at school the diminutive Lennox was enveloped in the customary crusty girl's uniform: a navy tunic and white blouse with a tie, and a black velour hat that *had* to be worn, with black lace-up shoes. 'Then there was a straw Panama hat in summer that you could only wear with a blazer, and in secondary school if you went downtown without a beret on you were in trouble. We all looked incredibly cute, but it drove my mother mad!' recalls Frances Penny.

The school placed a strict emphasis on training girls to be educated young ladies, teaching them how to curtsey and sit nicely at the table as well as pass exams. The bulk of the teachers were former pupils, and there was a cosy atmosphere, with just two classes in each year up to secondary school when the girls were divided into six streams from A–F. Girls took exams either at four or eleven to enter the school and many pupils then went on to further education, a system that created quite an academic hothouse.

Faced by the threat of being swallowed up in the educational stream, Annie instinctively found her identity in music and stuck to it, taking piano lessons and performing in school concerts. She was a moderate scholar, but she excelled at music.

In the 1950s and 1960s, Aberdeen ambitiously led the way in the teaching of music in schools. The scene was well organized with a specially established music centre that co-ordinated music teaching for all the schools in the area. Originally annexed to the girls' school, it then moved to Loch Street in the centre of town, with the principal teacher Mr Cutbush circulating his peripatetic staff around the city schools.

Annie took advantage of this arrangement, first learning the piano with Mrs Murray, a conscientious, patient character who had a penchant for hill walking. Right into her seventies, the old lady would tackle 'monroes' – hills or mountains over 700 feet. She taught the piano 'correctly', providing Annie with a good grounding in theory.

Also a major influence on Annie's early years was the eccentric, whimsical dance mistress, Marguerite Feltges, who specialized in a Greek form of dancing known as Eurhythmics – the inspiration, of course, for Annie and Dave's band, later deliberately mispelled to make it easier to read. Centred on a theory of harmony in bodily movement, Eurhythmics was devised in the early 1900s and adopted from original Greek formats and developed with music and dance into a system of education. Although such attitudes towards dance and education are now commonly held, in the 1950s this approach was considered strange and exotic. 'I can remember enjoying music and movement. Nothing was right or wrong, there were no rules, so you couldn't fail at it,' says Penny.

Former pupil Irene Burnett recalls how 'we floated about in little green skirts. I wasn't exactly Anna Pavlova, but we all did it when we were small.' This brisk, ebullient, bespectacled woman was later to be assistant administrator at the school. She remembers the days pre-1973, before the school became a mixed comprehensive and was renamed Harlaw Academy. Then there was room for the kind of teachers geared towards teaching girls of selective intake, dedicated women who were sometimes introverted, sometimes quirky, sometimes purely visionary, in an idealistic tradition immortalized in the Muriel Spark novel *The Prime of Miss Jean Brodie*. With her flowing mane of black hair, round figure and physical vivacity, Marguerite Feltges was one of this band, proud in her position while the school remained all-girls, only to fade away once the atmosphere was disrupted by the complex demands of mixed comprehensive education.

'At the end of the 1970s it was very unsettling,' says Mrs Burnett, 'There were pupils coming in with low IQs etc, and it took a few years to adjust.' Before the high school became Harlaw Academy it was a curious mixture of traditional and forward-thinking ideas. As well as the Eurhythmic dancing, Penny recalls that they 'sat in groups rather than rows in class' and had an experimental method of learning numbers, with a system of coloured wooden blocks known as Cuisinier Rods. Her primary report book illustrates how the school was concerned with turning out responsible as well as enlightened young ladies, with categories ranging from Number and Handicraft to Social Studies and Physical and Social Development.

Penny fondly recalls some of the teachers she and Annie had: Miss Sadler, a gentle old lady who was 'very kindly with the kiddies', the briskly middle-aged Mrs Mathieson, and a red-headed dragon with 'a touch of temper' called Mrs Kelly. The most eccentric was undoubtedly Miss Feltges.

Now dead, Miss Feltges reportedly remembers Annie as: 'a charming child. I taught her mime and movement, and I remember when "Waltzing Matilda" first came out, my pianist was playing it and all the children were dancing in a circle while I stood with my arms outstretched. Ann was the child who took my hands and danced with me.'

Annie built up strong relationships with her music tutors. Bill Spittle, the city woodwind teacher, began teaching her the flute when she was twelve, and guided her until she left school at seventeen and decided to go to London's Royal Academy of Music.

A short, pragmatic man from Tyneside, Spittle has been retired for many years. When I spoke to him over tea and biscuits in his Aberdeen flat three miles from Annie's childhood home, he recalled her with a sharp memory. He has been following her career over time, concerned that she never fulfilled her classical potential. 'She was a very promising young musician and showed flair from the start. She was a useful pianist and a proper singer, not the rubbish there is nowadays. Now they don't sing, they just bawl into the mike and there's no trace of pure voice. It's the biggest sacrilege of the day that people are getting away with so much money and having no ability. I suppose Annie wouldn't make any money if she did straight choral singing, but her background of musical training and ability always shows through.'

Phlegmatic and astute, Spittle is one of a dying generation of musicians who learned his trade in light orchestra. 'It was mainly theatre work, because there were so many musicals shortly after the war. There was a glut of them. Every theatre would always have one of fifteen or more orchestras – that's practically finished now.'

Spittle had a 'pleasant, easy life' playing clarinet, sax and flute for the Leicester Opera House and Coventry Hippodrome. These gilt-edged Victorian emporiums staged a variety of popular American musicals, from *Oklahoma* to *South Pacific*, *The Sound of Music* and *Annie Get Your Gun*, for a post-war audience keen to escape into showtime musical fantasy.

Times grew lean with the popularization of television in the 1950s. 'I foresaw it would do harm to musicians,' says Spittle. As an ex-serviceman he took a year-long refresher course that was open to him at Trinity College in London. A crash course in teacher training, it gave him the qualification to teach music, and in the early 1950s he made the leap from entertainment to education. 'I heard about a job in Aberdeen teaching at a school, and it seemed attractive to me. I thought I'd give it a run for two or three years. Forty years later, I'm still here!'

Spittle's light orchestra background was unusual for a music teacher at that time, and he is proud of the difference his contribution made to notions of professionalism and presentation in traditional musical teaching. Annie, in particular, benefited from his popular yet disciplined approach, when he led the school's orchestra in outside band concerts. She would always have been a musical achiever, but Spittle played a guiding role in the shaping of her musical ambitions.

'We had about fifty performers. We'd do some radio broadcasts and a lot of hospital work for people with nervous complaints, a little bit off their head and so forth. We played the popular music that schools didn't dare feature in their curriculum. I thought the lighter side was necessary to give people a broader outlook; I'd had the good fortune to do all kinds of work from tip top dance to theatre orchestra, whereas lots of music teachers come from a very narrow field, having been choirmasters or organists. They wouldn't let their hair down to play *South Pacific* or something like that.'

Under Spittle's direction, many of the youngsters learned stage presentation, as well as the logistics of playing in a band. 'Instead of sitting like little zombies playing a classical piece I'd get sections to stand up and feature themselves, to put on a show,' he says. 'Showmanship might be cheap to some people's eyes – but it became very popular. Whether it's overtures or operatics, I can size my audience up because of my profession. Experience outweighs anything else. You might have the ability, but if you don't turn the style on, what's the point?'

Despite the fact that Annie always claimed she wasn't interested in becoming 'a star', she displayed an awareness of public presentation from an early age. All the children from the neighbouring tenement houses would play together in their backyards, occasionally putting on a concert for the mothers in the area. An old sheet hung over a washing line would serve as a stage curtain, and each child would do a star turn.

Annie also spent her Halloweens dressing up and going 'guising', the old Scottish tradition where children disguised as ghosts, pirates, cowboys or monsters carrying lanterns made from old turnips would knock on doors and perform for their neighbours. Annie would sing, rattling her biscuit tin for donations. 'It got so full of money it wouldn't close,' she said. Her first proper public appearance came at the age of seven, when she sang a traditional folk song at the annual Schools Music Festival in Aberdeen, and two years later she won second prize singing the old Scottish song 'Marie's Wedding' in a talent contest while on holiday at Butlins.

'She wasn't swell-headed or inclined to think herself better than the others, but she didn't lack confidence,' says Spittle. 'She had a zest to do well. Her *ability* gave her self-confidence. She experienced what it was like to have a little attention as a youngster, so she could cope with the present day demands put on her.'

One of his favourite stories is about the time he went on tour with the high school orchestra. 'Annie was quite a live customer, a good sport amongst her pals. Anyway, we were in the Lake District, and she was in a little rowing boat in the middle of the lake, rowing on her own – I don't know why she hadn't joined the other party – and she was singing at the top of her voice, just going round in circles.'

Annie was a confident performer. Each year the British Federation of Music Festivals would organize a week-long festival in Aberdeen, and Penny recalls how Annie would inevitably be entered for several events. 'She was absent quite a lot from school when the festival was on, and she picked up a lot of certificates. I remember a school show one year when she and a girl called Susan Davidson sang solo. What stays in my mind is the difference in their voices – Susan's was thin and silvery whereas Ann's was much richer, a very golden voice.'

In 1963 a record was made of the Aberdeen music festival, and Annie was recorded singing and playing the piano. Even in the most unlikely places she is unworried about bursting into song, like the day of the Cannes press conference many years later when she performed an impromptu acoustic set for a crowd of cynical journalists. The musical tuition she received in Aberdeen at twelve years old merely consolidated a talent and commitment that was already firmly in place.

Annie had one flute lesson each week with Bill Spittle, and in addition to after-school orchestra rehearsals, she played in military bands and sang every Saturday morning in Miss Auchinauchie's choir at the Loch Street Music Centre. She enjoyed constant practice, but had an aversion to playing a piece she didn't like, often refusing to perform it at all. 'I was a bit lazy and could have worked much harder,' she says. 'But I always managed to get away with it.'

Bill Spittle prefers to see it that the more she proved herself musically, the more respect he had for her version of things. 'She was forthcoming and level-headed. She was wise enough that if she disagreed with me she wouldn't let us fall out. I wasn't an easy teacher, but I've had some good results, getting some kids in the top orchestras. On occasion Annie did solo, but I didn't like to make too much of individuals when there were so many learning.'

At ten years old Annie won second place doing vocal solo in the Aberdeen and North-East Scotland Music Festival, but her main passion during her teens was the flute, after one was made available in the school orchestra. Old and faulty, it had elastic bands fitted instead of springs, and was fondly personalized by Annie with the name Flora. When she first took up the instrument, 'pigtailed and precocious, the envy of all the potential Shirley Temples of Aberdeen', Annie was a carefree pupil, supported by parents who were excited about her potential.

After living in a mid-town block in Hutcheon Street, the Lennox family moved to the top of a modest skyscraper in the Mastrick housing scheme on the outskirts of Aberdeen. Although only thirteen floors high, Mastrickland looms large over the low roofs of surrounding houses. It was here one windy winter's day that Spittle came to discuss with Annie's father the buying of a brand new flute.

'We talked man to man. He was very sensible and level-headed, and I liked him very much. Annie's father had a good grip on her. She played piano and flute, and she had a stack of homework. She didn't get away with anything as far as her parents were concerned. I wouldn't say she was spoiled, they were kind to her, but thought enough of her to keep her on a tight rein – not like some who let their children go like scarecrows.'

Annie's parents were not seen in their own right as particularly musical or artistic, so this emphasized her feeling of difference and isolation. She had allies and admirers at school, but ultimately as an only child who didn't musically identify with her parents, she began to feel odd, a kind of mental misfit. Until her teenage years, Annie was happy being a good girl and an obedient daughter. During Annie's early school years, Irene Burnett remembers her as 'just a nice girl with long blonde hair in plaits. If we'd known she was going to be famous we'd have taken more notice of her!'

Early on, though, there were rumblings of a deeper sensibility. Penny remembers one morning in primary school when Annie had stayed up late to watch the TV play 'Culloden', the dramatization of John Prebble's book *The Highland Clearance*, focusing on an infamous battle within Scottish history which took place on Culloden Fields in 1746, in which a well-equipped English army under the command of the Duke of Cumberland slaughtered a rag tag army of 1200 Highlanders. (The Highland Clearances and Culloden occupy a critical place within Scottish history. It is the story of Culloden that provides the basis for the alternative Scottish national anthem 'O Flower of Scotland'.) 'Most of us weren't allowed to watch TV that late, so that was unusual for a start. I remember Ann being very disturbed by it; the subject had sunk in deep. There was also an incident once in the school cloakroom when Ann and another girl had a strong political disagreement about something. The girl's parents were well-to-do and moderately right-wing, while Ann was brought up in a left-wing family, and being children, the two of them were probably regurgitating parental values. It was way above my head, though, and I remember thinking "they must be quite grown up to think these things".'

By the sixth year, Annie was becoming more noticeable. 'I have a vivid memory of her playing Peter Pan in the school pantomime,' says Mrs Burnett. 'She was really good. If she'd gone for an acting career she would have done really well.' She may have flowered in her later school years, but inwardly Annie found the high school such a frustrating experience, so at odds with her working-class background, that the day she left she tore her beret in two.

'The school was by no means grand,' says Penny, 'but because of selective intake it was probably fairly middle class, and pupils living in smaller flats were a minority. Ann was a serious person – I never saw her double up or really giggle, but I find it hurtful that she found the school a place of non-contentment. Except for that one political argument there wasn't any positive antagonism, and I wonder, did I say anything to her? I remember her as part of a *happy* childhood.'

Whatever the reasons for Annie's disaffection, she kept her feelings deeply submerged, and once she started the arduous adolescent task of growing up and moving away from parental influence, she began to break out with a frustrated vengeance. Before Annie could cross over into the public pop world, she needed to free herself from doing what she thought was right and expected of her, to doing what she wanted. This habit would prove to be a tough one to break. As Bill Spittle says: 'I never thought she'd be famous. She's too nice a girl.'

CANNES, 1989

The sun was setting low over the hotel forecourt. An attendant, imperious and impassive, helped a well-dressed old lady remove her baggage from a taxi. A gold limousine wilted in the thick heat at the end of the day. There were cries from the swimming pool, a few splashes, the clink of glasses and people settling down to supper. From an open window above came the abrupt murmuring of CNN, the American cable TV news station.

The Hotel Majestic in Cannes in August 1989 exuded a solid cosmopolitan calm. A film crew from MTV Europe packed their equipment into the back of a van and sat down for one last ice cream before their trip to the airport. Inside the large high-ceilinged reception room there were a collection of tables that had been elegantly set at midday for a press conference buffet. Hours later they were strewn with opaque glasses, empty bottles and food remains. Chairs were flung back, with hotel staff clearing away plates of pâté and cheese. Steve Blackwell, small, neat, affable and unhurried, pop manager for one of the biggest groups in the world, sat amidst the debris, waiting for his female boss. Her soft, arresting voice came through the stillness.

'Most pop stars believe in their own hype, the fantasy world that's created for them. I've never believed in it. I've always known it's a kind of monster. In the end it's all a huge fiction. Some of it's partly true, and sometimes truth is stranger than fiction.'

These words emanated from Annie Lennox, a tall, tense-looking blonde sitting next to me at a table on the hotel veranda. Her hair was cropped short and she wore a crisp white shirt and beige trousers. Behind her obligatory pop star bottle green shades, she darted two kinds of look. One sharp, direct and clear, the other a sly sideways glance that effectively estimates a situation in a second. The first look was unambiguous, the second more beguiling. Both were instinctively defensive.

'I don't take the pop machine seriously,' she said, adjusting her shades with a protective move. 'That's not to say I don't take my music seriously. All the passion of my life and life's work goes into Eurythmics music. That's our sanctified area. The rest is just glorified nonsense, meaningless puffballs.'

Annie Lennox keeps her own inner world intact, occasionally uncovering a crystallized edge that illuminates a point, a personal truth, an aspect of her character. It is this scarcity of illumination that keeps an interviewer careful, probing, fascinated. As each piece is turned to the light, a whole picture can be constructed.

Like all pop stars, Annie's personality is refracted through a media that shamelessly invents and celebrates its own pop myths. This perturbs her when her definition of herself is so precise and considered. She has a spare, lean frame, and likewise in her psyche leaves little room for illogical excess or pop flatulence.

'It's my Scottish roots. By nature my feet are solidly on the ground. If anyone comes towards me with any element of insincerity, I have a tracker dog instinct that quickly cuts through all of that. It's difficult. I only ask for people's attention when I'm performing. I don't live in clubs, I don't invite people into our living room to ogle at our lifestyle. I'm not in love with the idea of living on the front page of the tabloids.'

The road manager, a tall, burly guy with a black tour T-shirt interrupted the conversation, asking if Annie would like a bite to eat.

'Oh, just a light salad. Something really light,' she said. Minutes later he returned, depositing with a flourish a dry cheese baguette.

'Oh, another one of those awful things,' she said with casual disdain, then immediately checked herself. 'Thank you, thanks anyway.'

Constantly monitoring her public face as well as her deep-seated emotions, Annie is faintly embarrassed by the obvious pop star trappings and the attentions bestowed on her by the Eurythmics entourage. She doesn't refuse it, yet claims: 'I have a detachment from the music scene. It keeps me very sane, aware of reality. It's not all just someone giving me a cheese sandwich right on cue. The rest of my life isn't everyone running around giving me tea. OK, it's a bit like that when we're on tour, only because when we're at full stretch it's so exhausting.'

The day had been very demanding. An entire planeload of chattering London journalists had touched down the afternoon before to cover the first date of Eurythmics' 1989 'World Revival Tour'. From the moment Annie stepped onto the outdoor stage at Juan Le Pins for a romantic beach performance, people were jostling for her words, her attention and her face.

Like someone who had learned how to become a long distance runner, Annie set her pace and stuck to it. She and partner Dave were present to publicize their tenth album *We Too Are One*, and she had no intention of wavering from that task. Sleek and pale despite the hot evening sun and tanned audience, she raced through a set that included all the new songs, as well as breathless renditions of former hits like 'Sweet Dreams'. Behind her Dave Stewart stoked the engine room of the band, keeping a lead on the instrumentation with his authoritative guitar. Backing singer Joniece Jameson and The Gap Band's Charlie Wilson carried the soulful edge, while a French audience clapped out of time to the gospel-tinged beat.

Some called the gig crowd-pleasing, taking care of business. Others criticized it as 'rabble-rousing bullshit', while many commended Annie on her triumphant return after two years' break from touring, paying tribute to a Eurythmics set that was '24 carat gold'.

In fact Annie's musuclar return to the fray was notable for its enthusiastic professionalism and a live performance that traded energy for energy with the captive audience. A job well done. Once the concert was over, Annie continued with her calm public face intact, gracing the after-show beach party in a pristine white suit. She chatted to some guests and satisfied waiting cameras on the dancefloor by cavorting carefully with Dave's wife Siobhan Fahey. After a decent interval Annie took her husband Uri and made a neat, discreet exit. Dave, meanwhile, partied until dawn.

The following day the European media crammed into the reception room at the Hotel Majestic for a lunchtime press conference. Among the earnest Dutch, German and French journalists, the British brigade turned out to be the most rabid, planting such difficult tabloid questions on Annie as: 'Would you support your friend Chrissie Hynde in her statement about firebombing MacDonalds?' and 'Do you have a message of comfort for any mother who has lost her child?' Fielding these questions with nervous aplomb she said first:

'Chrissie was only joking – she has a very individual and violent sense of humour that I appreciate. We shouldn't shy away from standing up for causes as collective musicians,' and then with icy politeness: 'I think couples who have suffered a stillbirth would take great comfort in hearing what I have to say about coping with it.'

It seemed as if the presence of the press denoted a constant battle. In a calculated attempt to defuse the tension and move onto ground that she knew best, Annie led Dave into an impromptu acoustic performance. His guitar and her voice wooed the crowd with stark simplicity. Some cynics groaned at the turn of events, but all were effectively silenced. After the media confrontation, the TV interviews begin, continuing till the end of the afternoon, with the same showbiz questions repeated again and again and again. Instead of becoming fractious and wilting, Annie had a studied concentration, a wish to keep talking, to analyse and above all, to keep calm. She didn't even sweat.

It hadn't always been this way, so structured and so clear. Much of Annie's pop star's life had been fraught with confusion, so the well-organized attitude she presented in Cannes came across as one learned and consolidated over time.

I asked whether her parents taught her how to be tough.

'I taught myself,' she said quietly.

Trial and error?

She gave a sly, sideways glance. 'Yes. Very much trial, very much error.'

She then moved into an explosive confessional monologue, one that was as oddly naïve as it was heroic.

'When we're younger we don't have the benefit of hindsight and experience, we're so eager to go out there and get burned. Experience *means* getting burned, going right to the bottom, getting your teeth kicked in and having the guts to stand up, admit you made a terrible mistake and get on with it again. People get destroyed through that. It depends on how many risks you're prepared to take.'

From the young, anxiously solicitous girl who had broken free from her background in Aberdeen to the smooth, poised pop star she personified in Cannes nearly twenty years later, Annie tenaciously clung to her dream of musical and personal perfection. Such a view would take her through emotional extremes, but it's that dramatic self-awareness that fuelled and gave the edge to whatever she produced.

23

2

The Reluctant Rock Star

'**I** never considered myself a pop singer. I never had this ambition to be a *star*. To be a good musician, that was my primary concern. I had no real desire to be rich and famous and I hated being the centre of attention, which is hard to believe when you see me on stage, but nevertheless it's true. I have a strong suspicion of the tag "star" – people can't be "stars" for six months, it has to be a gradual long term thing.

'I'm coming to terms with it, because in actuality I am a star now. But there's an awful lot of people who start from that premise, that's their ambition.'

TEEN TRIVIA

In 1967 the American anti-Vietnam protests were at their height. Radicals, yippies, hippies and Students for a Democratic Society fought for ascendance in well-mediated campaigns for peace. The Spring Mobilization Committee planned large demonstrations in the spring; 75,000 marched on San Francisco while 400,000 congregated in New York. Bands like Buffalo Springfield, Jefferson Airplane and the Doors captured the imagination of the stoned-out, anti-parent teen generation, while such figures as Bob Dylan and Janis Joplin were lauded as heroes and spokespeople, whatever their qualifications.

In Britain, the British Labour Government closed down offshore pirate radio stations, but in the ensuing national uproar were forced through the BBC to capitulate. In recognition of the part that pop music was beginning to play in everyday life for the young, the BBC launched Radio One, Britain's first pure pop station.

British pop in 1967 was entering its second phase of rejuvenation. The first wave came in the early 1960s, when beat groups like the Beatles and the Dave Clark Five reinvented American rock'n'roll and sold it back to the States. With the growth of psychedelia and hippy

24

idealism, pop expanded to blur boundaries between pop and rock. Fusions of blues, gospel and folk surfaced in bands like the Jimi Hendrix Experience, Cream, Led Zepplin, Procol Harum and Pink Floyd.

These sounds filtered through to Aberdeen on the North-East coast of Scotland, where thirteen-year-old Annie Lennox wore her fair hair long and experimented with a soft hippy style, opting for blue paisley and little bells. She regularly rummaged through thrift shops at the far end of town, taking her second-hand spoils home and spreading them on the floor with delight.

Bewildered at her daughter's burgeoning teenage identity, Dorothy Lennox would often remonstrate, 'I'm not walking down the street with you wearing those things!' Annie refused to modify anything for her parents, beginning a battle with them that would continue throughout her teenage years. Much of the conflict centred around her father's strict nature and her mother's compliance.

'When I met him Annie's father seemed like a nice, sweet old man,' says her friend and album sleeve designer Laurence Stevens. 'But he often rowed with her mother. After he met Dorothy he toned down a lot, but he was still very strict – doing things like coming in at six o'clock and saying "Where's my dinner?" Annie didn't totally respect her mum because she didn't stand up to her father. That's why Annie presented such a tough, fighting image in her career, as if in reaction to that.

'She's the opposite of her mother. Dorothy is a warm, shy, retiring woman who wouldn't say boo to a goose. She's what a mother should be – plump and grey-haired and always cooking, cleaning and worrying about Annie. It's really funny – Annie's face is now known from Bangkok to Brazil and her mum's oblivious. Dorothy says things like "Shall I put the potatoes here?" or "Do you want white or brown bread?" and Annie answers "It doesn't *matter* mum, make a decision!"'

Up to her early adolescence, Annie had been playing flute in the British Youth Wind Orchestra, singing in the Aberdeen Schools Choir and concentrating her ambitions on becoming one of a small chamber ensemble. Her musical awareness began to drift and grow as pop records made inroads into her psyche, and dating boys became an exciting prospect.

She would meet a group of friends every night after school to hang out in the centre of town, smoking the occasional cigarette, laughing, gossiping and eyeing the local boys. Coming from an all-girls school, boys – no matter how spotty or greasy they were – held a special charm. You could kiss them, be touched, feel wanted, loved, special, super-confident.

Each weekend she had a running battle with her father. She discovered Motown and boys, and he didn't like it. He was anxious for her to go to the Royal Academy, do her course and have a good career, while she continually pulled away from his influence. 'He was a working-class man who'd worked the whole of his life in the shipyard. Annie felt he was used, that he never really made anything of his life,' says a close friend, 'and that was why he was so strict with her.'

By the age of fourteen she was a fully-fledged dissatisfied rebel, fighting to assert herself in the face of parental concern. Although she was forced to be home by 10.30 p.m., she went to the Beach Ballroom every Friday night, a white seafront emporium situated between the docks and the gasworks that thumped out Motown, Stax and grinding soul – the other side of 1960s pop culture, far from the wafting delights of hippy psychedelia. The Beach Ballroom, along with the Salvation Ballroom in Perth and Kircaldy's Raith Ballroom, was part of a string of old Scottish dancehalls converted into makeshift discos. Geared to live music, they adjusted uncomfortably to DJs and often included showbands who performed rousing cover versions like the Temptations' 'Get Ready' or Wilson Pickett's 'Land of a Thousand Dances'.

Among the bands who toured the Beach Ballroom circuit in the 1960s were Lulu & the Luvvers, the Beat Poets from Glasgow, the Vikings from Perth who later became the Average White Band, and finally in the early 1970s the Glasgow group Salvation fronted by Midge Ure, who was later to join Annie in the ranks of the rock elite. At the Beach Ballroom, Annie danced to the Temptations, the Supremes, the Four Tops and Marvin Gaye, the sound of sheer ebullience informing her tastes for years to come.

She also heard the best of British pop – the Beatles, the Rolling Stones and the Kinks, ingesting their clean lines and clear melodies. She fell in love with the Moody Blues' 'Whiter Shade of Pale' and bought the record especially for a weekend party. When the kissing games started, the boys paired off with the girls and her smoochy hit was played over and over again.

At the age of fifteen, she focused her passion on her first boyfriend, a young lad named Clifton Collier. 'He was a nice guy,' recalls Annie's old schoolfriend Diane Mackie, who now works as a photographer near Aberdeen. 'He went to one of the public schools in Aberdeen, and his father had an advertising business already set up. Clifton's now a successful businessman.'

Clifton and Annie would meet after school to hold hands or visit the bowling alley together, yet the relationship was to be short-lived, and he apparently dropped her. Heartbroken, she sat in her bedroom alone writing privately with the first stirrings of self-analysis. 'At the age of fourteen I became very moody, very easily depressed,' she said. 'I *seemed* extrovert but I was watching the world trying to cope with who I was and really very confused about it.'

But just as emotional pain burdened her and made her introspective, it also gave her the spark to fight. She became more adventurous, and in tune with the wayward idealism of the time, more experimental. The impact of years of being caught between two cultures, working-class and middle-class, town and country, began to surface. She yearned for total independence yet simultaneously retained the goals of perfect wife and motherhood. Confusion and uncertainty dogged her decisions as she wavered between two worlds: one that was safe, academic, orientated towards school and her classical interests, and another that centred around the more undisciplined minds of the local hippy music scene. At sixteen, much to her father's disappointment, she hung out with a much older crowd. She didn't feel at ease, but learned a lot about her sexuality and sense of self as an individual.

'Ann was a very likeable person, very quiet, studious and into music. I remember her from very young going away with her music bag. She didn't socialize too much until she was sixteen or seventeen, because she wasn't allowed out. Her parents restricted her,' says Mackie. 'But we went out a lot as teenagers. We'd go to the Student's Union at the university to go to discos or see late 1960s bands like America. We weren't too hippyish, we were quite nicely dressed; I had an Afghan coat and we both wore long skirts and Indian tops. There was a group of us that used to go, and we'd hang out with students.'

Annie had several boy friends, including one several years older than her, a student called Bob Morroco. 'I didn't think that much of him to be honest,' says Mackie. 'He was hippyish, very serious and intense – a typical student.'

In pre-oil boom days there wasn't a great deal for young Aberdonians to do, and in common with small towns or country villages in the

North of Scotland, it is rumoured that many a party would end in an uninhibited orgy, with much swapping of partners. Dundee-born Billy Mackenzie certainly testifies to the sexual precociousness of the time. 'We were quite advanced. We were dating steady at twelve, and girls were wearing hotpants and platforms and having sex by the time they were thirteen. It was quite natural, if you didn't do it you were laughed at. It was very promiscuous at that time – remember it was glam, skinheads and suedeheads, and the atmosphere was very charged.'

Annie's old schoolmates Diane and Frances didn't mention orgies, but the latter does remember 'a lot of local dances. In pre-oil days Aberdeen was a lot smaller, more parochial and old-fashioned. If you went downtown on a Saturday afternoon you always saw people you knew. After the oil boom it became a lot bigger, with a lot more incomers, a turnover of people and more cosmopolitan wine bars and night clubs. Within one or two years everything changed very quickly, and there was suddenly more money.'

In 1971 the oil boom had yet to break fully. Until the oil speculators moved in to make it a boom town, Aberdeen still seemed careful, staid and limited in outlook to the ambitious seventeen-year-old Annie. Once she had explored her healthy interest in boyfriends, she began to concentrate on getting into one of the most prestigious music colleges in the country. She was a thoroughly competent if unspectacular student, passing her fifth-year exams in French, art, maths, history, music, biology and English language, and specializing in her highers in art, English and, in particular, music.

Her parents were keen for her to study in the best establishment, but when she was accepted for the Royal Academy of Music in London, they feared for her safety. Five hundred miles away seemed an impossible distance. Besides, it was in England, a separate, strange and seemingly 'sophisticated' country, where single girls lived in bedsits, took drugs and got pregnant.

It was unusual for Annie to go as far as London. In the 1960s and 1970s young people in Aberdeen tended to continue their education in local colleges or the university. 'Aberdeen served a large area for students,' recalls Penny, herself a pharmacy graduate of Aberdeen University. 'It had a very large catchment area, taking in places like Inverness, Elgin and Fort William. In my class one person went to Edinburgh and that seemed remarkably far-flung. It wouldn't have occurred to me to go down south, because at that time Aberdeen had a very parochial outlook, like, what do you want to leave home for?'

Annie stuck to her decision and started to save some money to supplement her grant. She took a summer job at the local Findus fish factory, filletting plaice for three months. It was hard, smelly work, paying £9.50 for a forty-hour week. Each night she stuffed her work clothes into a plastic bag and, on taking them out the following morning, nearly asphyxiated with the smell. She laughed and joked with her workmates, but while they had to stay and earn their living, she was glad to be able to leave, swearing that she'd *never* work in a fish factory again.

'It was strange when she left Aberdeen because so many people were going off to do different things. We'd been a very close-knit group, so it seemed like the end of an era,' says Mackie.

In September 1971 Annie crammed her clothes into an old trunk and a few suitcases and made the long journey down to a new kind of freedom.

TAKE ONE GIRL

'I thought it would be just like a series on TV called 'Take Three Girls' about these girls living in swinging London and sharing a flat together. I thought it would all be just like that – boyfriends with little white sports cars, wine bars, Kensington sophistication, parties, good times. Was I ever wrong!' said Annie.

On reaching London, her disappointment was intense. For a teenage girl moving far from her home in the far north of Scotland, London must have been a daunting experience. A difficult city to break into and feel at home, it was large, sprawling and polluted, packed with uniform bedsits and a shifting, impersonal population.

She had enrolled at the Royal Academy to study piano and harp-sichord, as well as the flute, with a view to becoming a professional classical musician. The audition had been tough, lasting an entire day, with close examination of her technical instrumental skill. One of the most prestigious conservatoires in the world, the Academy was founded in 1822 under the direct patronage of King George IV, and from George to Princess Diana, has enjoyed royal patronage ever since. Dating from 1830, the Academy's Royal Charter promoted 'the Cultivation of the Science of Music and the facilities for attaining perfection'. The college has consistently interpreted that as the pursuit of excellence, concerned that each student is equipped to play at the highest international level. Annie's acceptance into the Academy already marked her out for a place in the classical music elite.

From the moment Annie walked through the Academy's doors on Marylebone Road, near Regent's Park, she experienced a deep sense of foreboding. Inside this large seven-storey Edwardian building, it is dark and busy with students dashing up and down the main oak staircase. The sounds of different instruments and voices waft and intermingle from a warren of practice studios, while in the concert hall there may be the college orchestra playing, or a group rehearsing in the opera theatre.

The college walls seemed to close in on Annie, as she found this atmosphere stifling. She felt as if she was surrounded by prima donnas and found her fellow students to be highly competitive, practising six to eight hours a day on a single instrument. 'Just one look at those adolescent pimples and sports jackets and I knew instinctively that it wasn't meant to be,' she graphically recalls. 'All the boys were gay and all the girls thought they were Maria Callas. I had a huge row with my conductor because the whole thing just developed into a pose.'

Much to her dismay, opera singers walked up the stairs singing at the tops of their voices, in a show of florid indulgence that went against the grain of her strict Scottish upbringing. The mood of the college was stretched with the needle-point tension of competition and single-minded dedication, a combination that Annie found elitist and alienating.

President of the Academy Student's Union in 1990, Peter Mitchell is a rumbustious dark-haired opera student who, having finished his course, decided to move away from music and become an MP. He admits that: 'Competition is fairly fierce. By and large the students who come to the Academy are geared up to that. In music, as in all professions, people in institutions like this will want to hit the top and are prepared to compete in this field. Yes, you could say it's a hothouse, but there's also a great sense of camaraderie.'

Some students hold similar reservations to Annie. A bright, doe-eyed girl called Vicky who entered the Academy as a singer in 1987 says: 'If I'm down on any of my subjects, the tutor is always saying "shouldn't you be devoting more time to music?" There are other things in life apart from music. While it's important to be single-minded about your music, the college can often put out the wrong kind of person, producing very insular people who don't mix well with others.'

Orchestral playing, though, requires sociable rather than insular people, especially if the performer is on tour with a symphony orchestra for four weeks of the year. What Annie objected to was negative competitiveness. Although she was a confident and competent performer, the thought that she was being judged was inhibiting.

'Stress was high at the Academy because people there were very self-centred,' says Philip Sunderland, an Academy graduate and organist/choirmaster. 'The feeling when you gave a concert in the Academy was that you were faced by an audience not there to enjoy themselves, but to wait for you to make a mistake. The moment you made a slip you could envisage them giggling and writing it down. When you felt that you played well, you rarely found people coming over to congratulate you. They'd ignore you because they were jealous, whereas if you played badly they'd come and say hello!'

Annie's summary of her experience there has always been dismissive. Intimidated by the rigours of the curriculum, she felt that she had to become a mere extension of her instrument, a god-like object that seemed to enslave the student at the expense of his or her individual personality. For a girl motivated mainly by her own interpretations and musical ideas, this seemed too restrictive. The turning point came one day when she arrived at orchestral rehearsal without a piccolo. The orchestra began playing, but when the time came for Annie to play solo, there was dead silence. The conductor erupted with rage, Annie shouted back, and was then promptly thrown out.

'The place was an antiquated wreck,' she said. 'I was really miserable. I spent three dreadful years there trying to figure a way out. I worked hard to fit in, to understand my colleagues and tutors, but I felt they were so stifling, so rigid, so uninspiring. I found that classical music, despite the elements of emotion I loved, was so inflexible, too redundant in its formalism.'

Many feel that Annie has gone too far in her criticism of the place. 'It's a shame that Annie Lennox feels she has to knock the Academy. Obviously she didn't get from it what she wanted. She's been lucky and found fame and fortune elsewhere,' says Peter Mitchell. 'The institution, though, is exactly what you make it. I'd never call it antiquated and it's certainly not a wreck. She came searching for one thing and found she'd discovered something else, which turned the institution into an antiquated wreck for her.

'I think it's very forward-looking and exciting with a great future. I wouldn't underplay the fact that the Academy has a heritage, though I'd say any place shouldn't be run by the need to preserve its past. Too often the Academy has been guilty of looking to its laurels or preserving what was a great past in the Empire without looking towards the future. The Academy, though, *has* thrown away snobbish misgivings and changed its stance since Annie's time.'

Feeling distressed and isolated by the pressure to pass exams and achieve consistently high grades, Annie made many phone calls home to her parents in Aberdeen. They tried to persuade her to finish the course, finding it difficult to comprehend her unhappiness. The Academy was the best college in London; it would give her such a good training for an orchestra or chamber ensemble. To them an Academy honours degree offered endless possibilities.

The reality for many graduates was one of intense competition for places in the profession. Musicians went to orchestras or chamber ensembles whilst singers joined opera companies, maybe doing a summer season at Glyndebourne or applying to the BBC singers for work in light music. For many involved in classical playing, there were only occasional jobs and a lot of sitting by the phone. Some graduates ended up teaching, while others left music for good.

The week before her final exams, Annie anxiously decided to quit, unable to face the strain. 'It would have been hypocritical to sit those exams because I didn't believe in them,' Annie said at the time. Whether she gave up out of pure principle or because she had long given up trying is a question that has nagged her. 'I realize now that quitting was a very cowardly thing to do,' she said later. 'But at the time it seemed like an extremely dramatic and positive action and I was determined to make an impact.'

The Academy has changed in several ways since Annie's day. When she was there, the college had over 850 students, whereas by 1989 that number had been cut to 500, making the place smaller and more companionable. There was a recognition that many students coming straight from school didn't have the emotional maturity to cope with the rigours of the course, and its high degree of specialization. 'It had been pointed out by the Polytechnic & Colleges Funding Council (PCFC) that the Academy has a very high cost training, and the place was encouraged to take more post-graduates, because it believes in many ways it's rather an expensive way of undergraduates larking around, discovering themselves and their abilities,' says Mitchell.

Annie's problem was that she was more interested in singing than playing the flute, and didn't want to restrict herself to the classical idiom. It wasn't until fifteen years after Annie left the Academy that it instituted a full-time rock and jazz course, thereby acknowledging the growth and respectability of pop music. In the early 1970s, rock was still considered a vulgar commercial scam unworthy of anyone's serious attention, and it was only the classical sphere that turned out performers of real expertise. The irony is that the Academy has produced many acclaimed rock artists. As well as classical stars like the singer Aled Jones and percussionist Evelyn Glenny, its roster of former pupils includes Elton John, Joe Jackson, Jethro Tull's David Palmer and New Age supremo Michael Nyman. Unlike Annie, Elton John remembered the Academy with affection, donating a gold disc to the college during their 1990 Rag Week celebrations.

Annie's decision to leave her course meant further battling with her father, and this is probably why she reacted so strongly against the course. 'I saw Ann in Aberdeen once just after she'd left the Academy,' says Diane Mackie. 'She said she'd found it too clique-ish, and her parents weren't at all pleased that she'd left. At one time her future had been classical music, but by then she was on the verge of getting together with Dave Stewart. She said she knew they'd make it, and told me: "Look out for us!" '

Young and alone in London, hundreds of miles from home, Annie had found it hard to fit in and wanted to establish her identity separately from the experience of being a student. By 1974, she was free and beginning to forge her own musical direction. 'Much to everyone's disappointment and my relief I have to thank the Academy for giving me the opportunity to rebel against it so violently, because it led me to what I actually wanted to do. If I hadn't spent all those years practising and playing music then I don't think I would have ever had the ability and conviction to go for a career in rock.'

She got a job in a bookshop and moved into a flat with a fellow employee, Steve Tomlin. Delving into his record collection one day, she pulled out a copy of Stevie Wonder's 1972 album *Talking Book*. Listening to the first few bars of 'I Believe (When I Fall in Love It Will Be Forever)', she became transfixed. The plangent, emotive soul could have mirrored a faultline deep within Annie's psyche.

The song was revelatory as well as romantic, registering her love for a new kind of music unrestricted by the classical tradition.

'Stevie Wonder seemed to have a new definition of perfection, instead of the precision with the flute that the school had drilled into me,' she later recalled. 'Those songs touched me – the joy, the freedom, the form of expression. It made me realize that the person I was turning into liked *that* kind of music, not Hector Berlioz concerts.'

It was a significant choice, a kind of conceptual soul which bridged the Motown of her teenage days at Aberdeen Beach Ballroom and the more intellectual ideas of her hippy transformation. The Eurythmics' music has similarly bridged this divide, and ironically over ten years later she was to work with Stevie Wonder when he played an inspired harmonica for the track 'There Must Be an Angel (Playing with My Heart)'. To hear Stevie Wonder playing on a song that was dedicated to him anyway was heaven,' Annie said afterwards.

She also listened to Joni Mitchell, taking inspiration from the songwriter's articulate, complex structures. She realized that pop wasn't necessarily throwaway, that it had an intricate quality and emotion just as precise as the most rigorous classical piece. This fuelled her determination to create her own spontaneous response to music, one based on song writing and singing. Annie began to compose lyrics and sing them to her friends, gratified by their warm response. 'I discovered I could silence a room and have people almost moved to tears,' she said.

Having found her liquid soul voice, she concentrated less on flute playing, and took lessons with an Australian vocal tutor who told her somewhat dubiously to 'sing like a black nigger'.

'I didn't know about octaves and all that stuff. Everyone thinks I must know about all the female singers, like Bessie Smith or Lena Horne, but I don't,' Annie said to Max Bell at *The Face* ten years later. 'This tutor taught me how to sing with soul, with abandonment. *Thinking* about singing gets in the way of communication.'

Singing was the one form of musical expression that hadn't been beaten out of her by the Academy, and she approached it with relish. She took a job as a waitress, spending her spare hours writing songs and scanning the classified sections of music papers for singing work. Eventually she applied for a job with a folk-rock band called Dragon's Playground. Her Scottish folk-singing background stood her in good stead, and she was chosen from 250 applicants.

Excited at her first break, Annie was soon to be disappointed. The first night she sang to a completely inert crowd, more interested in beer and darts than the rock band disturbing their peace. She stuck it out for three months, touring pubs and working men's clubs, sandwiched between bingo callers and stand-up comedians. Annie's fragile sensibility soon began to wilt in the face of such indifference, so it was with renewed hope that she left and joined her second outfit, an eleven-piece socialist jazz-rock orchestra called Red Brass that gave her room to experiment with flute and percussion as well as sing.

Playing key venues such as London's 100 Club and going on a national tour gave Annie some vital live experience. It also allowed her to make clearer choices about the direction she wanted to take. Although Red Brass were an organized outfit who'd already recorded an album, *Silence Is Consent*, she didn't find jazz-fusion inspiring. To her the pursuit of pop was paramount.

After leaving Red Brass Annie tried vocal cabaret in a duo with another singer called Joy Dey. Having met through an advert in *The Stage*, they both knew they wanted to sing together, but their approach was naïve and haphazard, and they had little idea of exactly how they wanted to present themselves. Through an advert in the same paper they took on a manager who christened them the Stocking Tops, a corny showbiz name that they felt unqualified to resist. He set up gigs in South London nightclubs where most audiences greeted them with monumental indifference.

Joy and Annie braved it for a few months, travelling round the country in the former's rattling Ford Anglia, trying to get bookings. With just a few contacts and very little clout, they realized they were unlikely to make much progress, and decided to quit before they sunk in a mire of cover versions. Annie now recalls her 'chitlin circuit' days with a darkly judgemental backward glance. 'It was so tacky and sad. Although it was bloody awful I learned from it. There are thousands of no-hopers in those situations, still dreaming of stardom in some seedy, clapped-out pub doing Beatles and Simon & Garfunkel cover versions. God rest their weary heads!'

Annie continued her odd-jobbing, waiting tables at a West End health restaurant and then a Kensington wine bar, still nurturing an ambition to sing. It wasn't until she got a job waitressing at a health restaurant in Hampstead called Pippins that she finally came near to attaining her goal.

TOURIST TRADE

The process of musical exploration that began the moment Annie stepped out from the doors of the Academy was a long, slow, confused quest to find a stage identity and a unified sound. Annie began her musical career as a strictly classical student, intent on succeeding within the precise confines of orchestral work. For a long time it was the only approach she knew.

Quitting the Academy and taking up singing opened up a whole new vista, but it was still one that left her uncertain and struggling. Musical expertise was her primary interest, with the notion of stardom placed firmly in the background. When the time came for the Tourists to take off, Annie felt uneasy about the lead role expected of her and she became a reluctant rock star.

By autumn 1976, Annie was living in a small bedsit in Camden, waitressing during the day, setting up a second-hand clothes stall at the market every weekend with her friend Margo, and composing songs every night on her harmonium. It was a solitary, circumscribed life, with no defined goal apart from a love of music.

One Sunday Annie started talking to a guy called Paul Jacobs, who ran the nearby record stall. He recognized in Annie a kindred spirit, someone thoughtful, disaffected and totally driven by music. 'We seemed to have a lot in common,' he said. 'In a way we were both very lonely people.' They became close friends, and a few weeks later Paul asked to hear some of her songs. She performed for him in her bedsit, singing a selection of the thirty or so songs she already had stashed away in exercise books under her bed.

Jacobs was so impressed with her vocals that he decided to introduce her to an old musical friend whom he'd last seen running a record shop called Small Mercies, in Kilburn. Jacobs was sure that Dave Stewart, a bedraggled neo-hippy with a nifty guitar, would appreciate Annie's spontaneous musical approach, and he arranged a meeting between them in the Hampstead restaurant where she worked.

When he met Annie, Dave had already been through the record company mill, and was able to give her advice about a dubious contract she had been offered. He started his career as a sixteen-year-old folk singer in Sunderland, achieved a brief spurt of fame when signed to Elton John's label as a guitarist in the band Longdancer, and then sank temporarily into a world of drugs, busking, and intermittent session-playing for various bands, performing everything from acid rock to pure Afro-funk. When he met Annie he had been working on some demos with his old Tyneside friend Peet Coombes, and on the advice of a friend, the three decided to throw in their lot together and approach Logo Records, a promising independent company ran by Geoff Hannington.

A pragmatic, bespectacled man who smokes cigars and wears business suits, Hannington now works from his office in Holborn doing publishing and management deals. A London boy who began his career in the 1960s marketing for Philips Records, then the epicentre of the booming British music industry, Hannington proved to be a good hustler. Before long he became marketing manager at RCA, steering Bowie's career through the 1970s. The entrepreneurial bug bit, and he left the corporate structure to form his own publishing and record companies with his partner Olav Wyper. 'We bought Transatlantic Records, an existing label which was owned by Granada TV and had a lot of folk artists, like Ralph McTell, John Renbourne and the guitarist Bert Jansch. It also had the first folk-rock group, Pentangle.'

Transatlantic was the parent company for Logo Music and Logo Records, the latter quickly becoming identified with dependable mid-1970s rock- and folk-inspired song writing – a combination that was present in much of the Tourists' early material. The label was not high profile. 'We didn't want to develop too many bands at once,' says Hannington. 'Apart from the Tourists the only other big group we had was Meal Ticket, a good solid rock band whose first LP came out the very day the Sex Pistols happened. So everything changed immediately. Still, they were great guys, they went on to do three or four albums.'

Sifting through his post one day in early 1977, Hannington picked up a tape that had been sent to him by an unknown guitarist/song-writer called Dave Stewart. 'I thought it was good, and there was a woman's voice on it that I thought was terrific, so when I told him to come in I said bring the girl too.'

Dave, Annie and Peet Coombes marched into the Logo office in St Martin's Lane and performed a few numbers on acoustic guitar and piano. They were promptly offered a deal. 'I immediately saw they had charisma, and saw how good they were,' claims Hannington. 'We offered them a contract but they only wanted a publishing deal because they just wanted to be a song-writing team. We eventually persuaded them to put a record out and we'd see how it went.'

Broke and anxious for cash, Dave, Annie and Peet Coombes each accepted a cheque for £500 and a publishing deal that they would regret for many years to come. It was rumoured that the company was only interested in Annie, confident that they could mould her into a kind of white Joan Armatrading and they were prepared to drop Dave and Peet for the cheaper option of session musicians. 'Good Lord no!' says Hannington. 'We signed them up as a group of people that went through several formats.' Whatever the original plans were, Annie steadfastly refused to do anything without Dave. He was her partner, and it was with him that she intended to stay.

The three friends called themselves, rather uninspiringly, Catch, and in October 1977 released a competent pop record called 'Borderline' that stiffed everywhere apart from Holland, where it was a minor hit. 'They wanted Catch over in Holland to do TV promotion for the single,' says Hannington. 'But Dave and Annie weren't sure. They delayed it and delayed it until I had EMI distributors on the phone saying "What's going on?".

'The band then came to me saying they'd changed their minds, they didn't want to promote Catch and had decided to become a fully fledged band. Suddenly there were three new musicians and they'd changed into all this punk gear.' Annie was beginning to experiment with her appearance, and picking up on the eccentric energy of punk, she dyed a blue streak in her hair. At first Logo baulked at this change of line up and direction, but then went with the band.

Excitedly pursuing what seemed at the time to be a madcap musical adventure, the refurbished Catch decided to augment the band in order to go out on tour, and enlisted Jim Toomey on drums. A pragmatic Cockney who'd cut his teeth playing on the Continent with Colin Blunstone, Toomey was slightly taken aback when he first met Annie, Dave and Peet. 'I thought they were just a bunch of hippies at the time, you know. Real nutcases', was his original verdict. Essentially fun-loving rather than existential, he anchored the group's sound with a simple, loud pop drumbeat.

Two extra musicians, Chris Parren and Andy Brown, who had played on the Catch sessions, soon left – one to spend time with his family, the other to go to America. As replacements were urgently needed, Toomey rang his Malaysian friend Eddie Chinn, a quiet but thorough bass player with a mandarin moustache and a long pony tail who'd worked every kind of session from mad funk to commercial jingles. He played his first gig with the band at London's premier late

1970s punk venue, the Hope & Anchor in Islington, with the chord structure written on a piece of paper at his feet. He passed the test.

'They were a bit raw around the edges for their first live gigs, but that's to be expected,' recalls Hannington. With the group organized, their next priority was finding a new name. At that time, the full force of punk had broken and the live scene was scattered with countless short, sharp variations. After the purple poetics of the early 1970s generation which had spawned lengthy pretentious names like Barclay James Harvest and Emerson Lake & Palmer, or such abstract concepts as Genesis and Deep Purple, the punk generation opted for the simplicity of the 1960s beat groups with that unambiguous use of the prefix 'the'. After the Vibrators, the Sex Pistols, the Adverts, the Rezillos, and a bus ride past a Tourist Information Centre, the Tourists were born.

Already with a Logo publishing deal under their belt, the band signed a lengthy contract with the same company – a hasty move that left them locked in a six-album contract taking them up to 1984. At the time the Tourists had a pay-the-advance-now-think-later policy, a combination of naïvety and lack of attention to detail that would rebound on them once the band encountered difficulties. In the beginning they even asked Logo to manage them as well. 'We said, well we can't really do that because we're your record label and you have a publishing deal with us. A manager is supposed to negotiate with the record company. We gave them a list of possible managers – they went through two or three different ones over a period of months – none fitted the bill. Then they eventually joined up with Lloyd Beiny and Mike Dolan, that is Arnakata.'

At first it seemed deliciously simple. Annie was happy to hang out with her new male gang, dusting off some of those old songs and trying out her vocal performance in an upbeat power pop arrangement. The band spent the first few months of 1978 recording at Conny Plank's studio in Cologne and returned to London in April with a collection of songs and a well-honed determination to achieve chart success. Producer of the German improvisatory electro group Can, Plank had worked with Dave and Annie the previous summer when they recorded an offbeat song 'Exclusive' with a Crouch End eccentric, Creepy John Thomas. He gave their songs that light electro touch and powerful rhythmic feel. The lyrics and overall arrangements within the band, however, were not so focused.

The Tourists' approach harked back to the more hippy folk-rock Beefheart/Byrds feel of the late 1960s than to the mangled garage beat beloved of their punk contemporaries. This earned them immediate and unforgiving vilification. 'We were influenced by punk but we weren't a punk group. It was very difficult for us because I felt you had to conform – and if you didn't, people didn't bother with you,' said Annie.

With their amalgam of differing musical styles and mixed sartorial message, the Tourists played on the punk patch, but they were never taken seriously as part of the scene. Punk was direct in its requirements: short sets, skin-tight trousers, plenty of grit, humour and cynicism, no beards, no flares and above all, no namby pamby hippydom. The Tourists consistently broke these rules, yet were bewildered when they played punk venues like the Nashville in West London and were met with spikey hostility. One night they played there a bouncer laid into a Tourist friend with karate kicks and punches. 'We thought he'd killed him,' said Annie.

Another evening Scottish punk outfit the Rezillos spray-canned their dressing room with anti-Tourist graffiti, seeing the band as imposters. The Rezillos' vocalist and Scotland's leading punk singer Fay Fife apparently attacked Annie with a deliberately Scottish insult: 'I'm Fay Fife, where are you fae?' The girl from Aberdeen walked away in disgust.

The internal codes of British youth culture have always been strict, proud and emblematic, and in the late 1970s they became more confrontational than ever before. Despite the chaotic look of punk, its style and attitudes were stringent. Imposters were spotted a mile off, and treated with disdain. With Annie's day-glo jumble sale look incorporating everything from bright polka dots to stage vaudeville, she was lodged under the 'fun and quirky' end of punk. 'The trouble with the punk thing was that the music was great but so many of the people looked really drab. I was just doing my bit to try and bring a little colour back into things,' she said.

Jim Toomey, in his straight tie, straight suits and chopped hair, could have been taken for a mod, whilst Peet Coombes exuded the straggly hair and baggy jackets of a Northern Angry Young Man, and with an Oriental jazz-funk style Eddie Chinn looked like he had accidentally stepped into the wrong band. Dave's psychedelic jackets and cowboy boots, meanwhile, marked him out as a 1960s Sergeant Pepper reject. The combination was as visually confusing as it was eye-catching; a reflection of the disparate motivations within the band.

Annie also felt nervous at this time defining herself by a particular look, unsure about the image she wanted to project. 'It's all about fashion, isn't it?' she once said exasperatedly. 'If some kid catches me wearing one particular outfit on the street, they grab hold of me and ask, "What are you – a mod, or a punk or *what?*" They seem to need to identify themselves with fashions in clothes *and* music, to be part of something that's bigger than the individual.'

Musically she hadn't yet come to the fore with her song writing, and it was accepted that Peet Coombes would write all the songs, sharing lead vocals with Annie. A shy, moody individual, Peet was difficult to work with and difficult to fathom. His lyrics, likewise, were often abstract and impenetrable to the point of saying nothing. Words like 'Blind among the flowers/Nothing means nothing to me' or 'The useless duration of time', for instance, tended to leave the listener more bewildered than energized.

The Tourists' strongest point, however, was the blinding, driving power pop rhythm that swept along with swathes of light harmony and melody. Live they performed well, with Annie laying down the basis of her future stagecraft, ever-watchful of the audience, constantly challenging herself to make them move. While Jim drummed enthusiastically, Eddie mysteriously stalked the back of the stage, Dave occasionally swivelled his hips and Peet stood stock still staring into the mike, Annie traversed the stage as if she owned it, covering every square foot with a breadth of mime and intonation that made her an automatic focal point.

'Ours is eclectic music with no blinkers,' she said. 'If we want to do something we're not thinking about fashion. We're very pro getting good feelings across and getting people to react. It's got to be total commitment. Really.'

The initial reviews of their live gigs were favourable, and they received generous coverage in the press ranging from 'very catchy, very attractive tunes which they belt out with precision and confidence' (*Sounds*) to 'Their musical gift is of the rock'n'reel variety. File under infectious fun' (*NME*). Much of this attention was down to Annie's striking peroxide blonde image and her colourful wardrobe. Gone were the mousey fair-haired days of the Academy, those first unconfident years on the road. 'I was sick of sitting in my bedsit with my harmonium, and peroxiding my hair was a very dramatic thing to do. My hair was a different colour and I felt a different colour.' Annie was experimenting with a vengeance.

Having built up a strong fan following, the band returned to Cologne and recorded their eponymous debut album with Conny Plank. The release of *The Tourists* on 8 June 1979 proved to be a disappointment. Like many bands who generate a strong energy on stage, they were unable to duplicate that quality on vinyl, and many reviewers were equivocal. *Sounds* heralded it as a 'confusion' of 'misguided excursions', saying that Conny Plank's production made it sound 'as if they're playing in a deserted swimming pool surrounded by sand bags to muffle the echo'.

Veering between straightahead pop rock, mock reggae and Fairport Convention/Byrds-type folk inflections, the album lacks a unified charge, moving from punk to shades of Led Zepplin's 'Stairway to Heaven'. The humalong opening track 'Blind Among The Flowers' was released as a single, but failed to move higher than Number 52 in the charts. Its follow-up, a folk-rock strumalong called 'The Loneliest Man In The World' was slightly more successful, reaching Number 32. It was their next single, though, that launched them into mainstream commercial pop in a way that none of the band had anticipated or desired.

'They'd been in the studio, and of the eleven songs on their next album *Reality Effect*, only one wasn't their own – it was a Dusty Springfield song. I thought it was an instant hit and suggested they release it,' says Hannington. 'They came back to me saying "Yes, why not", and it became a huge hit.'

The Tourists' 'I Only Want To Be With You' was a cover version of Dusty Springfield's 1963 hit, recorded 'for fun' and released in an era when 1960s covers were decidedly unfashionable. It wasn't until the late 1980s that artists like the Pet Shop Boys and Marc Almond made 1960s hits cult material, actually working with the original stars to re-create a 1960s pop sound. In the throes of punk and New Wave at the end of the 1970s this was seen as a blatantly commercial, retrogressive move. 'This silly version of the Dusty Springfield classic replaces precocity with predictability,' wrote *Sounds* in a typical music press response.

Ironically though, the track has lasted as one of the Tourists' strongest: ebullient, bright and upbeat, its clapping, power punk instrumentation is the perfect showcase for Annie's bell-like voice. For the first time her vocals have been allowed to emerge. This, coupled with the band's first TV appearance on 'Top Of The Pops', where Annie spontaneously high-kicked her way through the song in a pair of stripey trousers, huge plastic earrings and a blonde beehive, remains welded onto public memory.

The record was a massive hit, reaching Number 4 and staying in the charts for sixteen weeks. Its follow-up 'So Good To Be Back Home' was released three months later, at the beginning of February 1980, with a similar inviting pop backbeat. Reaching Number 8, it was to be their second and last Top Ten success. The Tourists' star was as brief as it was bright, descending very quickly.

'We rose to fame on a song that came out almost by accident,' says Annie, 'We did it so casually at the time, but the press absolutely slaughtered us, and you can take a beating for so long – no one came to ask me what I felt like.'

Because of the single's success, the Tourists' second album *Reality Effect* sold well, getting to Number 23 in the album charts. For the cover the band went for a look that was suggestive and experimental: Annie sits down to tea wearing a white wedding dress, surrounded by her male cohorts, who are also dressed in white with lunatic expressions and liberally splattered with different coloured paint. The way-out cover didn't mask the uniformity of the 1960s-influenced power pop tracks inside. Although they possessed two strong ideas – a driving guitar and a sense of harmony – these became diluted in a muted, temperate mix. Reviewers' reactions, too, were mixed, ranging from 'totally forgettable slabs of posey sophistication' to 'clever modern meticulously produced pop'.

The Tourists built up a wide following, doing their first national tour in summer 1979 supporting Roxy Music, followed by a European stint in the winter and a large projected world tour the following year titled, prophetically 'The Last Laugh Tour'. Despite their mounting success, Annie's tone in interviews began to get defensive.

'I'm into quality. Good quality sounds with a quality message. Not just saying what everybody's said before. That's very unfashionable I suppose,' she said. Ever since she had left the Academy and become involved in mainstream pop, Annie felt uneasy about the frontwoman role ascribed to her, along with the hype about her being the British Debbie Harry. She rejected the uncomplicated star status so many other performers enthusiastically embraced.

The truth was that as a very able frontwoman who worked hard on stage to involve the audience, Annie was bound to be the centre of interest. She played that down by stressing that the Tourists were a *band*, not just a cute girl singer with a bunch of guys at the back. 'I'm a minor part,' she said, rather disingenuously. In attempting to minimize the impact of her stage presence, Annie was trying to control or curtail a public image that she didn't feel comfortable with. When a journalist asked her bluntly: 'How do you find being a rock star?' she immediately retorted: 'I'm not a rock star. Rock star is ludicrous. I detest the word star – it's a hackneyed phrase that belongs to Hollywood, it doesn't belong to nowadays. I would accept possibly . . . personality.'

Coming from an insular town in Scotland, and having studied classical music, a form of music that was aesthetic rather than glitzy and vulgar, Annie felt wary of the absolutes of the rock world, hating the constant attention and trial by media that came with the job.

'People think just because we did a Dusty Springfield song, that's an end in itself, y'know – stick on a label, *categorize*. They seem to think we're just a bunch of stupid thickos who're only in it for the money!' she said belligerently to a *Smash Hits* journalist in 1980. 'There's a great deal behind this group, and a great deal to be found out about this group. But nobody in the press ever gives us a *chance!* It's bloody unfair! Having bad press all the time limits our audience. Audiences really *are* affected by what they read.'

Although Tourists' concerts were packed out, people bought their records and they had a large faithful following, the band felt constantly aggrieved that they weren't being taken seriously. Headlines in *NME* like: 'The Tourists talk about suicide – Graham Lock wishes they did', had stung.

Not content with being seen as 'just a pop band', Dave, Annie and Peet were anxious for the depth of their abilities to be recognized. The problem was that the band didn't gel as personalities, and although each was musically proficient, they weren't clear about the group's overall direction. An act has to have a burning belief and conviction in its music to survive, along with an ability to pursue its own vision regardless of press opinion. If, deep down, the Tourists weren't fully convinced by themselves, they weren't going to convince a group of cynical hacks.

Part of the problem lay with the fact that Peet Coombes wrote all the lyrics, but was not a good communicator in interviews. Hence Dave and Annie were often put in the position of articulating his personal ramblings. 'What we're talking about is, like, human politics, personal politics,' Dave once said, unspecifically. 'We're singing about things from the inside – like a group from the 1960s – because the inside is where all the change is going to come from. We'd like to get people to think for themselves again.'

Their defensive reaction was an attempt to paper over the cracks and lack of confidence that were already surfacing between band members. Dave and Annie defended Peet's lyrics in public, but frustratedly, they were anxious to develop their own song-writing potential. At one point Dave acknowledged that they possessed an *ideal* of the band in their heads, yet found difficulty translating that into the actual music. In referring to the 'fantastic resonance' of the instrumental tracks played by a band like Talking Heads as his ideal, Dave admitted: 'I think we're at a stage where we know what we're trying to do, but haven't quite managed it on record.'

Meanwhile relations between the Tourists and their Logo record company were gradually deteriorating. The band had signed a management deal with Arnakata, two self-assured music businessmen named Lloyd Beiny and Mike Dolan, who wanted to negotiate them onto a major label.

The Tourists were at loggerheads with Logo. 'We wanted to develop them as a rock band like Fleetwood Mac,' says Hannington. 'But they wanted to go into a different direction. We never *forced* them to do anything, though – none of the discussions we had with them were about that.'

He also disputes Annie's suggestion that they were pressuring her to be a dolly bird frontwoman: 'At no time did I say anything that could've given her that impression, we never discussed anything like that. I had absolutely no creative input – I'm a record man not a Svengali. I found her to be a very nice, polite lady. She was the driving force behind the band. When she and Dave came to see me she did a lot of the talking, she had a very clear idea of what she wanted. Although Peet wrote most of the three albums, he was quieter, more introverted, more in the background.'

By this time the Tourists desperately wanted to leave Logo, while the company secured a court injunction that would prevent them signing to another label. Arnakata entered into protracted negotiations, with both sides refusing to compromise.

'Arnakata rang me saying, "We'd like to buy the Tourists from you and sign them to a major company." We replied that we wanted to keep them. By that time we'd invested a lot in them and wanted to see it through,' says Hannington. 'Beiny said, "Well in that case they'll leave anyway," and he sent a letter saying we were in breach of contract.'

Logo took Arnakata to court and lost the first round. They appealed against the verdict and won, gaining a court injunction that claimed Logo had a valid contract. 'From that moment on we just talked to the management, the Tourists wouldn't speak to us,' recalls Hannington. 'Beiny was anxious for them to leave because he was negotiating a big contract with CBS. After a few months of court cases, though, CBS were no longer interested.'

When Logo realized that the band might split anyway, a compromise was reached. Negotiations began with RCA Records, and a deal was structured between Arnakata, Logo and the Tourists whereby RCA acquired recording rights, buying everything except American royalties. 'I backed out then,' says Hannington, his opinion misty and mellowed with the benefit of hindsight. 'I wasn't bitter – more disappointed. I was very upset about it for a while because it's like a proper relationship breaking up. But you can't get bitter in this business, that's what the music industry's like. I was pleased that we launched such great talent. It's not often such talent walks through your doors like that.'

Once the Tourists had signed their major deal with RCA they went on a low-budget coast-to-coast tour of the States. The trip was recuperative and an escape from the prolonged, nagging anxieties they'd been through back home. They travelled in Dolly Parton's old tour bus, reviving their energies by playing forty gigs over a period of six months, finishing up in Montserrat to record their third album *Luminous Basement*. Produced by Tom Allom, it is louder and more authoritative than their first two albums. The American tour had left them aggressive, more determined to experiment than before, so this had the effect of pulling the band several ways, between forthright rock-out on tracks like 'Walls and Foundations' and such juddering format pop as 'Round Round Blues'.

Although Coombes wrote most of the lyrics, one of the few songs credited to Annie presages the emotional landscape to come. 'One Step Nearer the Edge' is moody, bleak and soulful, with a raw clumsiness in the lyrics ('It's so uneasing/To think you're with me all the time') showing her trying out a new, more personal style.

By the time they returned to Britain, the band realized that the Tourists bubble had burst. The critics trashed *Luminous Basement* as 'self-consciously quirky, a cloying mixture of platitudes and pomposity' (*NME*); 'So many of the Tourists best ideas were other people's ten or more years ago. I'm still not convinced that they *work* as purveyors of pop' (*Sounds*).

The beefy upbeat harmonies of 'Don't Say I Told You So', the single that trailed the album's release in November 1980, failed to ignite record buyers' enthusiasm, and didn't make it past Number 40 in the charts. Record company wrangling, press hostility and the absence of hits were taking their toll; as in the ensuing 'Luminous Tour', many venues were half-empty. The stage show included a woman cavorting in a body stocking, luminous graphics and back projection, yet despite the flashy presentation long-standing tensions in the group were beginning to swallow the Tourists' confidence. With one reviewer describing their stage set as 'an express train going through a five-bar gate', it seemed that what the Tourists lacked in depth they made up for with hurtling speed.

It's astonishing that rather than winding the band down in its closing stages, they wound the situation up by taking on an impossibly ambitious tour of Australia, Europe and America. Arguments that had surfaced during the recording of 'Luminous Basement' resurfaced on the road. Not only was Annie impatient with Peet's lyrical limitations and lack of communication, she and Dave were aware that Jim Toomey's proficient rock'n'roll drumming was not up to the more complex electronic rhythms they were beginning to explore.

'I think if Peet had had a band on his own without me, it would have been better and he might have been happier,' Annie said afterwards, 'I never found him easy to get along with and I always felt a bit intimidated by him – and I'm sure he felt the same about me.'

Glum and alienated, Peet didn't make a good travelling companion, while Annie, wrought by the internal pressures, put herself under an even greater strain. This manifested itself dramatically when halfway through the Australian tour she collapsed on stage in a seizure of exhaustion and hypertension. By then, none of the band were committed to keeping up the charade.

'I'm fed up,' Peet announced one morning.

'We're fed up too,' said Annie and Dave.

'Let's pack it in then.'

'OK.'

Peet played half the dates on the tour to keep up appearances, then returned to England leaving the Tourists to complete their stint as a four-piece. The news officially broke when the band reached Bangkok at the end of the tour in March 1981, and the music papers prominently featured Annie's unusually honest 'resignation' statement:

'Our musical attitudes were becoming polarized, as well as having to cope with our steadily deteriorating personal relationships. I'm greatly relieved at the decision and glad it's all over, but it was fun while it lasted.'

Peet went on to form a new group with Eddie Chin called Acid Drops. It wasn't a successful venture, and as Dave and Annie moved towards greater fame, he dropped out of the limelight and into obscurity. 'It's very sad what happened to him. I saw him ten years later, living with his girl friend in an awful house in Highgate,' says Hannington. 'He wasn't working, so he was very pleased to get an old royalty cheque from me.' Jim Toomey, meanwhile, returned to session playing like so many rock drummers before him, and then moved to Australia.

As well as the post-Tourist emotional debris, there were debts of £15,000 – Dave and Annie's share of the £38,000 still owed to Arnakata. 'The Tourists made a stack of money and a lot of people got rich, but not the band!' Annie said ruefully. The debts would prove to be a nagging problem for years to come, dragging on into their career as Eurythmics and leaving them with a determinedly protective scepticism in dealing with the pop world.

Despite a sour taste after the Tourists split, Annie kept in her mind the memory of the day she returned to Aberdeen to play her first gig. It had been a fancy dress college ball at the end of February 1980, with champagne corks popping and the air of a celebration. 'Hello Aberdeen, it's good to be back!' Annie had yelled, before they launched into a victorious live set. The place was jammed with fans and the local reporter could hardly contain his hyperbole: 'The return of the conquering hero!' he wrote in the *Aberdeen Evening Express*. 'Annie, like Samson, stood in the centre pushing the pillars of sound apart to project her voice to the fore.'

The following day the Lord Provost William Fraser presented the band with a Scotstar Award for 'Most Original Show', a music industry award in recognition of their sales of LPs and cassettes. By the time the Tourists had finished, their LP *Reality Effect* had gone platinum. Annie's decisions, first to leave Aberdeen, then to break with the conventional path of classical teaching to pursue a different vision, had now been vindicated.

She felt in a stronger position to reconcile and reinforce her relationship with her parents, whom she hadn't seen properly since the band took off. 'My parents are absolutely over the moon,' she said, 'because something is working out for me. I suppose if I'd said, "Look, I'm not going to stick at this and I'm going to have a husband, kids and somewhere nice to live" then they would be pleased. But only if it was what I wanted. I'm lucky to have good parents who just want me to be happy – but there have been struggles. I rebelled and found it hard to relate to them. Now it's led to a togetherness even though I might be hundreds of miles away.'

With the break-up of the band just over a year later, she would need their support again. Her time with the Tourists had been heady and tough, but once that network of distractions and interests disappeared, Annie had no one to fall back on but Dave and herself.

3

I Got You Babe

DAVE

'She was one of the most radiant and healthiest people I'd met in a long time. She looked completely different to a lot of the people I was involved with who were ashen and grey and lived by night. She has a different attitude. She was fresh and I was immediately knocked out by her.

'I'd been taking LSD every day for a year. That sounds lighthearted, but when I look back on it I was really lucky not to end up the way most people did. She was really the turning point because she was someone I wanted to be all right *for*. When I met Annie I was about as far off as you could be into orbit. She was my saving grace.'

ANNIE

'Just before I met Dave I had reached a point where I decided I was suffering too much. London can be a cruel, heartless place. I was ready to go home, to become a flute teacher. Then Dave walked in, and that was the moment that changed my life. He was the first person to take an interest in me.

'It wasn't so much attraction at first sight as a question of compatability with someone you feel totally at ease with. He's the kindest person I've ever met. I just fell in love with him. I felt there hadn't been anybody in my life. You read about artists and how they live, and the romantic way in which nothing really matters except their art. Well, Dave was the first person I'd met who was completely like that.

'When we first met I was really keen to write, sing and make records, but I hadn't a clue how to go about it. With Dave I could do all these things.'

IT TAKES TWO

One day in the early 1960s in a California recording studio, the pretty dark-haired teenage Cherilyn Sarkisian, nicknamed Cher, stood in front of the mike and opened her mouth to sing. Nothing came out. She was terror-stricken.

Her new lover, a rising young songwriter named Sonny Bono, was producing the disc independently. A tireless promoter of her career, he had met Cher in a coffee shop next to radio station KFWB when he was working for the great pop impresario Phil Spector. A kind of A&R man and jack-of-all-trades for Spector's recording sessions, Sonny had previous experience as a producer on the staff of LA's Specialty Records, and was able to persuade his boss to give Cher backing vocal work. He then managed to get him to produce her first solo recording, a single called 'Ringo, I Love You' on the Annette label which unfortunately flopped and caused Spector to lose interest.

Although she was young and inexperienced Cher had good pedigree, groomed for the stage from a young age by her mother, a minor Hollywood actress. By the time she and Sonny met, Cher's smoky good looks and perfect poise were in place, and all she needed to work on was her vocal presentation. Despite the lack of success in Spector's studio, Sonny remained convinced of her potential, financing the next record himself.

Aware that Cher's initial failure had made her nervous and given her a bout of mike fright, Sonny decided to sing with her to bolster her confidence. Their recording of 'Baby Don't Go' was the first time they worked together as a team, and although the song wasn't a hit until they became famous a few years later, it established Sonny and Cher as musical partners.

It was in 1964, when they got married and signed to Atlantic Records' Atco subsidiary, that their career began to take off. At first it was mainly Sonny's song writing that paid the rent, but in August 1965, Atlantic released the record that was to become their anthem: 'I Got You Babe'. Arriving with a burst of bouncy optimism, the record announced Sonny and Cher as a husband and wife team, a model of togetherness and hippy excellence. Their stark image – she dark, him fair – was compounded by the clothes they wore, an unusual amalgam of bobcat fur jackets and multicoloured stripes that they had designed themselves. In 1964 their earnings came to a total of $10,000, but after the success of 'I Got You Babe' singles and accompanying album sales catapulted, making them an estimated $2 million the following year.

At first they attracted a huge teen audience, before successfully making the transition to a more adult, supper club market in the late 1960s. This image of them as a pop couple maturing together enabled them to secure their own TV show in the early 1970s. 'The Sonny and Cher Show' on CBS became prime-time TV, a showcase for their musical, comic and vocal skills.

As Cher began to record more and more on her own, and Sonny developed his off-stage interests, the couple grew apart. In February 1974 their marriage dissolved, and 'The Sonny and Cher Show' was cancelled. The pair tried to continue their TV careers with two separate shows – 'Cher' on CBS and 'The Sonny Comedy Hour' on ABC – but neither did well. They were brought back together for another Sonny and Cher series, but the magic had gone and the show soon came off the air. Cher went on to become a top rock vocalist and award-winning actress, while Sonny stayed in the backrooms of entertainment before opting for a political career, being elected Republican mayor of Palm Springs in 1988. He also moved into catering, opening a restaurant and salad bar in LA.

Sonny and Cher were successful as an entity only as long as they were together as a romantic couple. With album titles like *Look At Us* and *The Two Of Us*, it was obvious that their pop marriage was the selling point, one that they skilfully marketed and played to the hilt. The wide public profile of such a pop couple was unprecedented.

It had been established as an example of excellence in the movies, with Bogart and Bacall, Ginger Rogers and Fred Astaire and later Burton and Taylor, but the pop industry was uneasy about creating superstar couples. The portrayal of sexual tension and romance on screen needs two protagonists, whereas in pop music, the emphasis is on the single performer. Pop legends tend to be built around an individual idol, one voice and one style. When Elvis sings 'Don't Be Cruel' or Buddy Holly whoops 'Oh Boy', the listener enters into a kind of emotional contract, with the song providing for the fan a direct one-to-one personal articulation of feeling.

Even in a group there is one person, usually the lead vocalist, who becomes the focal point. The singer occupies pop's most powerful position, taking that pivotal place in music where emotions are put into words. Two lead singers inevitably dilute the impact, hence McCartney and Lennon taking it in turns to sing lead vocals in the Beatles. Pop's strongest duos, such as the Everly Brothers or the latter-day Scottish outfit the Proclaimers, are usually twinned and interchangeable, so there is no room for confusion in the record buyer's mind about the image they are consuming.

Pop couples are risky. Movie partners attract a more healthy box office status because their on-screen personas are enduring and permanent, glamorously fixed on celluloid. In the music industry the star couple is more of a novelty, less bankable and not so easy to market. A teenage fan wants to feel that an artist is singing personally for him or her, and the knowledge that someone is attached elsewhere breaks that illusion.

Sonny and Cher's response to this problem was to play up their romantic status rather than disguise it, a gamble that worked. Their success was built on a complementary stage act that incorporated elements of comedy and an image that projected their personalities *outward* – any hint of exclusivity or insularity would have lessened their popular appeal.

The music industry is full of husband and wife teams, but usually one is in the background, with the other featured upfront. A common dynamic is the man in the background acting as a mentor, with the woman singing and taking on the bulk of the stage personality. With Ike and Tina Turner, he recruited her as top Ikette for his raucous Kings of Rhythm revue, while Phil Spector liked to think he was a production Svengali for his Ronette wife, Ronnie (Veronica Bennett). Later, in the 1980s, Emilio Estefan courted and married Gloria, the lead singer of his band the Miami Sound Machine, and the two built up a solid musical identity based on a new Latin-pop scene in Florida.

Pop couples create a special form of energy while they last, galvanizing each other and concentrating their creative potential; but the pressures of touring, promotion and stardom place an impossible strain on the relationship. As well as the love affair that supposedly binds them, there is the pull of competition, jealousy and insecurity that inevitably affects their musical output. In Sonny and Cher's case, the marriage broke up as Cher began to pursue a more independent career, and for Ike and Tina Turner, while Ike was initially content for his wife to sing upfront, the more her funky talent was singled out, the more possessive and abusive he became. She escaped through divorce and after many painful years alone on the road, forged her own phenomenally successful musical direction. It is rumoured that the reclusive Phil Spector, too, felt threatened by his wife's position in the limelight, keeping her hidden away in his Los Angeles mansion. His relationship with her became a gruesome pop legend that was fictionalized in James Robert Baker's bizarre 1986 novel *Fuel Injected Dreams* (Signet, US).

Pop relationships need strong negotiations and a clear personal contract to endure. John and Yoko are another rare pop couple who weathered intense relationship difficulties and still remained together on a public level. Although a little mawkish, their image as a couple was the controversial inspiration for a generation. Putting forward their (literally) naked coupledom as a symbol of 1960s and early 1970s peace and love, they went much deeper than Sonny and Cher, taking the latter's hippy ethos to its logical extreme.

By the late 1970s the idea of pop coupledom took a new, more calculatedly commercial turn, when the Swedish pop group ABBA turned their real life marriages into video soap opera. While Bjorn and Agnetha and Benny and Anni-Frid were together, their strong rapport provided the ballast for the band's record-breaking hit potential. The combination of two couples focused entirely on the creation of an international pop ideal proved to be formidable. Within four years of winning the Eurovision Song Contest in 1974, the group were one of Sweden's fastest growing corporations, amassing a yearly gross of over $16 million.

When marital strife beckoned, rather than hiding it, they brought it into their songs and videos. The internal strains and stagnation, however, meant that by 1983, ABBA had lost its creative edge, and group members went their separate ways.

When Dave and Annie entered the business at the end of the 1970s, they had no intention of placing their partnership upfront. As far as they were concenred they both loved music and they had just fallen in love. Music was primary, and to the outside world, their romance was peripheral.

HAMPSTEAD 1976

They met one autumn day at the small health food restaurant called Pippins in Hampstead, where Annie worked as a waitress. She was twenty-two years old and he was twenty-four. She had been down from Scotland since she was seventeen, but was only just getting used to London life, establishing a group of friends separate from the Royal Academy classical circle. Now writing her own songs in private, she was looking for a publishing deal and a place to showcase her voice.

The quiet of her careful existence was shattered by the entrance of Dave Stewart, who walked through the door of the restaurant that night and into her life with a chaotic bang. He was brought in by her Camden stall friend Paul Jacobs and introduced as 'the guy who can help you out with a record contract'. Annie took one look at this dishevelled man of uncertain age wearing a huge overcoat with a furry collar and Tony the Tiger sunglasses, and in her pragmatic Scots way, mentally marked him down as 'a complete nutter'.

Despite his straggly goatee beard, gaunt face and bleeding earlobe where his ear had recently been pierced, Dave came across as a personable enough man. He had a congenital urge to talk and smiled benignly at Annie from behind his ridiculous shades. His voice was cheeky with a Sunderland lilt, his gaze vulnerable. 'Will you marry me?' he quipped.

On her way to the kitchen the restaurant manager hissed: 'I hope you don't know those two. They look like drug addicts!' Graciously ignoring him, she attended to her two guests, who waited until the end of her shift. Later in the evening she relaxed a little, pleased to discover that although he looked like he'd been dragged through a hedge backwards, Dave possessed a warm sense of humour.

He asked to hear her songs, so the three of them made their way back to her bedsit in Camden, talking animatedly about their musical ambitions and the intricacies of getting a foothold in the business. Back at the flat, Annie nervously made a cup of tea before getting out her harmonium. Then with a concentrated cough she launched into a series of songs, self-penned lyrical essays on pleasure, isolation and pain, some filled with vigorous adolescent angst, others resonating with a new kind of poignancy.

Transfixed by her quiet charisma and the clarity of her words, Dave felt as if he'd never encountered anything so pure in his life; devoid of pretension, artifice, wastage and indulgence, a complete antidote to the drug-filled numbness that had been recently dogging his existence. He could imagine in his head the accompaniment to those seriously wrought words, a swirling mix of folk and pop.

The two experimented with some melodies before Dave suggested going for a late drink. They moved on to a local club, and Paul left them there, drinking lager and talking furiously. After an hour Dave and Annie decided to go back to the flat and try out more musical ideas. They played till early morning, inventing melodies and telling each other scraps of their life stories. Fired by a mutual attraction, they collapsed together on the bed and made love. To Annie, it felt as if she had come home.

Dave was always a great enabler, encouraging Annie to realize her potential. While he is very work-orientated and confident about his role in pop, Annie is less sure of her ability. This has led to inevitable speculation about Dave having a Svengali-like influence in their relationship.

'When I try and analyse the band I always think of him as Rasputin and she the Queen. Her Alma Mater. A Svengali, yes,' says her friend and Fleet Street photographer Joe Bangay, a bluff, brusque music fan who moved into photography after a career in the RAF. His judgement is based on a hard-nosed yet affectionate view of the business.

'I first met Annie in a record shop when she was a Tourist,' he says. 'I thought what a very difficult, neurotic girl she was and decided to dislike her for the rest of her life. Then later I got to know her, doing photographs with Eurythmics, and grew to like her immediately. I realized she was very unhappy, but she and Dave had obviously suppressed their differences to be professional about it. They still do. Annie's very resolute about her business. They realized they *had* to stay together – she needed him for his emotional support, he needed her for her brilliance. She could put his music into sound.'

Annie always refers to Dave's influence in their relationship, placing him on a musical pedestal, which maybe in turn inhibits her personal output. 'Dave works like an editor for me,' she said in 1989. 'We work together lyrically; I usually say what I've written is rubbish and he looks at what I've done. I don't know about working separately. I've never done anything on my own. I'm willing to have a bash to see where my weaknesses lie and where I can turn weaknesses into strengths. I don't know what I'd do, though, without Eurythmics.'

Bangay, too, voices doubts on the effectiveness of Dave and Annie as separate artists. 'Now he's stopped pulling strings so much because he's with Siobhan, things are going wrong. I don't think they've done any good work since he married Siobhan. I thought that Dave was doing all the organizing.'

At one time Annie recorded a duet with Dundee-born Associates star Billy Mackenzie. He feels that she should experiment in working with someone else. 'She still has a competitive spirit and she genuinely loves music, but Dave gives her a real blanket of security,' he says. 'Outside that Eurythmics' womb she's not got as much faith in herself as I do. I'd like her to meet some of my musicians – I think she'd freak! She feels things acutely. I'm different, as a boy, no one could intimidate me musically.'

Annie would often take the back seat in discussions about album covers or general video ideas, but when she had decided on something she was very forceful. 'At first Annie would let Dave bung ideas in, and she might not say anything until she saw it on paper. She could see it then, whereas Dave would imagine it more in his head,' says Laurence Stevens, their sleeve designer. 'He was like a modern-day Magritte. People would always say "Dave's a bit weird, a bit strange", and in certain senses he plays up to that. He said to me once, "You don't spend a year on acid without having some of it lodged in your brain." He can throw out endless stupid ideas because of who he is. Annie's persona came more upfront once they'd sold more records. She became more confident, had more of a say.'

The Eurythmics' first press officer, Sheila Sedgwick, remembers how important Dave was in Annie's life: 'She relied on him for so many things. He'd always give her something else to think about. She relied on him emotionally, certainly to start with.'

While Dave contributed a great deal off-stage, Annie was promoted upfront. As a star vocalist with a strong image, she was the selling point of the band, and her coolly sensual persona encapsulated the *concept* of Eurythmics. 'Right at the beginning I was aware that any serious personality input from me would just capsize the Eurythmics "thing",' he said shortly before the release of his first solo album, *Spiritual Cowboy*, in 1990. 'In Eurythmics it's always Annie's psyche that's kind of on display. I'll play a counterpart – like in videos – to help diffuse it sometimes or to build it up. If you notice early press shots there's Annie right up front and a bit of the back of my head somewhere.'

Their Logo Records boss Geoff Hannington remembers Annie as being *more* forceful than Dave in their discussions during the days of the Tourists, and rumour has it that when Dave was in hospital in 1981 with a collapsed lung just after the failure of Eurythmics' first album, Annie barged into the ward, sat on his bed with a mini-computer, played the blueprint for 'Sweet Dreams' and said:

'*This* is what we're going to do.' Whatever the later power balance in their relationship, though, Dave began with the upper hand.

When they first met Dave and Annie were in their early twenties with barely two years between them, yet Dave had had a great deal more streetwise experience in the music business. She was grounded in a solid classical training, but was only just learning how to apply it to the rock sphere. Having left the Academy, she was scraping together a living while trying to get a record deal, whereas Dave had already been through the record company mill with his band Longdancer and was looking for the next step. He was in a vulnerable phase, recently separated from his wife and constantly taking acid. He swears that Annie was the person responsible for weaning him off drugs; her brisk, clean attitude to life favourably influenced him.

Both were in precarious circumstances, yet their relationship thrived on difference, and as they grew together their complementary opposite natures became more pronounced, almost mythologized. Sonny and Cher blended together with the outward face of harmony, while Dave and Annie forged for themselves a public persona based on discussion, debate and business – a very modern coupling. They are regularly written about as dynamic opposites, two in a 'salt and pepper relationship'.

'Dave embodies a spirit of total optimism. It doesn't matter what the circumstances are, he seems to be undaunted by anything. He has that ability to float up again,' says Annie, almost wistfully. She gallantly gives him credit. In 1984 she said: 'The magazines may stick me on the cover by myself, but I'm proud of both of us because I wouldn't be on those covers without Dave.'

'I know loads of people, I'm always out, my phone's always ringing. Annie's very quite – more into solitude,' counters Dave. Annie is very rigorous, disciplined and concise, while Dave approaches work and relationships with a more haphazard, intuitive feel and a basic strength of self-confidence that has often shored up Annie's insecurities. 'I definitely couldn't form Eurythmics with another girl, and I don't think, if Annie went, that some other bloke could try to do what we do,' says Dave. 'It's a mixture of our personalities . . . It's weird how the two of us fit. We're on a similar wavelength.'

With his garrulous, light-hearted social side, Dave plays the bluff soldier to Annie's more reticent, tortured musician image. Their difference in approach goes right back to their respective upbringings: Annie came from a strict Scottish Communist working-class family, whilst Dave's parents were liberal middle class, his father, Jack Stewart, an accountant, and his mother Sadie passionately interested in unorthodox child psychology.

Born on 8 September 1952, Dave's imagination as a boy was given free rein. His father was an obsessive music fan who rigged up every room in the house with a sound system, so Dave and his older brother John would often wake up to the sound of *South Pacific* or *Oklahoma*. Sadie Stewart experimented each week with different ethnic dishes and colours, claiming that Dave sometimes sat down to blue porridge or green mashed potatoes. She believed in teaching her children to cope with frustration in a practical way, encouraging them to sleep in a tent in the garden during the summer, and she didn't turn a hair when Dave at the age of ten ran off to the station and spent his pocket money on an exploratory train trip to Glasgow.

Brought up in Sunderland, a strongly working-class town in the North-East of England, Dave's privileged upbringing could have set him apart, but his open, sociable nature made him adaptable and popular. 'They'd always call me "richie" and whack me on the head with a cricket bat,' he said. Passionate about sports, particularly soccer, he became captain of the school football team and would have continued with the game if it hadn't been for the cartilage injury that hospitalized him at thirteen. Bored and frustrated in bed, he taught himself guitar – in much the same way as nearly twenty years later he laid down the first Eurythmics tracks on a keyboard sequencer from his hospital bed.

Once out of hospital and recovered from his cartilage injury, the teenage Dave bought himself a leather jacket, a stack of blues albums and a new guitar, and religiously posed in front of the bedroom mirror. 'I was so crazy to be a pop star, I used to phone up the local radio station and sing down the phone,' Dave claimed. He would borrow his brother's Stax singles and copy the raw R&B sound note for note on his guitar, a raw soul influence that would remain with him until the days of Eurythmics. He was identified with music to such an extent that a representative of Bell Records approached him as a schoolboy, wanting to turn him into a British David Cassidy.

This, thankfully, never happened, but Dave became so obsessed with the idea of becoming a pop star that the night after going to his first rock concert, he stowed away in the group's transit van and ended up with them in Scunthorpe. The group, a medieval folk outfit called Amazing Blondel, took him on for the next three months as an informal roadie, teaching him about life 'on the road'.

At sixteen, Dave felt independent enough to live on his own, and moved into a flat with his best friend Eddie Fenwick. The two of them would court the girls from the local comprehensive, while Dave eked out a living teaching guitar and playing solo folk gigs. His dreams of becoming the new Bob Dylan were squashed somewhat by a stint at local castle banqueting events where he dressed as a minstrel and sang folk airs to people on works outings.

Stardom soon beckoned in a peculiar kind of way when Dave teamed up with Sunderland folk musician Brian Harrison to form a successful song-writing duo, Stewart & Harrison. By autumn 1971, the duo grew into a fully fledged band called Longdancer, with a line-up that consisted of Dave, Brian, and two other local lads, Steve Sproxton and Kai Olsson. Their contemplative acoustic folk rock marked them out as a new Lindisfarne, and within a year they were being courted by London music business executives. Elton John eventually signed the band to his new label Rocket Records, more, it is rumoured, as a tax loss than a commercial proposition.

The band released two sweet-sounding LPs – *If It Was So Simple* and *Trailer For A Good Life* – that were affably received but instantly forgotten, and played a disastrous tour of Europe that ended with internal acrimony and abuse. After beginning life as a close harmony vocal band with a larger than usual advance, Longdancer dabbled in too many drugs, mutated to uneasy rock, and experienced an identity crisis, with Dave screaming for a higher T Rex-type electro pop profile while the rest of the band looked on in complete incomprehension.

Not surprisingly the band split, and in 1975 Dave was on his own again. Regularly taking acid, he would come home to Pam, his childhood sweetheart whom he'd married at twenty, and spout LSD-driven nonsense at her. He joined the all-female satirical cabaret crew the Sadista Sisters and ended up running off with the lead singer Jude Alderson. This, together with three car crashes that left him hospitalized and poverty-stricken, led to the collapse of their marriage. Pam admits now that they married too young and should have just lived together. 'I learned a lot from Dave and I value the time we were together because he was so fantastic to be with,' she said. By the advent of Eurythmics they had recovered enough of a strong friendship for Pam to run the first years of the fan club.

Before he met Annie at the restaurant in Hampstead, though,

Dave was an undisciplined mess. With his private life in shatters, he and another Sunderland song-writing friend Peet Coombes (with whom he later formed the Tourists) toured aimlessly round Europe, living in squats, busking cabaret in cheap clubs in Germany and being deported from Holland. In 1976, Dave returned to London to open Small Mercies, his record shop in Kilburn. Dazed, confused and run-down, he was playing small pub gigs at night, desperately looking for a new direction. In the calm, deceptively quiet persona of Annie Lennox, he eventually found it.

Dave and Annie are fond of emphasizing the extra dimension in their relationship, pointing to a telepathy between them that makes their work seamless and an other-worldly ESP quality that makes them special. With the benefit of hindsight Dave and Annie have given their relationship a powerfully rosy glow, an idealized view of themselves as a couple. Constant reiteration of the importance of their relationship, though, has also been an effective defence: presenting a wholly united front to the world provides protection against those who want them divided, and therefore less powerful.

'Dave and I have a very unique bond,' Annie told *Rolling Stone* journalist, Brant Mewborn, in 1985. 'Our partnership . . . there's something about it, you can't see it, it's an invisible thing, and I find it quite mystifying that there is this connection between us that is so powerful. People around us feel it as well. I'm always very touched by that.'

Within days of meeting each other Annie and Dave were completely infatuated. He persuaded her to give up waitressing and sign on the dole, so she could concentrate wholeheartedly on music, while she asked him to come and live with her in her new flat. Paul Jacobs, the friend who had brought them together, was opening a new record shop in Crouch End called Spanish Moon, and he had asked Annie if she would like to rent the flat upstairs. When she lumped her suitcases in, Dave and his belongings came too.

For the next few months Annie and Dave lived in blissful coupledom with just £11 per week between them. The flat was derelict, with a bathroom full of rubble and a kitchen they could never keep clean, but while things were going well their limited existence acted as a spur, making them resourceful rather than depleting their energy. Paul had set up a small recording studio in the basement that he rented out to Dave and Annie for a minimal fee, and this enabled them to commit their ideas to tape.

Before long they had thrown in their lot with Peet Coombes and signed to Logo Records as the song-writing team that would form the basis of the Tourists. To Annie, this pop lark was totally new, a career that gave her licence to dress up, experiment with her face and explore a stage presentation that was entirely her own. Instead of the bands she had previously guested with, the Tourists belonged to her, Dave and Peet, as their prized creation.

After their first accidental chart hit, the cover of Dusty Springfield's 'I Only Want To Be With You', and their first press slagging, the gloss began to wear off. By the time they were locked into a dispute with Logo Records, Dave and Annie's initial excitement was replaced by stress, tension and a profound malaise. When Annie collapsed on stage in Australia at the end of the Tourists' ill-fated final tour, she began asking herself what had gone wrong, how the dream she and Dave had nursed so religiously in that Crouch End flat had begun to turn so sour.

Part of the problem lay in the simple adage: two's company, three's a crowd. The initial nucleus of the Tourists was a threesome, with Peet Coombes taking the song-writing lead. A morose, complex figure, he had been on the dole for six years playing in a little-known Sunderland band called Peculiar Star before he teamed up with Dave. A slothful spirit, his presence soon began to grate on the brisk-minded Annie. She felt herself influenced by his moods and resented it.

Dave and Annie were brimming with musical ideas that they did not yet know how to put into practice. For most of the Tourists' brief life, Dave had been content to play guitar, and Annie had allowed Peet's song writing to dominate because she, as yet, was unconfident of her ability. As the situation with the Tourists worsened, the couple grew closer and closer together, distancing themselves from the rest of the band. When the time came for the group to split, Dave and Annie were well on their way to the independence of a new sound and a new concept.

There are many parallels in their experience with that of the other great 'New Wave' couple, Debbie Harry and Chris Stein of Blondie. Because she had dyed peroxide hair and sang lead for a guitar pop band, Annie was constantly being compared to Debbie Harry, cited in the popular press as the 'British Blondie'. Although Annie's personality and musical direction are very different, she greatly admires Debbie, acknowledging her as a major influence.

'She for me was so enigmatic as a performer. Not a great singer, but as a *popstress* she had this unique quality. She's never been given the recognition she deserves. It's too easy to dismiss Debbie Harry. Stylistically, she was unique,' says Annie.

Debbie's circumstances mirrored Annie's in that she had a boyfriend in the band, a factor that initially gelled the group in the first place, but with the pressure of success, created a marked internal division.

Blondie began in the early 1970s when Debbie, a former Playboy Club bunny, beautician, and waitress at New York rock'n'roll club Max's Kansas City waiting for her big break, met Chris Stein, a New York area guitarist. The two founded Blondie, and after initial line-up changes, settled with Gary Valentine on bass, James Destri on keyboards and Clem Burke playing drums. By 1976, along with New York artists like Patti Smith and the Ramones, Blondie had a record deal and were playing major hip venues like Max's and CBGBs, the garage punk club in the Bowery.

After signing to the British label Chrysalis, they were successful in Britain first with 'Denis', a pop cartoon cover of Randy & the Rainbow's old hit 'Denise', but it was the disco sheen of 'Heart of Glass' in 1978 that broke them the world over. Among their albums, *Parallel Lines*, *Eat To The Beat* and *Autoamerican* yielded strong hit singles and the group headlined major auditoriums around the world. With her puckered lips, bright blonde hair, sensual kooky style and endorsement of designer jeans, Debbie was inevitably the focus of constant media attention.

This caused deep resentment within the group, with other band members insisting that they were more than mere backing musicians. In fact a promotional campaign was instituted with the headline, 'Blondie is a Group'. Chris and Debbie formed a strong, stubborn axis, and began to distance themselves from the rest of the band – particularly when they took the unpopular decision of using disco producer Giorgio Moroder on their *Eat To The Beat* album.

By 1981 Blondie were running out of steam, especially as Debbie focused on separate solo projects, such as her less-than-successful LP *Koo Koo* recorded with Chris Stein and Chic. After the release of the last Blondie album *The Hunter* in 1982, the band split, and Chris became seriously ill with a rare genetic disease called Pemphigus. For the next three years Debbie was out of the music business, nursing her boyfriend. While being part of a couple in a band was a vital source of strength, once the band split up, it became problematic, with Debbie searching for her own identity. 'It was a sad, unhappy and scary time,' she told an *LA Times* reporter in 1985, 'We had been working and living together for eleven years . . . so I really couldn't leave. When someone gets that sick, you can't carry on with your job.'

Once the Tourists split, Annie too found it a great strain when in 1981 Dave was hospitalized at London's Royal Free with a collapsed lung, and the pressure on the pair of them became unbearable. Both of them were at a low ebb. While Annie was having difficulty coping with depression, Dave had been forced to completely re-evaluate his accident-prone life. One of his lungs had previously collapsed due to years of drug taking, and after the Tourists split he was involved in a car accident that collapsed the other one. He was critically ill and nearly died during the operation.

'After that I took time to repair myself,' he said later. 'It was a pretty wretched time. I kept collapsing in the flat. I'd broken up with Annie who thought I was completely nuts and I was alone in this place really weak.'

Even though Dave and Annie split as lovers, they stayed together professionally. Likewise, Chris Stein is very much involved with Debbie Harry's career. Although Debbie has pursued her own acting and singing career with a lead role in the film *Hairspray*, Chris played on her critically acclaimed solo LPs, and still accompanies her on tour. During their London gigs at Brixton Academy in 1990, they were very much the nagging showbiz couple, occasionally bickering between songs and giving each other loaded looks.

The couple is a formidable unit, the very strength of its togetherness sometimes becoming too tight and strangling what started out as healthy. Dave and Annie have often used their togetherness as a power base. When hiring and firing musicians their tactic sometimes is to withhold information about the line-up they want until just before the beginning of the tour. This ensures that no one musician becomes too powerful or constant in the Eurythmics line-up; the focus, after all, and the selling point, is Annie and Dave.

Some of their employees found this difficult. 'It wasn't real. They had a feudal system, like something out of the Middle Ages – they were the King and Queen and you were the serfs,' says a former engineer who used to work at their church studio and now makes his living in Los Angeles. 'I didn't enjoy it at all. Despite their professional image they treated everyone badly, especially the musicians. They were incredibly self-centred.'

Annie and Dave could use their togetherness as a couple to

manipulate those around them. While Annie promoted their relationship as an example of 'the good association going on between men and women, something totally healthy and very special', some found the power base they created a little intimidating.

The positive side was that Annie and Dave strove to work together with professionalism, and he was often the foil for her more difficult moods, calming down anyone she may have snapped at in frustration. 'Couples in groups can lead to fraught situations,' says Vic Martin, their keyboardist on early tours. 'But Dave and Annie were unusual in that they could work so happily together, there were no weird dramas. They were more like brother and sister.'

Within a group the couple are often the focus of publicity, a romantic hook for a media story, and this creates its own particular pressure. Early on in the Tourists' brief career, RCA offered that if Dave and Annie got married, they would hire a ship and fly journalists out to it for a huge reception. 'We considered getting married and then starting divorce proceedings the next day, but it didn't seem worth it,' said Annie.

Resolutely in their own private world, Dave and Annie never embraced public pop coupledom when they were together as lovers. 'If someone else came into the room, it didn't seem real,' Dave later recalled. 'The only reality was us. We'd be writing these great songs and making love. And we were just so wrapped up in one another that there was no room for anyone else in our lives.' It wasn't until they split romantically and made Eurythmics the focus of their partnership that the two felt safe to reveal their relationship to the world.

The transition was a painful one, though. Dave and Annie may have engineered an image of professional perfection, but their private emotions were awry. 'When Annie split up with Dave she was at a very low ebb emotionally. We used to go and have tea together, and she'd have the odd cry on my shoulder,' says Bangay who, like several men who've worked with her, became a platonic father figure. 'Ideally you'd love them to get married and live happily ever after. But Dave's not that sort of character. I'm amazed he's married, frankly.'

Annie was twenty-six when she and Dave split, so theirs was a passionate but young relationship. Both of them were growing and changing as individuals, and therefore bound to separate or at least be forced to redefine the parameters of their affair. The break-up of the band in the end of 1980 had a direct effect on this.

After the demise of the Tourists, the press and record company were not interested in Dave and Annie. RCA kept them on a contract after the Tourists, but there was little motivation within the company to develop the couple, forcing them to fall back on their own resources after years of international touring, limousines and audience accolades. Profoundly depressed by the wranglings within the Tourists, Annie was exhausted and unsure of herself. As she and Dave made plans for a new band, they felt suffocated by the dependency that had grown between them, yet were ambitiously striving for the same musical partnership and mutual spark of ideas that had brought them together in the first place.

'Our relationship was too consuming, too frightening to continue,' said Dave. 'Sometimes we'd be together and one of us would have to leave the room. We'd each know what the other was thinking and found that the margins between us became blurred.

'We'd have to fight really hard to retain our individuality, it was terrifying. When we decided to form Eurythmics we accepted that we couldn't continue our relationship as well. It was us or Eurythmics and Eurythmics was too important to ignore.'

Such a decision seems too conveniently cut and dried. It doesn't take into account the conflict that Dave and Annie also had in their relationship. 'You'd see them one day and things would be fine. The next week they wouldn't have spoken for three days. It had a real venom and volcanic feel,' says a close friend. Within relationships there is always a power struggle; it's extremely rare for a couple to have the complete rational agreement that Eurythmics like to present to the world. In making music they often fight fiercely, each sticking to their own point of view until they agreed to a compromise. 'Sure, we argue,' says Annie. 'We have tremendous clashes of personality. When we were recording the *Revenge* album we were yelling and screaming. It's not a childish thing, it's just the mix of two different temperaments.'

Dave and Annie are a difficult couple to fathom. They look and behave so differently, it is hard to see their physical sexual chemistry. Most of Annie's lovers since Dave have been tall and dark with a certain elegance, whereas Dave is more of a bright, brotherly shaggy dog. Much of their initial attraction was based on a musical compatibility rather than outstanding physical lust, with the emphasis on forging a career as well as a romantic liaison – in fact the romantic dimension was *part* of that career.

They were used to living and working together twenty-four hours a day. With both of them musicians and both in the same band, there were few moments when they could really relax and be apart. Being in business together, particularly their type of business, meant that inspiration could strike at any time, creating between them an overheated intensity. 'Even though you might not be performing or writing songs in the studio, you always think the way of a musician; you can't stop it,' says Dave. 'You can't say "Between six and ten I'm not going to think about anything creative." By seven o'clock you might suddenly start doing something. That's the way Annie and I worked. It was never a normal relationship.'

By the end of 1980, Annie was prepared to leave the four-year relationship that had sustained her. 'We'd spent so much intensive time together, been through so many changes – I felt I needed a chance to find out who I really was, separate from Eurythmics and Dave Stewart. When I went and was on my own living alone it was very traumatic. It felt like I had my legs cut off, like someone had put plaster legs on me and I had to learn how to use them again.'

Annie moved out, but it was one of the hardest decisions she forced herself to make. 'She loved him for a long time after she'd left him,' says Bangay. 'She couldn't stand it any more, and he got other women. She found it really upsetting, having been with him for so many years – he did tend to flaunt women in front of her. I was there when they shot the "Who's That Girl" video. Dave was playing himself, parading in with as many girls as he could muster. I think that affected Annie even more . . . here was this bloody ex-boyfriend trotting in with all these beautiful women. I think all her misery and trauma produced better music, though.'

Being alone meant that Annie could rediscover her musical ability without being so closely involved with Dave. The act of living apart immediately freed their ideas, so that each was able to come to the working partnership with a fresh perspective. It has been suggested that Dave and Annie were more compatible as friends than lovers, as they were able to work together after they split up – a feat that many couples totally immersed in the idea of an all-consuming great love cannot manage. For Dave and Annie their break-up in 1981 aided rather than held back their professional lives, and it was out of these tentative beginnings that Eurythmics was born.

They'd begun to explore new rhythms when the Tourists were in Bangkok on the last leg of their final tour, and Dave and Annie started recording street noises and sounds from the TV onto a tiny Sony recorder. These experimental techniques were a stirring cultural amalgamation that left them excited and inspired, a far cry from the pastiche 1960s pop they'd been accused of making with the Tourists. 'We were doing the opposite thing to punks at the time,' said Dave, 'getting more into sequencers and the mixture of soul feeling with electronics.'

Once free of the shackles of a band, they evolved a new concept whereby they would form the nucleus around which various musicians 'subject to availability and compatibility' would work. Whatever the input from other invited musicians, Dave and Annie would have ultimate control over the sound. In time, this grew to control over management, marketing, even merchandising, with the couple acting as a wholly professional unit.

Initially they focused on the musical concept, landing on the name Eurythmics after Annie recalled the Eurhythmic dancing of her youth. A discipline adapted by Emil Jacques Dalcroze, a professor of harmony at the Conservatoire of Music in Geneva in the 1890s, it shifted a child's appreciation of music from the intellectual to the physical, incorporating free-wheeling elements of rhythm and movement. Dalcroze's philosophy of encouraging students to listen to music with their 'inner ear' neatly sums up Dave and Annie's approach, with its combination of intellect and intuition.

The band had a troubled conception, forged at first by a rag bag of sounds, samples and an exuberant idealism. Although RCA had kept Dave and Annie on a contract after the Tourists' demise, the record company were extremely sceptical about an odd couple babbling on about experimental pop with the totally unsaleable name of Eurythmics. Dave and Annie would have to do a lot of persuading and get many people on their side before the label took any notice and invested a sizeable amount in them. Until then, they became their own cottage industry, writing their own press biographies and getting friends to do photos.

COLOGNE, 1981

At this time, Dave and Annie were also listening to German electronic bands like Kraftwerk and DAF, and took the chance to work again in Germany with Conny Plank, arriving at his Cologne studio in February 1981 with banks of tapes to record the demos that turned into their first album, *In The Garden*.

Annie had recently played keyboards and helped Conny to produce the *Latin Lover* LP by vocalist Gianna Nannini. It was the first time her production capabilities had been recognized, and after the frustration of the Tourists, where she felt she was treated as 'just a girl singer', Annie was keen to develop with Conny the more technical side of her musicianship.

Attracted to the clean complexity of synthesized sound, Dave and Annie moved right away from the Tourists' guitar pop to embrace a modern European feel. Kraftwerk remain the main inspiration for the synthesizer bands of the early 1980s, and that includes the dulcet electronic tones of the emergent Eurythmics. By the late 1970s, Kraftwerk founder member Ralf Hutter was declaring that the guitar was a relic of the Middle Ages. 'Why limit yourself to only six strings when you can play a synthesizer and get sound waves from 20 to 20,000!' he said.

Their most successful albums, *Autobahn*, *Trans-Europe Express* and *Man Machine*, rewrote contemporary pop, influencing everything from disco to David Bowie. It was synthesizer music with a philosophy: the contract between man and machine. 'Kraftwerk basically means "power plant"; we plug our machines into the electrical system and create transformed energy,' Hutter told *Hit Parade* magazine in 1978. 'The Human Machine means that we plug ourselves into the machines also. We play with our brains, our hands, our mouths, our feet . . . the machines should not do only slave work. We try to treat them as colleagues so they exchange energies with us.'

The other element influential in Kraftwerk thinking was the idea of a clean pop slate, an entirely new post-war music spurred on by the upheavals in twentieth-century Germany, where Hitler had dispersed the German artistic community in the 1930s and the Second World War shattered what was left. 'We have nothing to do with the past because we were stripped of everything,' Hutter said. 'In this vacuum we were able to start something really new. All you had was space, and the after-war generation could do with it what they wanted. It is a most interesting cultural climate.'

To a band intent on eradicating their troubled past, Kraftwerk's electronic impulses and radical attitude were an inspiration, and much of the early Eurythmics' sound touches this base. Recorded between February and June 1981, their first LP, *In The Garden*, has a faintly dreamy, psychedelic quality, its warmth cut through by the cool harmonies of the synth. Much of the dislocated electronic feel comes from Holgar Czukay and Jaki Liebezeit, two members of the German avant-garde electronic rock band Can, while Robert Gorl from DAF and Blondie's Clem Burke added their sound on drums.

The album has a serious, studied air of deliberate musical mismatch and muted vocals, Eurythmics' first teetering steps towards something more complex and evocative than a vague Tourist guitar lick. The LP cover is shot in a rich, green English country garden, with Annie and Dave dressed in funeral black wafting in the foreground. Sporting small round shades, a goatee beard and cropped hair, Dave's image has moved from Sergeant Pepper to post-punk beatnik, while Annie's peroxide hair is longer and has been dyed a mottled orange.

On record it is as if she is trying out her voice for the first time, with sweet, careful harmonies and a few operatic twirls. Already her lyrics show the angry alienation that was to become her trademark, with dramatic lines like: 'Cold clean glass and a razor blade', or 'I need to play with the ones I hate/I like to see them suffer'. She has yet to bring out the strong soul intonation in her vocals, that bell-like edge that can transform a melody line.

Dave's burgeoning studio wizardry is kept in check by Conny's careful production, so on experimental tracks like 'English Summer', the sampled sounds of police sirens, shouting children and dripping rain just sound melancholy and wistful, rather than disturbing. A reflective LP, it was Dave and Annie's opus for change, using the garden as a cyclical image of birth, decay, death and rebirth, a mixture of Eurythmic optimism and pessimism. 'There's a lot of beauty in the sound, but with a touch of something disturbing, a bit sinister,' said Annie, a statement that sums up the Eurythmics' agenda.

The first release from the newly formed Eurythmics came out in July 1981. Awash with Czukay's mournful french horn, the regal sax of Timothy Wheater and Dave's unexpected guitar turns, 'Never Gonna Cry Again' is a paen to post-punk cool. Annie sings with soft, robotic vocals.

The record was tentatively well received, fluttered into the charts at Number 63, and then moved no further.

The next try came a month later with another track from the album: 'Belinda'. A rush of mystical surf pop with clapping drums, it didn't stand out against the defiant designer pop that was emerging at the time from bands like Spandau Ballet, Duran Duran and Heaven 17, and flopped. The release of the album in October was a similar non-event, though it garnered some good reviews of the 'soothingly evocative' and 'delicately hypnotic' variety.

It was time for another rethink. Dissatisfied with other people's production techniques, and wanting to branch out fully on their own, Dave and Annie began to look for their own studio. They made a few live appearances – the first on 11 January 1982 at the Barracuda Club in London, where Annie sang in a curious long black wig, a million miles from the British Blondie image of the Tourists.

Rock legend has it that some enthusiastic fan reached up and pulled her wig off, to reveal to a gasping audience her shorn hair. By April she was sporting her carrot-coloured crop at the London nightclub Heaven, and was beginning to move towards her own powerful image. Their stage set was industrially sparse, with the duo playing to backing tapes, finding it cheaper and more flexible than a full-time band.

With the press making encouraging noises about their live gigs, Dave and Annie decided to record another single. Looking to rely more on their friends than the record company, they teamed up with ex-Selector bassist Adam Williams, a new friend who was conveniently moving to London from Lancaster with his own studio facilities. Impressed with the potential of *In The Garden*, Williams threw in his lot temporarily with Eurythmics, setting up his studio with them in an empty building above Falconer Studios picture framers in Ferdinand Road, Chalk Farm.

In buying extra studio equipment, Dave donned a suit and persuaded his local bank manager at Barclays in Crouch End to give them a loan. 'A determined young man with a good head for business' was the verdict from manager Geoff Williams, granting the money that would enable Dave to experiment to his heart's content in the small eight-track studio.

As the band gradually grew more independent, they distanced themselves from the Arnakata management team. Although good at negotiating deals, Arnakata were less in tune with Dave and Annie's creative potential, and the two camps parted company, leaving Dave to manage the band himself. The next year was one of the most taxing for Eurythmics, as they struggled financially and creatively to gain the confidence of their own record company, let alone the record-buying public.

Their next single, 'The Walk', with a more soulfully strident sound than previous offerings, was released in June 1982, but failed to make the charts. The twelve-inch 'This Is The House', likewise, made no impact. No one outside the music business knew who Eurythmics were and, convinced that the band wasn't commercially viable, RCA refused to spend a generous sum promoting them. In the ensuing lull, all the emotion and insecurities that had been troubling Annie since their unfortunate cover version of 'I Only Want To Be With You' rose to the surface. Like a delayed reaction to the Tourists' debacle, Annie finally let go and experienced a nervous breakdown.

BREAK DOWN TO BREAK OUT

RCA's intransigence, together with the embattled legacy of the Tourists, battered Annie's already fragile ego. Although assured of her accomplishments as a musician, she was less sure of herself and her ability to handle the more hostile demands of the pop world, along with the scathing scepticism of the punk-inspired music press.

An old friend and one-time designer for Annie, Carol Semaine, recalls: 'In a way I used to think she was much too sensitive as an artist to be able to handle pop. At one time I thought it might destroy her. Although she's very strong, she does have that fragile quality about her. Like a little bird that could really easily be crushed. That's why it worked having Dave, because he took a lot of pressure off her, stopped her freaking out completely.'

In the final days of the Tourists and those first years trying to get Eurythmics off the ground, Annie spent many hours crying. Her classical education, acutely sensitive temperament and small-town roots had not given her the veneer of toughness required for the record business, and when relations faltered with her romantic ally, Dave, she was overwhelmed by panic. 'It shocked my system. It was a struggle to say, Wait! I *do* think I have credibility: I do think my ideas are far-reaching. So I'll just have to use them to make music people can identify with but which does reflect my ideas about life,' she said to *NME*'s Cynthia Rose in October 1983.

The split with Dave affected her self-confidence. Although it was supposedly mutual, once Annie moved out he was searching through his address book for blonde distractions and relentlessly filling the gap with new girlfriends. She too embarked upon affairs, having a brief liaison with Eurythmics' first drummer, Robert Gorl. Tall and fair-haired with a bubbly, ambitious personality, Gorl has been described by a friend as being like 'a German male Marilyn Monroe'. His enthusiasm is sometimes greater than his talent, though, and his affair with the rigorous Annie soon petered out.

With an uncertain future ahead, she lost her self-esteem and sense of direction. For over a year, Annie had to struggle to get out of bed every day, and some days she didn't succeed. Unable to make the simplest decision, she sank into depression and began to suffer from agoraphobia.

'I can never stop questioning things, I can never accept face values. I even question tangible things like the tarmac on the road and the fact that we're alive. I wish I didn't think about things so much, it gets to be a burden. I can become very alienated by it. I often think that my making is also my downfall.

That's one of the reasons I had a nervous breakdown, thinking about things too much. I couldn't leave my room, couldn't get on a bus or a tube train, I felt so isolated. It was a delayed reaction to what happened to us in the Tourists, my own self-esteem hit rock bottom and that period of panic attacks lasted a whole year. It was a grey shadow with me every bloody day. It first happened when I was on stage in Birmingham and I got through the song by pinching the side of my leg so that I'd concentrate on the pain and not panic. When it happened on tour in Australia, I was actually carried off stage.

After Dave and I parted I tried to form new friendships but all I did was frighten people. People shy away from you when they think you've gone nuts. In the end you realize that you are devastatingly alone in this world.

I lived on the verge of suicide. I don't mean that I'd ever do away with myself, but it's as if I did toy with the idea for a long time. Everyone, though, is vulnerable. No matter how much you want to get out of that sort of thing, it's a very hard thing to crack. And in the end it has to come entirely from within yourself, you have to start thinking about your own self-preservation.

With a bit of luck, though, and a *lot* of grit, you can turn these bad experiences into something creative. I do believe in self-improvement and don't think one is always a victim, not at all.'

Dave proved to be an invaluable source of comfort at this time, hauling Annie up by her bootstraps, getting her out of bed in the morning and encouraging her to keep on working. While her response to stress was psychological, he broke down physically. His hospitalization with a collapsed lung in 1981 placed an intolerable strain on their relationship, but although they broke up as a couple, he remained loyal and concerned, determined that Annie shouldn't let go of her musical potential.

Friends were supportive, but the sheer tenacity of Annie's black depression led her to seek outside help. Suspicious of tranquillizers, she decided to opt for a psychotherapist. Annie was not impressed. 'She didn't help at all. She just sat there and looked at me while I got more and more tongue-tied. I was more freaked out when I came out of her office than when I came in.'

Although the therapist did not seem to help, the very fact that Annie made the positive move to change her situation meant that she was on the long road to recovery. Ironically, it was probably the therapist's mute silences that helped Annie release her anger, irritation and strict Calvinist exasperation. 'Well if she can't help me,' Annie thought, 'I'll just have to help myself!'

Several years later she returned briefly to psychotherapy when she was in Los Angeles and found it was the best $500 she had ever spent. An expensive sum, but: 'I was fortunate, I went to a woman I could really talk to about all my fears. To have an unbiased opinion from someone who wasn't overawed by who I was was fantastic.' The therapist reassured Annie that she wasn't going insane, that social circumstances often have a part to play, pointing to her rather extraordinary role as a pop singer, where self-doubt and paranoia can be multiplied a hundred times.

'We are living in this crazy, super-fast hyped-up society. There's this superconsciousness which we never really had before. We just did what we were doing and didn't ask too many questions. Now we're full of self-doubt. Neurosis is a common disease. We used to have scurvy, now we have neurosis.'

Annie's strength lies in her ability to channel much of this pain into her song writing, finding a valuable release in music. She speaks of a madness within her that she gives free rein to when on stage and in the studio. 'That's where it's allowed to express itself, that's where it's most at home. But I don't like it rearing its head too much because when you have to cope with getting buses and doing the shopping it becomes too surreal. You have to keep it in control. I think anyone who's creative has to acknowledge and explore the madness in themselves — it's just the subconscious being allowed a little more freedom than it would have conventionally.'

Her experience in relationships forms the basis, directly or indirectly, of much of her song writing. Annie was always looking for the perfect love and invested a great deal in her relationships. Already plagued by insecurity, the unpredictable nature of her pop career tended to make things even more uncertain, so she has intuitively chosen men who could provide solid support. Some close to her maintain that she was looking for a father figure, the archetypal strong, silent man who would make sense of her problems. She wasn't about to give up her career, so it had to be someone who was prepared to put his work second and accompany her wherever she went.

'She needs to be loved because she's got a lot of love to give,' says Joe Bangay. 'She was very fond of Dave for a long time.' Her intensity of feeling has created some of the harshest and sharpest images of modern pop, from the cynical prostitute to the derailed housewife to the enigmatic figure in a business suit. Annie's awkward yet starkly effective image in the early 1980s cut through pop's clutter with an immediacy never seen before.

Although she started out in a Sonny and Cher-type partnership with Dave, the emphasis had to shift before she could work out her role as an individual performer. After his marriage to Siobhan she made sure that they kept in contact professionally rather than socially. They had been growing apart, anyway, since 1986 when Dave embarked on solo production projects, working with rock heroes as diverse as Mick Jagger, Tom Petty and Bob Dylan, and Annie went off to record a soul duet with Al Green — 'Put A Little Love In Your Heart' — which became a chart hit in 1989. Dave and Annie's attitude towards the rock'n'roll lifestyle became fundamentally different. While he loved living it up at media bashes and throwing ostentatious parties at one of his many homes, Annie preferred to keep quiet and private. Dave wanted them to tour endlessly and make it big in America, while Annie was satisfied with the level of respect they had already attained. 'He wants mega-stardom, she wants credibility,' says their friend Laurence Stevens. By mid-1990, Dave was working on his first solo LP, *Spiritual Cowboys*, a release that marked the move away from Eurythmics as a sacred unit.

In their separation as a romantic couple at the beginning of the 1980s, Annie discovered her voice and a new persona. She also had to endure long years of experimentation and uncertainty to find out what she *really* wanted. She had to break down to break out, eventually to finding her own happiness in life without Dave.

4

She's No Lady

'I wanted to see if I could get rid of the woman completely, and killed Annie of the Tourists stone dead. I knew it would cause a few raised eyebrows; there's something subversive about it that I enjoy. To think of someone kissing their ideal projection of what a man should be, but to also be that man, was great.

'I recognize in myself that I am a woman, both as a performer and as a representative of my generation of women. But there is this double-edged thing about sexuality. Like most women today I am taking control of my own life and you can see my clothes as an expression of that. I like to wear trousers because they give me freedom of movement.

'There was a rumour that I used to be male and have had a sex change. That's not a bad rumour! My personal style is not ripping off Grace Jones at all, that would be far too simple, it's more complicated than that. She's an entertainer in her own right and she's incredible, but don't forget that she was a product of Jean Paul Goude's imagination, whereas I've just taken the liberty of wearing more masculine clothes.

'It's more a visual joke. Something taken to an absolute conclusion. There's nothing new or shocking about androgyny, look at Bowie and Boy George. I think the papers wanted me to be the equivalent of Boy George — that's wishful thinking, I don't fit that bill. If you have any intelligence you need to find a balance between acknowledging your sexuality and not conforming to a stereotype. I chose suits not because they were outlandish but because they were neutral. We wanted the strongest symbol of normality we could find.

'I've had a few gay girls come on to me, but just for the record, I'm not gay. Because I choose to wear practical male dress, though, I'm always being mistaken for a man. A disco bouncer once shouted at me when I went to the toilets, "Excuse me lad, that's the ladies." I told him, "I am a lady, fatso, even though I don't walk around half-naked like the rest of them." I'm happier to be compared with a man than a woman. In a funny way being neither male nor female widens your scope.

'I'm a very female person, but men seem to want to call my confidence, my positive awareness of myself, aggression. So many men still can't cope with the idea of the non-submissive female. Being in a middle place that's neither overtly male nor overtly female makes you threatening, it gives you power.'

VIDEOLAND, 1983

In videoland anything can happen. The video can transform your desires, concoct fantasy images, bewitch and falsify. A flickering, intense, throwaway medium, it has a rough, hurried quality set apart from the relaxed unrolling of film. Sometimes it is merely a cheap marketing tool, a three-minute music business ad, at other times it captures a pop moment and relays a faultless urgency.

Annie stands in a record company boardroom hitting the desk with her fist. She is wearing a sharp black suit, white shirt, grey tie and black gloves. Her hair is severely cropped, dyed orange, and bristling with integrity. Her eyes are rimmed with black Kohl and her lips are faintly pink, the only concessions to femininity.

An element of magic appears in this businesslike atmosphere when she takes a black wand, slaps it on her hand and then uses it as a teacher would, pointing at a spinning globe. 'I travel the world and the seven seas,' she sings. 'Everybody is looking for something.' She is businesswoman and adventuress, charting unknown territory, waving over the limitless boundaries of her ambition. With magic, mysticism and hard business sense, she aims to conquer, taking the man in a suit as her partner, to stand by her side as an equal.

Surrounded by banks of computers and video technology, they advance into a New Age of commercialism. She and Dave sit in front of a wall of gold discs with red tantric spots on their foreheads, meditating karmically, the spiritual symbols appearing odd and eccentric when set against their asexual uniformity. Her suit is a defence against exploitation, a signal that she, too, is entering the game. 'Some of them want to use you,' she sings. 'Some of them want to get used by you/Some of them want to abuse you/Some of them want to be abused.'

Her costume changes when she appears on a riverbank wearing a regency dress and black masque, vigorously playing the cello, like an outlaw from a masqued ball, lost, smiling and triumphant. She salutes the power of sweet dreams, moving back again to the image of the suit, the boardroom and the sense of playful surrealism, as she and Dave lie on the desk and a herd of cows plod past the table. In this scenario, anything is possible.

Another video, and Annie appears again in a suit, her hair slicked down, her gaze menacing. She is waiting for her prostitute, the love she has demanded and bought. 'I want you,' she sings, her finger pointing like a threat, '. . . it's an obsession.' She runs a comb through her tight, shiny hair and puts on a pair of mirrored shades, hiding behind their chilly reflection.

A different place, a different shot. A nightclub this time, and Annie is a blonde-haired chanteuse singing of love betrayed. She is watched silently and closely by herself, a woman disguised as a man with a dark suit, dark hair, sideburns and stubble, sitting at a table at the back eyeing up her own feminine image.

Outraged by the presence of her lover (appropriately played by Dave) who enters the room with a parade of different girls, Annie the singer throws away her chair in anger, leaves the stage and meets up with Annie the man. The unlikely couple leave the nightclub, she prancing forward with new-found freedom, 'he' walking beside her with an exaggeratedly masculine gait.

They turn towards each other, and she, as a man, kisses herself as a woman. With this disturbing narcissistic touch, she has entered a forbidden world, transforming and transcending her sex.

GIRLS WILL BE BOYS

LONDON, 1890

When English music hall star and male impersonator Vesta Tilley crossed the boards at the turn of the century wearing men's clothes, nobody thought she was strange. Tilley came from a long and illustrious theatrical tradition of female cross-dressing, appearing herself from the age of five in top hat and tails at her father's music hall.

By the age of sixteen she was a popular attraction, christened the 'London Idol'. A sharp and impeccable performer with a smart comic touch, the diminutive Tilley researched all her roles, from soldier to city gent to priest. During the First World War she played 'The Bold Militiaman', while in peacetime she sang the irreverent 'Burlington Bertie' and 'Algy – The Piccadilly Johnny With The Little Glass Eye'.

Despite her unusual stage persona, this national heroine was a respected establishment figure, marrying former music hall owner and MP Sir Walter de Frece and leading a long, successful career in Britain and the States. Tilley represented the professional side of female cross-dressing, an accepted comic tradition that had its roots in masque balls and street festivals. When Annie Lennox appeared eighty years later in a businessman's suit, what she was doing was nothing new. It was how she re-invented that image for the pop process that counted. Like the best music hall impersonators, Annie took her performance to its logical extreme, and in doing so shook accepted pop stereotypes to their foundations.

References to female cross-dressing abounded in popular song, plays and operas throughout the centuries. In the masque ball, a woman disguised heightened the erotic tension, while during carnivals and street festivals it was common for women to dress as men and run amuck – stealing, smoking, swearing, and fighting. Free to go out without a male chaperone, they could explore a wider urban world that, unless they were literally streetwalkers or prostitutes, had normally been denied them. For a few days once a year the streets were theirs.

'Trousers make a wonderful difference in the outlook on life. I know that dressed as a man I did not, as I do now I am wearing skirts again, feel hopeless and helpless,' said Valerie Arkell-Smith, a woman who lived much of her life as a man under the pseudonym Colonel Barker, in 1929. In outwardly changing her gender she pursued male freedoms and priorities, even to the extent of marrying another woman.

Apart from dressing up in a festive spirit, female cross-dressing has historically had other more practical uses, such as escape from poverty, prostitution or an unhappy home life. For women tied up in domestic drudgery, dressing as a man gave them access to male occupations and a life of adventure. If a girl was single and alone it provided a way of protecting herself, and a drastic solution to personal problems.

Ever since Joan of Arc strode across the battlefields of Compiegne, women have disguised themselves to enter military service, whether through a fervent sense of patriotism or sheer love of excitement. The penalties on detection were high: Joan of Arc was convicted of wearing male clothes, considered then an offence against the church, and burned later as a heretic. In later years, women suffered prison, penury and humiliation, yet at the same time they were eulogized and celebrated in ballads and plays. To men it seemed imitation was the sincerest form of flattery; to women, other women's bravery was a source of inspiration.

The Russian Women's Battalion of Death was admired at the time of the Revolution for its heroic nationalism, while the British Flora Sandes was honoured after she swapped her life in a closed Victorian suburban drawing room for that of a soldier and diplomat on the Serbian front line. During the First World War a headstrong young journalist, Dorothy Lawrence, joined the Royal Engineers in order to file reports from the battlefield with the rest of the foreign correspondents, while one Emma Edmonds turned herself into 'a smart handsome lad' to become a soldier in the US Civil War. Dating from the Amazons, the female warrior is a popular, even conventional heroine.

There have been frontierswomen like Annie Oakley and Calamity Jane who rebelled against their sex, female pirates Anne Bonney and Mary Read, and adventurers like Mary Reiby, an eighteenth-century Australian woman who disguised herself as a boy to enter the male world of business and finance. There were the literary heroines – Shakespeare's Rosalind facing a moral dilemma in *As You Like It*, and female novelists like Collette and George Sand who dressed as men so they could record life from Parisian bars.

Cross-dressing was also an effective way of avoiding marriage, postponing the time when a woman had to become a man's property. As long as a woman in disguise was chaste, she was safe, but once she became sexually active, her male charade was shattered. It is interesting that when she started in Eurythmics, Annie presented a determinedly asexual image that was far away from the blonde dolly bird look she was pressured to provide as lead singer for the

Tourists. By occupying a middle ground between male and female, a sort of boyish Peter Pan no-man's-land, she was able to avoid the pop illusion of sexual availability. She never allowed her sex to make her vulnerable.

'When I knew her she was very very anti showing any part of her body for effect,' says her former stylist Carol Semaine. 'She had this strict Scottish attitude, and certainly didn't approve of flaunting yourself – no matter what the reasons were behind you doing it.'

Many women cross-dressed in the past for financial gain. Even though some may have been poverty-stricken, to them prostitution was a very last resort. Annie herself has strong, curiously moralistic views on women's capacity to exploit themselves, calling Madonna's unrestrained sexual aura 'whorish'. In 1986 she condemned a video where Madonna rolled around on the floor in a wedding dress showing thighs and garters, saying: 'It was like she was fucking the music industry. It may have been parody on her part, but I thought it was very low.' A few years later she criticized late 1980s pop 'bimbos' as 'complete pornographic pop. It's all "show us yer tits dear",' she said. 'I don't choose that life. Those girls have to live with that. They'll probably find a rich Lebanese prince to marry or live off their earnings in a nice little cottage in Cornwall or somewhere. It's money, fame and pure escapism.'

Annie's gender-mixing was a temporary switch that enabled her to reach certain goals, to exude an air of autonomy and authority that was rare for women in pop. Once she was established, she felt free to experiment with more feminine images, even to the extent of flinging off her bra on stage during the 1987 *Revenge* tour, but in the early days of Eurythmics she was seeking serious credibility, regardless of her sex.

'Dave and I thought very carefully about how I could present myself to the public without narrowing myself down to that pure conception of woman-as-sex-object, and in that sense I played with my sexuality, brought it more towards the masculine side, which gave me power,' says Annie. 'It made me sexually – although I don't like to use that word – androgynous.'

The initial impetus behind the idea was to promote a uniform neutrality, regardless of the sexual overtones. 'Me and Dave liked to think of ourselves as twins,' said Annie. 'Quite some time before this gender bender business we both went to a very ordinary gent's tailor and had identical suits made. It made us feel like a unit.' Although the point of the project was to *de*-sexualize herself, Annie's image attracted women as well as men with its stark ambivalent power.

Cross-dressing has also historically been a way for women to express love for other women. In previous centuries, sex without a man was inconceivable, so a woman taking on a male identity to pursue her female lover provided a kind of 'acceptable' sexual solution. This grew into the lesbian 'butch-femme' role-playing tradition, one immortalized in the slick hair and tweed jackets of cult gay novelist Radclyffe Hall. Her controversial 1928 book *The Well of Loneliness* bemoaned the lot of 'inverts', while she herself was the leading light of a fashion for lesbians to don men's tailored suits, watch-chains, cufflinks and carnations.

This image was later compounded by the 1960s film *The Killing of Sister George*, where Beryl Reid and Susannah York indulge in a little lesbian role playing and gender mixing. It is not surprising, then, that when Annie chose to dress as a man she attracted a huge gay audience, and there was speculation about her sexuality. She fielded this by asserting, almost over-enthusiastically: 'Just for the record, I'm not gay. I'm not threatened by men and they shouldn't feel threatened by me. I *love* men!'

Annie has publicly chosen heterosexual love and marriage, but the resonance of her besuited image and cropped hair still reverberates throughout the lesbian world, especially since her 1985 hit with Aretha Franklin, 'Sisters Are Doin' It for Themselves'. When Eurythmics presented their dance music at Heaven, London's premier gay nightspot in the early 1980s, there were rumours about Annie being bisexual. She had a sexual ambivalence that Aretha Franklin apparently picked up on when Annie came to Detroit for the 'Sisters . . .' video shoot. Producer of the video, Jon Roseman recalls: 'Annie had just had a photo session and the woman photographer was gay. Aretha has this thing about gays and assumed Annie was a lesbian. She more or less ignored her throughout the entire session.'

Aretha's official version is that she, Annie and Dave 'had a ball. Working with them was fun,' she said. 'They are very technically minded and professional. I found out that Annie liked baked potatoes so I ordered some for her and got me some of Detroit's finest ribs and everyone was comfortable. Hey, we just did it up!'

Roseman found the event to be less impressive. 'God, could she eat those spare ribs! She ordered tons,' he says. 'There's Aretha Franklin, songstress extraordinaire, tearing into this meat. Really yucky. The

Detroit studio was in a really dodgy part of town, and she arrived in a limo, while her manager drove a posh Excalibur. There was no reason for him to drive it – she just wanted to let everyone know she had one. After the video Annie didn't want to speak to Aretha; the atmosphere was strained between them.'

Tina Turner was originally favoured to do the duet with Annie, but was unavailable at the time. It is interesting that after she'd come into contact with Eurythmics, Aretha went the way of Tina Turner, making the no-nonsense rock album *Zoomin*. Produced by Narada Michael Walden and released in 1985, the album went platinum in the States. 'I told Michael before I started recording it that I wanted to do a younger sound, to make music that kids could bop to.' Much of the inspiration to take that direction had come from Dave Stewart.

Although they appeared in the video as spiritual soul sisters, Aretha and Annie were two opposites. Annie sang in 1980s' fashion with clear-cut melody line, while Aretha soared in her old soul style, embellishing her sound with florid, decorative swirls. While Annie represented a forward-looking vision of womanhood, Aretha stressed, 'I guess I'm old-fashioned, I like a guy who knows how to romance a girl. I like to be wined and dined, all that good stuff.'

This caused a little conflict in the interpretation of the song. Aretha was loathe to sing the line: 'The inferior sex are still superior', thinking it was a little strong. The next line was 'We've got doctors, lawyers, politicians, too,' which to Annie attached the meaning – 'look, we're really on equal terms'. Aretha refused to buy it, so the line was changed to something softer: 'The inferior sex have got a new exterior/We've got doctors, lawyers, politicians, too . . .'

'Annie's very moody and Aretha's very moody,' Dave said in an attempt to explain their differences. When asked what she thought of Aretha, Annie said politely, 'What can I say, Queen of Soul, a living legend. I learned so much from her.' Then her reservations peeped through when she admitted, 'To be honest, I'm embarrassed to say this, but I'm not that familiar with Aretha's records.'

Aretha obviously wasn't sure about Annie's besuited look, a video image that made people uncomfortable, particularly in the States. 'It would be easy not to understand her if you look at the videos. She seems quite hard, and in America people think she's a bit weird,' says Nathan East, bassist for the 'Sisters . . .' session. 'I didn't know what to expect at first, so I was happy that she was a sweetheart, a regular person and as nice as can be.'

The most powerful twist to Annie's career has been in her manipulation of video images. Female transvestism also has a rich and colourful history on screen, with top movie stars from Marlene Dietrich to Greta Garbo, Gloria Swanson and Katherine Hepburn opting for the power of this disguise. While Madonna has opted for more obvious images of female glamour in her videos, aping Marilyn Monroe for her song 'Material Girl' and a cast of thousands for her 1990 hit 'Vogue', Annie has been able to plunder a more risque, satirical Hollywood tradition in which women wear the trousers.

In the 1930s, Dietrich exuded a towering presence on screen with her black tux, top hat and elegantly poised cigarette in the film *Morocco*. She then changed it for a glittering white tuxedo in *Blonde Venus*, and full pristine navy regalia when she sang 'The Man's In The Navy' for the 1940 film *Seven Sinners*.

Female cross-dressing in films shows how women get into forbidden areas, whether it's runaways opting for a life of crime, film *noir* heroines disguising themselves to escape detection, or girls going for employment in the big, bad city. Sometimes it's for comic effect — like Bette Davis doing a spoof on Groucho Marx, or Madge Bellamy in blackface impersonating Al Jolson, while in other cases it is the central moral theme.

The 1949 courtroom drama *Adam's Rib*, for instance, poses a gender dilemma, where Spencer Tracy and Katharine Hepburn play husband and wife lawyers on opposing sides of the same case. During the trial Hepburn accuses Tracy of male chauvinism in his hard treatment of her female clients, and, to prove her point, asks the jury to look at each woman and imagine for a moment that they are men. Judy Holliday and Jean Hagen in Brylcreemed hair and Prince-of-Wales check provide one of the most enduring screen images of women in drag. The illusion only works if the details are exactly right, a point that Annie noted in her precise adaptation of the businessman or the low-life male seducer roles in her videos.

A woman in drag bumps against the margins of social respectability: she's one of the teenage girls who dons tie and tails in the 1917 film *The Amazons* to crash an all-male club. She's continental star Dolly Haas hitting back at misogynist men through a boxing glove in *Girls Will Be Boys*. She's Lil Dagover with male attire and monocle, performing German decadent cabaret in *Dr Mabuse, der Spieler*. All Annie's androgynous images contain this element of aggressive visual parody, with the sense of a sweet pre-Nazi

Germany decay softened at times by her self-conscious, satirical smile.

The tradition of theatrical cross-dressing extended from music hall through to cabaret and Broadway musical to pre-war pop. In the 1920s and 1930s, singers like Ma Rainey and Bessie Smith welded jazz blues to showbusiness with their raunchy attire, while the sparky vaudeville star Josephine Baker high-kicked her way through a variety of mischievous disguises.

After the Second World War, however, when pop music became more institutionalized, women performers tended towards taffeta skirts, sequins and a modest, demure sophistication. Singers like Connie Francis, Ruby Murray and later 1960s stars from Sandie Shaw to the Supremes were not noted for their wicked gender bending. In the mid-1960s, British girl singer Polly Perkins was a one-off. Openly gay, she dressed in collar-and-tie and Carnaby Street pinstripe suits, and sang songs like 'Superdyke'. Her novelty act was a small rebellion against the restrictions for 1960s pop girls to be skinny, straight and sweet.

By the early 1970s the proliferation of progressive rock and hippy values led to the creation of the straight-ahead, groovy rock chick. This was concurrent with a revival in the singer/song-writer scene, where female artists like Carly Simon and Carole King relaxed into a reassuring 'natural look'. For a depressing number of years, long flowing hair and flared skirts were in, theatrical artifice was out.

The entrance of 1970s glam rock set the precedent for a new vogue in gender switching. With his skintight metallic costume, high, laced hunting boots and orange feathered hair, David Bowie created his powerful futurist alter ego – the mythical rock star Ziggy Stardust. Flaunting gender boundaries, this glittering pop creature made androgyny fashionable, spawning thousands of Ziggy lookalike fans. Ten years later when Annie appeared on stage with mannish clothes and her face painted in puce zig-zag stripes, there were inevitable comparisons to Bowie.

While many male pop stars had experimented with the drag element of glam, wearing wigs and spangled make-up, women were not encouraged to be so adventurous, and Annie was one of the first to go that far. On a woman, androgynous glam just looked weird rather than commercial, a fact that Labelle's Nona Hendryx had to suffer when her semi-androgynous space-age persona was passed over by the record industry in the 1970s. As always, she was a woman ahead of her time.

The noisy bawdiness of punk opened up new possibilities for female artists, and many performers from Poly Styrene to the Slits and Siouxsie Sioux seized the time to turn dress codes upside down. Punk revelled in asexual ugliness and sartorial chaos, a confrontational style of dressing that threw out an array of combinations – a vague female cross-dressing being just one aspect of that trend. Poly Styrene's little drummer boy outfit and Siouxsie Sioux's tails were more to do with anarchistic punk pantomime than serious cross-dressing.

What is striking about Annie's pose is its clean-cut edge, and her desire to visually *become* a man, rather than simply adapt bits and pieces of male clothing. The clarity of her image made most impact by coming right on cue, at the beginning of the designer video boom of the early 1980s.

Annie's precursor was Grace Jones, an agile Jamaican New Yorker whose career in top international modelling had schooled her in the power of certain styles and dress codes. She exploded from the disco underground in Paris in the late 1970s with a bizarre bullet-shaped flat top and an angular figure accentuated by starkly androgynous clothes. In her videos she blurred the distinction between male and female, more often than not aping a man in her stage suits and robotic moves. 'The more different you looked, the more attention people would pay to you,' she said. 'I saw that people were fascinated by my aura. But that's just me. It's something that comes from my grandfather . . . People are afraid to approach him, he's got this independent "I-don't-need-you" attitude, and I'm like that too.'

Jones' hit albums *Warm Leatherette*, *Nightclubbing* and *Living My Life* marked her out amongst the risque disco set, and she received worldwide recognition for roles in movies like *Conan The Barbarian* and the James Bond odyssey *A View To A Kill*. In the realm of pop, though, her appeal was one of notoriety and eccentricity, austere on the level of image, but not so hot when it came to actual musical ability.

Annie's strength lay in the way she combined visual prowess with astonishing vocal talent. Less severe than Grace Jones, she was still more effective. Her cross-dressing guise was well thought out, with a definite purpose: for Annie it was important to make her mark in a male-dominated sphere with control over every part of the business, not just on the visual level.

TWO MEN IN A SUIT

In the early 1980s Annie and Dave formed their own company and became partners in crime. The perfect pop couple turned themselves into two men, appearing on the 'Sweet Dreams' video in business suits, exuding a thoroughly corporate image. Such meticulous organization was a reaction to the days of the Tourists, where they felt themselves controlled by the record company and at the mercy of a distant management. Forming their own limited company was an exercise in control. 'I learned everything from maintaining a studio to how much equipment costs, to video budgets, to paying trucking companies,' said Dave. 'We had no manager, even when 'Sweet Dreams' was at Number 1. Just everything you could imagine to do with running a group, I found out about it.'

Early on Eurythmics parted with Arnakata, and apart from a stint with a friend and Coventry Art School teacher, Alan Harrison, a man 'emotionally involved but you have to keep control of it to get results', Dave assumed total management responsibility. Envisaging a kind of Beatles Apple set-up without the headache, Dave concentrated as much on cash-flow as flowing musical concepts. When the Beatles flung open Apple's doors in the 1960s in a spirit of mutual co-operation and independence from the record company, a generation of hippies nearly bled them dry. Although seeking a similar loose association of musicians and performers under their umbrella, Eurythmics tried to keep a sharp eye on the accounts.

Starting out with a small advance and little backing from RCA, Dave negotiated a bank loan in order to buy production independence, setting up the Chalk Farm studio above a picture framer's shop with his friend Adam Williams. It was here that Dave and Annie recorded *Sweet Dreams* on a cheap, cheerful eight-track, constrained by very basic recording techniques, yet forced to be inventive in recreating the sounds of the latest sophisticated pop technology.

Constantly having to keep costs down meant that Dave and Annie gravitated towards people who were young, enthusiastic, new to the business and therefore not too expensive. They were also people prepared to hustle some radical ideas, like the graphic designer Laurence Stevens who came to Eurythmics fresh from the London College of Printing, to invent the sparse, ground-breaking design of their record sleeves and posters.

'I was extremely lucky. I was there at the right time with the right idea and they were willing to give me a chance,' says Laurence, speaking to me one day in his bright, comfortable, impeccably organized West Hampstead studio, where we drank tea from vast yellow china cups. A perceptive, precise man interested in fashion and music, he recalls how as a graduate he wanted to combine those two aspects in typography. Intuiting the designer-led 1980s and the self-conscious manipulation of pop as a business, he invented Dave and Annie's 'D&A' company logo.

'I came up with the Palace script logo D&A; it was like a product stamp. The band Ultravox had the UV stamp that Peter Saville had given to them. It was an important cosmetic image, signalling music with irony. There was new technology with drum machines and synthesizers, it was no longer five guys like the Clash – this was a proper production business, hence the business suits. We'd laugh about the logo being like retailers C&A.'

The *Sweet Dreams* album cover Stevens designed features Annie holding a heart-shaped box of chocolates. The luridly wrapped box is a commercial product that contains the group's Sweet Dreams. By emphasizing the box and the typography, the point was made about Eurythmics being a small business, not just a rock band. The severe sweep of their early images was borne out by the design ideas that surrounded them, echoing the controversial fascination that bands such as Joy Division and New Order had with Nazi imagery.

'I made it look authoritative with that Fascist feel. I'll always remember seeing a postcard with a black swastika, white circle and red background, with the words underneath: "Don't underestimate the power of a strong institutional image." I try and do that with logos. With Eurythmics I was going for something clean, with precision and lots of white space, giving it a strict, stylish sit-up-and-take-notice-of-me feel. This was in contrast to punk, which was all torn paper, splashed paint, pins and people making funny faces.'

The sensational use of quasi-Fascist design – such as punk's anarchic use of the swastika, and the rigorous imagery of labels like Factory Records – was at times irresponsible and open to misunderstanding. Although Annie summoned up spectres of Nazi cabaret in the austerity of her cross-dressing image and parodic S&M innuendos, she was more concerned with stirring up people's preconceptions than giving offence.

'I don't want to give you the wrong impression,' says Stevens. 'It was a design based on the German Bauhaus in 1926, the foundation of all modern design. Everything was linear, pure forms, and fussiness and filigree work were no longer needed. It's all at the level of symbolism. The swastika was an ancient symbol that originally meant "peace", Nostradamus called it the "crooked cross". The letterheads of the Third Reich must have looked fabulous. You look at six guys in SS uniforms, they look clean-cut and perfect, no matter what they're up to. Hitler used it like Hollywood – Nuremburg with all those columns, it was like a film set. Product design doesn't look dated. Fashion dates, style doesn't.'

Stevens took the unusual step of including gold in the album cover lettering, adding rich, classic overtones to the muted yet elegant design. The radical subtlety of this effect was not well received by the American record company, accustomed to bold, obviously saleable images, and they sent back a design proof that 'annihilated the original idea' with plain grey and the chocolate box stuck in the middle. Luckily Eurythmics had another young Turk on their side in the form of a thoroughly committed junior A&R man, Jack Steven.

'At that time Alabama were a big act for RCA,' he says. 'So I got a pair of scissors, chopped up an Alabama record, stuck it on paper with bits of photos here and there and sent it to the guy who'd ruined Laurence's work saying, "this is what we'll do with the new Alabama album, I hope you find it credible and modern". They got the message, and eventually went with the original design.'

In the beginning, Dave and Annie needed people strategically rooting for them, and were selective about who they trusted. Jack was an ideal hustler for them. A music business maverick with flashing eyes and a wayward head of hair, he now runs his own management company in Marble Arch, schooling bands in the importance of 'music quality as opposed to the façade of being a pop star'. Formerly involved in music publishing, he was attracted to A&R work because it was 'the front line'. RCA noticed his risk-taking verve, and decided to employ him to bring a young contemporary front to the company.

'My brief was to go and look through the roster, to pick up acts on the list and sign new ones. At that time they had Eurovision winners Bucks Fizz – everyone laughs at Bucks Fizz, but they effectively gave the money for Eurythmics to develop. They also had the amazingly boring Sad Café and heavy rock groups like Alcatraz and the elderly Steve Gibbons. Bowie was their only real contemporary artist. I found a band called Eurythmics who'd done an album called *In The Garden* and were being dropped. I said to the managing director, "If there's one act I want to keep, it's Eurythmics . . . get rid of the rest." They said, "We don't understand what you're doing, but go ahead".'

Jack's thinking was in tune with Dave and Annie's new independent business attitude. His motto with regard to record companies is 'You don't work for them, you're there to inspire them to work for you'. From the start he encouraged the band to remain slightly aloof from RCA, to work from an autonomous base *within* the record company. 'If you want to be successful, you have to control your own destiny. Look at Spielberg; he doesn't associate with any one film studio, he remains autonomous from them,' he says. 'You have to understand who, what and why you want to use people.'

Eurythmics didn't stray from this concept of control. When they scored a hit with 'Sweet Dreams' they built their own studio beneath The Church in Crouch End, a building that originally belonged to a strange religious sect, apparently called The Aggepemonites. 'They were like a religious group in the 1800s who had all these ideas on free love and sex. They were a bit weird,' says Dave.

D&A became a parent company, spouting several different off-shoots that were all ultimately answerable to Dave and Annie. After they became successful and Dave had to hand over the management reins to someone else, instead of being guided by an outside manager, they employed their friend Kenny Smith to do the job from The Church. Smith has since moved with Steve Blackwell to bigger premises to form the subsidiary company Hyperkinetics, still managing Eurythmics, but now dealing with other acts as well.

Dave also owns his own production, publishing and record companies (Eligible Music and Anxious), while Annie has the Oil Factory, a video production company run by Dave's brother John. Owning all these industry outlets, with twenty people on the full-time payroll by 1989, has now given them almost complete artistic independence. They liaise regularly with RCA over promotion and distribution, having successfully commandeered their career from the moment 'Sweet Dreams' took off.

'Why should someone else have the power to interfere with what you've done?' Dave told *The Observer's* Dave Hill in 1986. 'It's like baking a cake, then letting someone else put the icing on. All the way down the line they're trying to put stickers on the things . . . You've got to watch everything, the bigger you get.'

Although D&A became a close-knit, family-type organization, Dave and Annie's obsession with control had its downside, making the rest of the staff sometimes feel insecure.

'The Church set-up was OK when it was good,' says a former engineer who worked in the studio there. 'But there was no continuity, it was a careless operation . . . and the staff didn't know from one day to the next what would be happening. Because of that a lot of people left who were very good. Eurythmics was a very calculated thing, a calculated image. That might be a way of dealing with the market but I don't think they believed in it at all.'

The concept of D&A was fine in principle but the day-to-day workings of an organization that thrives on tight-knit independence means that the set-up can become intense and claustrophobic. As in any small pop organization there is pressure on the staff members to conform and show absolute loyalty. Dave and Annie find criticism difficult, and therefore try and protect their organization from outside influences. Some who have worked with them say that either you were 'in' or 'forever excommunicated'. While in one way their desire to take on young, enthusiastic and inexperienced people is laudable, on a practical financial level it is also cheaper, and if decisions are centrally controlled there won't be too much opposition.

'That's not what I'd expect working with modern artistic people in the field of rock'n'roll,' says a former employee. 'Some pop stars are just as bad, others worse, but you expect the Eurythmics to be different.'

Although Eurythmics inevitably have their D&A disaffected, their concept of total control meant that the impact of the band was undiluted and highly individual. From the start of Eurythmics, Annie was concerned about keeping her hard-won control. Constantly seeing the process in terms of a battle, her armour was literally the male suit she wore, an outward sign of her mental resolve.

'Before when we worked with other people within the record company, someone was forever coming in and saying "this is the guy who's doing this for you",' she says. 'And it never turned out right, because the ideas all came from us, but then they'd be taken out of our hands.'

Although Dave and Annie were confident about the direction of their career, RCA were sceptical. 'Nobody actually knew who they were. They thought Eurythmics was some kind of toothpaste,' says Jack. 'It was a struggle all the way. We took a massive risk, but no one was prepared to back them. On one level Dave and Annie were incredibly naïve, a pair of innocents about the business and life in general. But when you talked to them a bit further there was an immense cynicism.'

At first RCA would not put up the money for a video, so Jack had to commission the initial promos 'behind the record company's back'. He had to fight for decent-sized posters, a budget and a tour. When 'Love Is A Stranger' became a dancefloor hit, the label conceded that there might be something there. Thumping his fist on the desk, Jack said: 'There's no *might* be about this . . . it's going to happen. Don't rely on what's happening in the street – do this thing for yourselves. *Make* the fucking thing happen!'

Annie, too, was combative. One day she was taken by record company promoters to dinner to meet producers at national Radio One. A powerful group in the pop industry, whose decisions on the playlist in the 1970s and early 1980s could make or break a record, they were used to being treated with kid gloves. Any young female pop performer faced with sexual or sexist innuendo from a stray DJ or producer simply had to bite her lip. Annie, though, was prepared to fight back, however undiplomatic it might appear.

Sure enough, one of the established producers, renowned in some quarters as 'a dirty old man', made unwarranted advances towards Annie. Her response was to turn round and slap him hard on the back, so he went flying off his chair. She stormed out, and in the ensuing commotion one of the promotions guys who had brought her said angrily: 'Look, in the Tourists you had it. In Eurythmics you don't. You might as well just give up.'

Another time Annie sent up the stereotypes of the music industry when she went to an official music therapy luncheon in a huge wig and a mini. 'I looked like a groupie because I was *being* a groupie,' she said, 'and these men were patting me on the head saying, "Oh! your hair is so beautiful!" *Really*! I looked the epitome of a prostitute and they were leering and winking. It was a joke. It wasn't style.'

There was much about the pop business that caused Annie to panic, but once she got over the upset of an occasion like the Radio One dinner, it hardened her resolve to keep on trying. 'She was very confused and emotional at times,' says Jack. 'But that was partly to do with all the appalling things she and Dave went through. There was an immense determination on her part – not to become a star, but to express herself.'

Expressing herself effectively meant continuing with the androgynous image, even when people objected to it. Most obvious incomprehension and opposition came from America, which under Reagan was undergoing a renaissance in 'wholesomeness'. There was a return to apple values where boys were boys and girls were girls, and, wary of the censurial force of the popular moral majority and its anti-rock offshoot the PMRC, the video channel MTV requested a birth certificate as proof that Annie Lennox was really a girl and not a decadent transvestite.

Dave and Annie regarded this with hilarity, but there was an edge to their response. When Eurythmics were invited to appear on the 1984 American Grammy Awards, Annie decided to resurrect Earl, her male alter ego from the days of the 'Who's That Girl?' video as a subtle form of revenge. 'The record company wanted us to make an appearance because they thought it would be prestigious, but we were very reticent about it,' Annie said later. 'We felt our stance was not in the bosom of the conventional music scene. We wouldn't have been comfortable simply playing our latest hit.

'If we'd refused to be on it the company would have been really upset with us, so we had to think of a way of satisfying them but at the same time to do it on our own terms. There had been a lot of talk about sexual ambiguity that year, so we decided this would be a perfect way to kind of put it back in their faces . . . a way of saying: "You want me to be a gender bender? Here I am".'

After a long make-up job, Annie appeared behind stage at the Grammys with her famous greased black hair, pocked chin and sideburns. While waiting for the curtain to go up, the stage manager anxiously looked for Annie Lennox, expecting to see a cool blonde. Then he realized that the scowling man waiting to sing was Her. After falling onto his knees in shock, he rolled around the floor, screaming with laughter.

John Denver was in front of the curtain, introducing Eurythmics with adulatory showbiz pomp and circumstance. Then the curtain went up, he turned round, saw Annie, and his jaw fell. The band began performing their song, but soon realized that their elaborate joke had been a little too effective.

'You know you're doing something weird because instead of looking at you, the audience are all talking to each other going "what the *fuck*",' Dave later recalled. 'When we stopped, instead of applause there was just loud *talking*. So they turned up this canned applause, quick.'

Infuriated and tense, Annie the man walked off stage and promptly punched the guy who was operating the monitors. 'We're fucking professionals, why aren't you?' she blasted at him, compounding the gender confusion with her explosive aggression. Although a sensitive soul, she can turn on the toughness if it is needed.

The hard thing for Annie was that her gender blending was far more threatening than the male pop stars who decided to cross-dress. When performers like Prince and Marilyn mischievously mixed gender, it was considered pretty and risque, pop fun in the camp tradition stretching back to Little Richard with his pomaded hair. Boy George in particular elicited more affection than dismay in his boy-meets-girl garb, especially when he made that off-quoted reassuring statement: 'I prefer a cup of tea to sex.' Hailed as 'the most outrageous character since Elton John and Liberace', his camp style and cross-dressing were pure pop pantomime, perfect fodder for the tabloid press.

George Alan O'Dowd rose on the crest of the New Romantic wave. Along with other puff-sleeved bands like Duran Duran, Depeche Mode and Spandau Ballet, Culture Club celebrated an early 1980s British club culture that welded fashion to music with the emphasis on gender confusion. Boys wore lipstick, long hair and clown's outfits. Clothes were designed on softer, flowing lines in accordance with melodic soul synthesizer-based music, a reaction to the harsh, luminous, discordant days of punk. Punk was full of macho heroics, whereas New Romanticism made prissies of us all, blurring the sexual roles with flamboyant attire.

A refugee of 1970s glitter-rock, Boy George combined the spirit of that style with punk and reggae to come up with a vivid dreadlocked hybrid. With his Hasidic hat and ribbons, and Annie's clipped, cropped mannish style, they presented an exercise in contrast, epitomizing the adventurous styling of new designer pop.

He and Annie were singled out as figureheads of the new androgyny when they appeared on the cover of *Newsweek* magazine in 1984 under the coverline, 'BRITAIN ROCKS AMERICA – AGAIN: From the Beatles to Boy George and Beyond'. Twenty years after the British beat groups invaded America, spearheaded by the Beatles, a sweep of pop-soul synthesizer bands arrived via the early 1980s American national fad, MTV. With bright designer image as much the selling point as their music, bands like Duran Duran, Culture Club and

Eurythmics wooed the States. Boy George and Annie Lennox were convenient polar opposites, both experimenting with gender roles, but one cheeky and chirpy, the other exuding neutral cool.

To a nation weaned on regular straight-up-and-down rock guys and girls, these British images were a risque revelation. 'A heady sense of adventure, irreverence and playful passion', said *Newsweek*. 'Forget about nostalgia for the earnest pop optimism of the '60s and face the era of cramped hopes and wild style.'

Annie's cross-dressing wild style was brief, yet explosive in its impact. When the device was no longer useful to her, she abandoned it for fear of becoming typecast. The fashion press, though, eagerly embraced her as an example of androgynous street style. In early 1984, *The Times* ran a feature on 'the girls and guys of King's Road, Chelsea, who are mirror images of each other, slowly walk the length of London's famous peacock parade wearing identical clothes'.

They focused on Annie as the heroine of girls in razor-cut spiked hair and military caps. Designer Vivienne Westwood, too, was hailed as an inspiration, with her genderless collections. Even Calvin Klein's Y-fronts for women got a mention. 'We are experiencing the breaking-down of traditional barriers between the sexes,' eulogized *The Times*, 'and can perceive these changing mental attitudes reflected in street fashion.'

Disliking any form of categorization, Annie began to make her escape. 'Unfortunately, the media being the animal it is, it's necessary for them to slap a label on you very quickly, hence I became gender bender. I realized I'd escaped one box (the dolly bird singer) only to be in danger of being locked into another one.'

By the end of 1984, Annie had modified the extremity of her image, opting for a variety of new styles and looks – from ballgowns to the leopard-skin pill box hat. 'Now I don't need to assert that kind of masculine sexuality as much,' she said later, 'I'm allowing the feminine side of my sexuality to come through and I'm more comfortable with that. Now I've established a certain persona, I can move into something a little softer.'

By November 1986 she was claiming: 'I am not the androgynous Annie Lennox. I never was. I used it for something else.' A year later she was experimenting with a female-in-drag look in the video for the single 'I Need A Man'.

Aggressively made up with a gargantuan blonde wig and a skintight dress, Annie sings in Rolling Stones' pastiche. Many took the record at face value and considered it a retrograde step for Annie, crudely singing the praises of men. She was flamboyantly taking the opposite tack to those early cross-dressing days, yet still intending to appeal to her gay audience:

'It's like a woman dressed as a man dressed as a woman,' she told *The Independent*'s Marek Kohn, 'so there's a lot of sexual ambiguity in the whole thing. It's almost a homosexual statement as well. It's a song that gay men could and will identify with very strongly. That's the beauty of it, that it can be really perverted in a sense.'

Annie's transvestite style opened up new avenues for women's visual presentation in pop. By the end of the 1980s, women in the commercial mainstream felt freer to wear more masculine or individualistic clothes, though admittedly this was at the more 'intelligent' singer/song-writing end of the rock-pop spectrum. Many women who started their pop careers with a more masculine look did so in order for their music to be taken seriously.

Sinead O'Connor, for example, began her career in 1987 with loud and forthright interviews, and a shaved head and Doc Marten boots to match. For her first album, *The Lion And The Cobra*, which she wrote and produced herself, this determined stance was necessary. By her second offering several years later, *I Do Not Want What I Haven't Got*, she was married with a child and a string of hits behind her. The more she became established and respected within the business, the more she felt able to ease up and bring out her feminine side.

Similarly, US singer/song writer Tracy Chapman made her debut on the strength of her songs rather than her sexuality, dressed in old combat trousers and a baggy T-shirt. After the phenomenal success of her first eponymous album, when she became the darling of the high profile benefit circuit, her image was slightly softened and smartened with airbrushed Herb Ritts shots.

Folk pop artist Michelle Shocked, too, doesn't deny that her tomboy style complete with urchin's cap was a form of protection, particularly in her hitch-hiking days. 'If there had been a more realistic attitude towards women, I wouldn't have had to go to what appeared such an extreme. To face the risks of travelling alone, I had to dress like a boy. The same with music . . . If there was a more realistic image of women in pop I maybe wouldn't have been such a nihilistic punk with a mohawk and a ring in my nose.'

By the arrival of her critically acclaimed third album, *Captain Swing*, Shocked was taking the unheard-of step of appearing in videos with red lipstick and tight lycra dresses. Although that sartorial step was deliberately humorous, she didn't take it without a certain amount of guilt. 'In the course of life I want to find a middle ground. I carry a sense of responsibility – I have an opportunity to defeat existing media stereotypes. If I soften the edges, whether I need to personally or whether it's being imposed on me, I feel I'd be letting down the revolution!'

The Canadian country star k d lang found that although her deliciously butch female Elvis persona gave her greater autonomy, it meant she was also shunned by Nashville. USA's home of country music likes its women with the perms, skirts and lip gloss, not the duck-billed haircut. k d often recalls a story when a man was handing out leaflets in the street, giving blue ones to men, pink to the women. He was clearly confused by k d. 'I decided to put him out of his misery,' she says, 'so I took a pink one.'

While Michelle Shocked and k d lang gained widespread popularity in the late 1980s, their task would have been much harder at the beginning of the decade. In terms of image Annie unwittingly became the spearhead for a female pop revolution, even though she doesn't want to be viewed as such. 'The music industry often goes against *men*,' she says. 'If you have a woman she'll be given a great deal more attention than a man, because she happens to be female. Very often that goes against male musicians.'

The attention that women are given, though, is not often the kind that they want, a fact that Annie had to bear in mind when she first started. Until the mid-1980s, unless she was a groupie or a gimmick, it was very difficult for female pop artist to get serious mainstream respect. A lot of women came through during punk rock, but they were systematically destroyed by a music industry that marginalized them. In terms of financial investment, for many years women were viewed as loss leaders, despite the fact that a large proportion of record-buyers are women. Annie emerged after punk, when challenging female performers had been forced to retreat and leave the stage to lip-glossed MTV idols like Laura Brannigan, so Annie's image, as calculated as it was uncompromising, was a deft stylistic stroke that reverberated through pop's hallowed halls.

Her careful professionalism and visual gender experimentation have acted as an inspiration for many women – and men – ever since.

'I met Annie in the basement of the BBC, at "Top Of The Pops",' recalls premier rap singer Neneh Cherry, whose Buffalo style symbolized much of late 1980s tough girl chic. 'I wanted to talk to her. We kept trying to get together in LA, but I felt a bit shy. I've got a lot of respect for her. She's one of the women who's been a real guiding star; she was completely provocative, the first women to do that. Unfortunately, a lot of women I respect have to wear dungarees to be taken seriously, but she was both sexy and tough. People would love to classify you as a bimbo if they could, like they're testing to see if there's anything there.'

Another long-term music industry admirer has been her former A&R, Jack Stevens: 'What attracted me about Annie was that she meant what she said in terms of her career. Most women in the music industry struggle for one reason or another: (a) because it's a very chauvinistic business, and (b) women immediately tend to be regarded as second rate anyhow. Annie would never compromise, she was determined to get on in terms of her own intellectualism rather than being a floozy or a stupid girl. As a result of that she had greater insight creatively and was prepared to take the heartache. Very few women are.

'Working with Annie subsequently showed me that a woman determined and serious about her career is a better proposition than anything else. Everyone talks this crap about female wobblers, but you actually get more with men than you do women. There was none of those stupid games or silliness – with Annie, it was just straight down to business.'

By dressing as a man Annie took men on at their own game, turning the suit into an anarchic gender weapon, as well as something smart and chic. It's an achievement that has given her an enduring image – when people think of Annie Lennox, they return time and time again to the Amazon in a tie beating her wand in 'Sweet Dreams', an image that crystallizes a classic moment in 1980s pop.

5

The Female Gaze

'I'm amazed by the power of make-up and costume. I see image as a wrapping, something to play with. There's fifteen thousand different Annies. Within the one person there are a million types of abilities and personas according to the environment you're in. When we started Eurythmics Dave and I wanted to represent ourselves in a visually intelligent way, not by some cliché that would limit us for years. We wanted to give ourselves longevity by making sure we were allowed to change.

'But at the same time, there is only one Roxy Music, there is only one David Bowie, one Smokey Robinson. When people reach the peak of their musical achievement they've defined their own territory, they typify themselves. Really great groups find out what really represents them and then bring it to a peak . . . It's like the monkfish that lives deep down in the water. It has a light connected to its head. As it swims about, all the little fish floating nearby get attracted to the light – and all the time the monkfish has its mouth wide open.

'People relate to each other very much in terms of what they're wearing, a sense of personal style. Image is always a thing that fascinates, and in pop music it's a great vehicle for the imagination. Yet clothes are very misleading. The essence of what people are is contained within them, not in their clothes. You can package a *projection* of me, but not the *essential* me.

'Although I'm terribly vain, I'm not afraid of looking unattractive. I want to set new limits on what women in the music industry are allowed to do. I can look beautiful or dreadful, and like to play with those two extremes.'

ANGEL

Annie appears in Restoration theatrical costume, wearing a long white flowing gown and a golden wig. Little boys and girls resembling cupids

100

dart in and out as she sings: 'There must be an angel . . .' Her voice is trilling, coy, sweet and innocent.

Another later shot: this time Annie is dressed in pure white, wandering through a house disrupted by a seance. The atmosphere is forbidding, with unseen spirits knocking on doors, injecting terror into the group seated at the table summoning up souls. Wearing her ghost white, Annie runs panic-stricken through the hallway, caught in slow motion before she is relentlessly consumed by fire.

HOUSEWIFE

Annie acts the dowdy housewife in a demure, flowery blouse, preparing the evening meal. She is tense with frustrated emotion, anxious that her house should be kept spotless, yet constantly overcome by the urge to tear it apart. She fusses, moralizes and makes judgements, weighed down by suburbia's heavy calm and strangled by its expectations. She listens to Beethoven, and awakens the little manic girl inside her, the one who wants to unravel everything that has gone before, to become *bad*. There is also a third entity, a shadowy asexual personality that stands in the corner waiting to strike.

WHORE

Perched on the back seat of a car, Annie is the sophisticated prostitute being driven to an assignation in a large house in London's St John's Wood. Wearing furs and diamond earrings, she gives a sly, cynical smile before ripping off her wig to reveal slick, cropped hair. She changes into black leather erotica to become the stereotypical Lady Dominatrix, conquering all her foes through the force of her desire.

Another shot: this time in a suburban living room Annie plays a frenzied woman in a low-cut chintzy dress painting her face in a Valium-induced haze. She staggers into the broad daylight and makes her way down to a run-down theatre. Here she snatches the stage, the mike and some temporary limelight. 'I need a man,' she sneers, with a convincingly blank stare.

CHAMELEON POWER

More than any other woman in pop, with the possible exception of Madonna, Annie has projected a breadth of images that are stunning in both conviction and visual challenge. Her stark beauty and severely styled hair has led to countless offers of lucrative work, from a reputed £3 million modelling for Vidal Sassoon, to the cover of *Vogue* and various modelling or advertising contracts. In 1985 *Playboy* magazine voted her one of the world's sexiest women.

'I don't sell myself as a product,' she maintains, not accepting what she sees as a 'sell-out'. Unlike Madonna with Pepsi-Cola, Annie wants to create a series of images that are enigmatic and aloof rather than commercially connected to brand names and styles. Both women sell their personalities: Madonna's is rooted in what journalist Julie Burchill termed 'honest to goodness blood, sweat and lipgloss'; Annie's projection of images is more carefully cerebral.

Her pop career has been built around a series of themes, starting with the businessman in a suit, graduating to a female androgynous Aladdin Sane figure, to move to every point on pop's sartorial compass – from the glitter suit to the rock chick to suburban satire and back again. Her visually controversial approach is theatrical rather than welded to current fashion tastes. It is one that she has had to refine and learn, working by trial and error, searching through bargain basements and theatrical outfitters as well as designer styles in order to create something unique.

'I'm not sure she necessarily had a good eye for clothes at first. She wasn't confident about her image, and that came out in the way she dressed. She had strong ideas about what she wanted, but it didn't always work,' says Carol Semaine, a young designer who made clothes for Annie in the days of the Tourists and now runs her own shop called Modern Art, situated off Tottenham Court Road. A textile design graduate from Middlesex Polytechnic, Carol met Annie in the last furious days of punk, when the former was running a clothes stall with a friend at Camden Market and designing clothes for punk bands like the Vibrators and Generation X.

One day Annie arrived at the stall and asked Carol if she would make her some clothes. 'At that time she was in the Tourists and really broke, with the band trying to get out of their contract. The band were all bound by the fact that they had absolutely no money. You can't have a sleek image – unless you wear tuxedos or something –

if you're living hand to mouth. Annie would get old curtains and I'd cut them up to make into trousers and skirts.'

With a resourcefulness that Julie Andrews would be proud of, Carol attempted to meet Annie's sometimes bizarre specifications. 'She had some very unusual styles. I made an outfit for when she signed the Eurythmics' contract. It was a top and trousers in pea green lycra with a black lace frill round the yoke and a Peter Pan collar. I didn't really like it but when you're making clothes for other people you don't say anything. She wanted something vivid that no one else had.'

When she was in the Tourists Annie was still finding her feet stylistically, and her image then was a jumble sale amalgam of bright colours and odd combinations. 'At that time everyone was wearing second-hand clothes and putting it all together,' says Carol. 'Annie was really anti-black. That's another reason why, although I could appreciate her clothes, it wasn't my style. It was too busy and colourful for me at the time.'

At that time Carol teetered around on stilettos and plastic trousers in a version of 'sugared-up punk', invariably dressed in black. It's not surprising that she and Annie were on different wavelengths. 'Annie would tell me what she wanted and I'd say whether it could be done or not. I remember she asked me to do some trousers skin tight. I made them skin tight. Then she said "Oh, I don't want them *that* tight." I thought – what am I supposed to do now, and said "That's it I'm afraid!" My idea of skin tight then was so you couldn't breathe. If someone asked for something skin tight, they'd *get* it skin tight! We just had different interpretations.'

Although Annie loved experimenting with style, at first she wasn't so confident about explaining what she wanted. 'I don't think she always realized how clothes were going to turn out,' says Carol. 'A lot was in her head – if she had come with a picture from a magazine I could've done that. Billy Idol used to bring pictures he'd torn out of *Vogue* and say "I want one of those but with chains all over it." That way you'd get a definite idea.'

The very individuality that marked Annie out later in her career held her back in the beginning. A former classical music student, she had to spend a period acclimatizing herself to the rigours of image in the pop marketplace. To create the most impact, a performer has to pick up on, articulate or invent an almost cartoon-like youth style, wearing larger-than-life signals that fans can immediately identify with. Tina

Turner has her red lipstick, Neneh Cherry her huge trainers and Madonna her platinum blonde hair. For Annie her trademark was to be the orange crop and suit.

'She wasn't really a punk,' says Carol. 'She didn't belong to a youth cult. She really was an individual. That added to her feelings of insecurity because she knew she wasn't conforming – while she didn't want to, she also felt she didn't belong anywhere.'

In searching for a set of images that suited her, Annie constantly battled with the implications of revealing her sexuality. Her reluctance to show any flesh was part of a refusal to trade in the more vulgar areas of pop, with a self-consciousness that inhibited her during the days of the Tourists. She later turned that stringent self-awareness to a strength as, growing increasingly confident with success, she invented an elaborate system of pop disguises.

'I don't think she realized at first how stunning-looking she was,' maintains Carol. 'Either she didn't realize or she knew but couldn't handle it. That went hand in hand with her not wanting to flaunt her body. You'd *never* see her in a low-cut dress. If she was whistled at in the street, it'd really make her hackles rise.'

Now with a long video history behind her, Annie is confident about the chameleon power of her image, and can relax with her sexuality. 'In a subtle way she's experimenting with the effect it's going to have on people. It's a very well-thought-out game, and I don't think the average punter realizes it. She's extremely intelligent and sensitive – things like wearing a bra top, lot's of people would think "Whoah, that's a sexy thing to do", but it goes a lot deeper with her.'

Changing her image from cute lead vocalist in the Tourists to serious-minded Eurythmic was a long haul for Annie. In the small RCA team that initially showed Eurythmics any interest was a young dedicated press officer called Sheila Sedgwick, whose success with the band earned her an industry award and peach position as Head of Press at MCA Records. Having taken a break from PR since then to travel, Sheila still vigorously recalls the process Annie had to go through to find her famous style.

'When I first met Annie, she didn't quite know about her image. There was a transition period between the Tourists and Eurythmics, as the two bands were so different. The Tourists were a bit retro, whereas Eurythmics were in a very forward-looking mode. It took ages for Annie and Dave to work it out,' she says.

Early Eurythmics photo sessions threw up an array of images, from the bizarre Gered Mankowitz shot that featured Annie on a cube wearing a bra, a binliner and a bunch of fairy lights, to the picture of Annie in a mannequin shirt dress during Eurythmics' Kraftwerk phase. She dyed her hair a variety of shades, from brittle peroxide blonde to soft red, and wore stark black wigs. The problem for the press office was in helping Annie find a coherent image that they could promote. The media was still hostile towards Dave and Annie since the Tourists debacle, so the pressure was on to come up with something utterly startling or simply unique.

'It was one of my toughest challenges as a PR to turn the whole hate campaign round. It was a *serious slog*,' recalls Sheila. This, coupled with RCA's indifference towards the band, meant they had an uphill struggle.

Dave's outlandish imagination coupled with Annie's magpie love of different clothes led to a bewildering range of ideas that had to be honed down. It was very gratifying to Sheila that Eurythmics were pragmatic and professional, prepared to engage in endless discussion about the direction of their promotional campaign. Although Annie was sometimes confused about *how* to project what she wanted, she was always definite about the approach.

'She had an interesting way of not being a bimbo fashion vehicle,' says Sheila. 'She had a very strong personality, an aura. Before I met her I had a coloured impression, as rumours had been circulating that she was a "difficult artist", and we had to be very careful. I was on my guard the first time she walked in the room. It sounds so clichéd, but everyone knew she was *there*. When she speaks, everybody listens, she's not a jabbery girly female. We ended up having a good working relationship because Annie's attitude was straightforward: "This is a problem, so what can we do to get round it?"

'She has an interest in details, clothes and style, not necessarily fashion. She wants to be unique with something that will shock people slightly. She's not an outrageous Wendy O'Williams type, it's more thought-provoking.'

After intense discussions Dave and Annie moved towards the stark, suited image that chimed with their burgeoning D&A organization. It was her neutral cross-dressing look that proved to be a major turning-point, both in the way they were perceived by the press, and the positive reaction from within RCA ranks. To coincide with the release of the 'Sweet Dreams' single in February 1983, pictures went out showing Dave and Annie in business suits, Annie facing the camera with her wrists tied (suggestions of sado-sexual bondage), Dave turned away. It was a stark, decisive shot that summed up a new trend in pop – design-conscious, stylized and materialistic.

The editor of Britain's biggest selling pop glossy, *Smash Hits*, rang Sheila for a transparency of Eurythmics that he could put on the magazine's cover. This together with the critical recognition that accompanied the *Sweet Dreams* album made the record company decide to get behind the band.

'You had two characters who could really perform as *stars*, as opposed to being seen as slightly weird, bizarre, difficult artists – which is how they came across at first. Nobody could see any direction for them,' says Sheila.

Eurythmics' luck had begun to change five months previously when their fifth release, 'Love Is A Stranger', tickled the upper reaches of the charts at Number 54, and they shifted their recording base from Chalk Farm to The Church in Crouch End. Although it wasn't a hit first time round, 'Love Is A Stranger' served to introduce Eurythmics' distinctive sound: synth as a bass rhythm with clear soul vocals on top.

Their A&R cheerleader at the time, Jack Steven, remembers what attracted him to the band in the first place. 'It was really interesting seeing a *white* vocalist who could really sing with amazing feel and a quirky little personality in the background doing the job of a complete band. In those days it was unheard of. They played pure techno – long before the Yazoos and all that. I never imagine that technology can create soulfulness, and to this day I still don't. I think Dave's very talented in the way he *can* put those combinations together.'

The second Eurythmics' album, *Sweet Dreams (Are Made Of This)*, was a much more focused affair than *In The Garden*, with Dave joyfully fusing studio technology to a live feel, and Annie directing her song writing into clear themes of obsession and emotional addiction. Her chillingly dramatic analysis of love and loss gained an edge and a poignancy when delivered against such sweet melody.

Hailed as 'an immaculate post-disco view of urban romance' (*NME*), 'the peak of heartbreak' (*Sounds*), 'captivating aural experience' (*Rolling Stone*) and 'one of the most important albums of '83' (*Melody Maker*), *Sweet Dreams* gave Dave and Annie the credibility they had been fighting to establish since the Tourists.

It was the stylistic leap they made in terms of video, too, that consolidated the impact. In the early 1980s, Britain led the way, manufacturing slick, innovative and eye-catching videos that were exported worldwide, particularly to the States. In the same way that they absorbed and articulated new music technology, Eurythmics gathered a coterie of video-makers around them who were keen to experiment on a shoestring with startling images or unusual film techniques.

Chris Ashbrooke was the enthusiastic director who assembled images like Annie's cross-gender kiss with herself in the 'Who's That Girl?' video ('I animated it like a cartoon,' he said), while Jack Steven contributed many ideas from his sound grasp of European cinema, and Jon Roseman oversaw each early operation as producer.

A tall, burly Jewish man with a dry sense of humour, Roseman now runs his own film and video agency in London's West End. He began his career as a whizz-kid arts graduate working for London Weekend Television, and was promoted rapidly before he left to form his own production agency. He remembers how difficult it was to get record companies interested in video throughout the 1970s.

'It took a long, long time before video became remotely relevant. I worked with Rod Stewart and the Rolling Stones in the early days. It was all shot in mute, you didn't have playback, so you'd just have a woman floating through the woods and that was your lot. "Bohemian Rhapsody" broke the back of that because it was *commercial*.'

Queen's 'Bohemian Rhapsody' sat at the top of the British charts for nine weeks in 1975, a rock-operatic melange that was noteworthy as much for the accompanying video promo (the first of its kind) as the song itself. This paved the way for pop as a three-minute TV commercial, a factor that the Americans were uncharacteristically slow to pick up on.

'There were only two TV shows in the States that used any kind of video: one was a rock show, the other a midnight special. I used to go to America to hustle for work, and I'd often go to places where they didn't have a TV set in the entire building. Nothing whatsoever,' recalls Jon.

'I used to have to go back to the house I rented, put a TV and video in the back of the car, bring it in, tune it all up, bang in a tape, and they'd say: "Yeah, that's really great, Jon. If we were ever to make videos – which we don't – we'd be sure to call you". Americans were really slow. But then when MTV happened, you had the American attitude of going way over the top.'

Being a comparatively small country with a tight national TV network, Britain had a head start in the video age. Pop's New

Wave of the late 1970s grew up knowing the importance of video for them, whereas in the States there wasn't the same exposure for a band. With a vast disparate collection of TV stations in the States, the visual promotion of pop could not be properly co-ordinated.

All this changed on 1 August 1981 when Warner Communications' MTV opened for business. Within two years the first American cable music channel Music TeleVision became second in importance only to radio as a music industry promotional vehicle. The station provided twenty-four hours of rock videos, music news, interviews and gossip, catching the American video-less record industry on the hop. British videos were imported to plug the gap, thus paving the way for the 'Second British Invasion' of the early 1980s.

Britain's strongest pop export at that time was designer irony, with bands like Heaven 17, Spandau Ballet, ABC and Culture Club manipulating the pop process with a vivid mix of streetwise image-making and coded melodic pop/soul. In 1983 Eurythmics spearheaded this renaissance, with Annie being the only woman at that time to break through and break the mould alongside the style-conscious male bands.

Similarities have often been pointed out between Eurythmics and that other major 1983 synthesizer duo Yazoo. Both were odd polar opposite couples, and both Annie and Alison 'Alf' Moyet presented images that went against the grain – Annie the bullet-headed cross-dresser, Alison uncompromisingly overweight singing bluesy mainstream pop – yet the latter never experimented with her image in the same way as Annie, and once she went solo she slimmed down, softened and airbrushed her look.

Annie's penchant for theatre recklessly displayed itself in her videos, with a selection of female characters and archetypes thrown up in order to bewitch her audience. Her desire for dressing up was given free rein within Dave's fantastical storylines, mini-narratives that liberally mixed metaphors. His ideas provided the framework of a particular video, while Annie worked on the costume or image she wanted to present.

Eurythmics' use of video evolved to such an extent that they were among the first bands to introduce the concept of the 'video album' or V-LP, a form that has its own aesthetic demands.

The whole litany of visual style the Eurythmics draws on owes much to an awareness of European art cinema and film history. Dave Stewart is an avid film enthusiast and his brother John, a director of their Oil Factory video company, previously worked as the TV officer at the British Film Institute.

Jon Roseman swears that in the beginning, though, there was never an overall plan. 'The videos don't really have complex plots. I think a lot of it's down to the fact that Dave did acid for a year. The cow in the record company boardroom, for instance, in the 'Sweet Dreams' video. Someone suggested "how about a cow?" It wasn't "let's get esoteric about the meaning of life". Maybe I'm demeaning Dave's genius in a way to say things just happened – but there wasn't any great *raison d'être*. We just saved what looked good in the edit.'

Even if much of Eurythmics' visual presentation was down to Dave's lysergic haze, that doesn't detract from the surreal power of their videos and album covers, or the confidence of Annie as a leading player. 'You stick a camera in front of Annie and she would always look fabulous,' recalls Roseman. 'She's not like some of those grungy rock guys who stand there with a guitar.'

Top lighting cameraman Chris Asbrooke found her challenging to work with. 'She's got the sort of face which can look either terrible or wonderful, and it's a real pleasure to make her look wonderful,' he said. 'The contradictory thing is, if you look at the 'Who's That Girl?' video when she's dressed up in a long blonde wig, she hates herself like that. But everyone says "doesn't she look good!"'

Annie's selection of pop personas act as a filter for her own personality, so, through the medium of disguise, she can present different aspects of herself to the public without becoming vulnerable. Each character reflects and distorts conventional feminine images in a kind of moral pop pageant, a latter-day pop *Canterbury Tales*.

The album *Sweet Dreams* acts as a blueprint for the themes that resonate throughout her career, starting with the sleeve shot that shows Annie naked with her back turned. Nakedness is a strong motif for her, denoting something pure and elemental. It was symbolic on *Sweet Dreams* as a way of showing how Eurythmics stripped their music down to the basics before building it up again. 'I like working with no clothes on. I don't mean showing your breasts for the sake of it; it's just a really neat way of being who you are,' she says.

Lewis Ziolek, the young fashion and music photographer who shot that particular session, remembers Annie being an ideal subject. 'Annie definitely thinks about the personas she projects. Often when you work with people you have to keep suggesting ideas, whereas the Eurythmics were spontaneous. I don't remember telling her to do a back shot with no shirt on – that would've been embarrassing – she just decided to do it herself. At the time it didn't seem unusual.'

Annie took her bare image a step further on the cover of the next album, *Touch*, a Peter Ashworth shot that features her close up flexing her tanned biceps with a menacing sideways look. Her black leather mask and lurid orange hair highlight the sharp aggression of the shot. She summons up the image of a female wrestler in the same way that Neneh Cherry six years later symbolized a female boxer with wrapped hands on the cover of her debut album *Raw Like Sushi*. 'I'd turned the previous album picture round the other way, so the heart had gone, and it was almost a stance of defiance,' Annie says of *Touch*.

She appears naked for the third time on the cover of their 1986 album *Revenge*, standing next to Dave who is fully clothed in Puritan black and white. Both gaze straight at the camera with a pose that is clear, uncomplicated and touching on a cherubic cleanliness. They duplicate this sense of innocence later on the video collection for the LP *Savage*, where for the song 'Shame', Annie and Dave lay entwined like two uncorruptible star twins while the flotsam and jetsam of the decadent twentieth-century world spins around them.

Throughout her career Annie has returned time and time again to the image of the angel, a natural choice for someone who was born on Christmas Day and recorded her best songs in a church. It's there in the innocence of *Sweet Dreams*, especially the song 'Jennifer', which tells the story of a young woman who has drowned, conjuring up an image of a sweet, ethereal Ophelia. It's there as a bare asexual being on the cover of *Touch*, and it's there, gloriously triumphant two years later, in the song 'There Must Be An Angel (Playing With My Heart)'.

Usually Dave came up with the ideas for videos, but 'There Must Be An Angel' was Annie's creation from start to finish. In this she trills in her long golden hair and white gown, surrounded by pillars, vestal virgins and little children dressed up like tiny playing cupids. Dave's presence as a decadent, feasting King Louis XIV gives the proceedings an air of high camp festivity.

The tone becomes more serious for their 1990 release 'Angel', which is shot in stark black and white until Annie meets her angelic destiny and the video flashes into colour. Here Annie explores a deep, unnerving spirtuality, placing herself at the centre of a seance. With her high-collared white gown and dramatically blanched face, she exudes a disturbing other-worldliness.

Annie sings, her angelic persona wanders through the ragged wind-blown drapes and ruins of an old house, summoned to the spirit world. After wading past the flying autumn leaves and ancient dust she reaches a kind of heavenly nirvana, singing madly as she is consumed by flames. In a prosaic white suit, Dave runs after her and tries to save her, but already she has transcended this world.

Here Annie reaches the peak of her angelic dream, assuming its role as divine attendant or messenger, a spiritual alchemist that symbolizes an invisible, positive life-force. Annie has always identified with the purity and mystic protection of this image, one that is in tune with her pursuit of an abstract concept or an *idea* of perfection. Not surprisingly, her favourite word is 'sublime'.

'There are so many mythological beings that have been written about and painted throughout history, the angelic figure being one of them,' she told *NME*'s Stuart Bailey in 1989. 'We have no angels in our time. I have never met an angel, but there's this idea of a fictitious being that is somehow connected to a higher creative source, and that might be a protection for us you know.'

She admitted to a frequent longing for such a protective figure in her life, its very purity making it invulnerable. That's an attractive prospect when you're working within a pop industry that renders nothing sacred.

Completely opposing this image is its other archetype: the whore. Annie often makes reference to prostitution in moralistic, almost biblical terms, setting it up as the dark, sleazy opposite of the whiter than white angel. The prostitute amplifies and caricatures the bad girl in her, the girl that likes to play around or play for money: kooky, knowing, amoral and free. She first makes her appearance on the *Sweet Dreams* track 'Love Is A Stranger', sitting self-satisfied in the back of a chauffeur-driven limousine.

Wrapped in white fur and diamonds and wearing a magnificent blonde wig, Annie's whore is a glamorized, smiling creation. She would never get ripped off or run over; she is in control. Before reaching her destination, she pulls off her wig to reveal the slick short hair underneath. She then changes into her final costume, appearing in the black and white tiled bathroom wearing a black wig, black leather skirt, studded belt and fishnet tights. Now the Dominatrix, the sadistic stereotype, she fingers a pair of open scissors. She trades in obsession, buying and selling a destructive love that's like an addiction.

The whore is an icily beautiful, unforgiving, threatening character. Annie wanted to make the connection between the prostitute, pusher and junkie explicit with the use of hypodermic syringes in the video. That, of course, would not have endeared the band to a 'Top Of The Pops' audience, so it was wisely left out. There is still a strong sense of one of Annie's most pervasive themes – that the trading of pop fantasy at a basic or superficial level involves a pimp/prostitute-type relationship, with the female star exploiting herself for male management or a male audience.

'She liked wearing leather, PVC or slightly erotic clothes,' says Annie's early photographer Joe Bangay. 'Maybe she wanted to be noticed. She did it to be slightly outrageous. She's got tremendous presence in front of the camera, she learned about lighting very quickly and she knew all her best angles.'

Annie's tarty bad girl turns up again on the *Savage* video album singing 'I Need A Man'. Here there is an emphasis on cold drag, with Annie's breasts hugged tight in a pencil-thin purple dress, her head covered in ridiculous blonde curls and her face slashed with make-up. She sings a parody of a Rolling Stones' number in a crusty old theatre, leering at the camera with an almost macho style.

'It is a song that gay men can identify with very strongly,' she noted. The 'tranny Annie' image was presented as the deliberate opposite to her stereotyped housewife persona on *Savage's* opening track 'Beethoven'. 'We had two polarized characters,' said Annie. 'Both heightened clichés. We were so fond of them.' The neat, ordered housewife sequence was filmed like a TV soap opera, with all normal expectations subverted by Annie's transformation from housewife to bedraggled, decadent chanteuse.

'Annie liked the incredible feeling of voyeurism,' the video's director Sophie Muller told *City Limits* in 1987. A 1983 graduate of film studies at the Royal College of Art, Muller was hired by Eurythmics because her offbeat camera angles were considered perfect for the spinning, fractious quality of *Savage*. She did a startling job, and has remained with Eurythmics' Oil Factory video production company ever since. 'I'd spent a lot of time struggling and this was my big break,' she said.

More of a serious film maker than a pop video fan, Muller brought a quirkily trained eye to Eurythmics' visual dimension. 'Eurythmics' songs are not profound,' she said. 'But then most pop music isn't. They are deeper than average though – and it's very suggestive stuff. For me, the spur was what they do with the *sound*.' For the track 'Do You Want To Break Up', the sound was jaunty rather than sad, appealing to Muller's deep-seated sense of irony, and she mischievously turned Annie into a Julie Andrews figure for the song.

'When Sophie and I get together, our humour is really quite cruel. We both have a black sense of humour. She can be a terrible Führer,' said Annie.

Although Muller's approach is dead-pan and wry, she retains a great respect for Annie as a performer. 'You can't go wrong with her. She's a strong character – it's not like you do a video and she's just going to fit in. But we did work together very closely [on *Savage*] . . . Probably it was somewhat easier because she was female and we were dealing with female conceits.'

Much of Annie's stance involves an insider's commentary on the excesses of pop, particularly for women. There is a thin line between her prostitute persona and the other favourite, the starlet or rock chick. The starlet first appears during the *Sweet Dreams* era in the 'Who's That Girl?' video, sitting on stage in a velvety nightclub, wearing a little black dress and demure blonde wig. As she sings, Dave plays Annie's unfaithful lover, parading in with a variety of well-known girls from Bananarama to Kate from Haysee Fantaysee, Hazel O'Connor, the beautiful male cross-dresser Marilyn and a Meryl Streep lookalike.

Annie as the mournful and manipulated starlet suffers this humiliation until the spell is broken by the appearance of her alter ego, a male stud who stares at her, chewing a matchstick. In a defiant gesture, she throws down the chair and leaves the club with her male self. She then engages in an empowering screen kiss with herself.

Annie's starlets are never straightfoward kewpie dolls; she delights in adding a twist to their tale, or even deforming them, as in the video for 'I Need A Man'. She is uncomfortable with an overt expression of sexuality that isn't somehow undercut with ironic parody. The *Savage* starlet turns into a rock chick, demanding sex and saying she wants her man to be a *man*.

Annie takes this a step further in the video for 'King And Queen Of America', a breathless costume-changing extravaganza that incorporates a series of characters parodying the sleazy dominance of American popular culture. At one point Annie wags her backside, dressed in fishnet tights, short mini skirt and long black Cher-like wig.

She is the glam-rock superstar, the rock chick incarnate, representing a vulgar part of herself that rarely gets an airing.

'Sometimes I think I'd like to make exquisitely beautiful, sublime music that's almost rhythm-less. At other times the most frenzied angry club music you'd ever heard – what I think Heavy Metal *could* be but never is,' she says. 'It could be very powerful, but the subjects they choose to address are inevitably inane, so it never gets further than being moronic.

'Heavy Metal is very clichéd and sexist, with a chauvinistic swagger. Well *I* would like to have a chauvinistic swagger too. I think I could do it better than any of 'em!'

Annie's parody of macho behaviour took its most extreme and logical form in the character of the businessman in a suit, a major presence during the *Sweet Dreams* era. Once she was taken seriously and became established in the music business, the device was no longer necessary. Shades of cross-dressing appear in later videos, notably for 'Sex Crime: 1984' where there is an appropriately Fascist feel and Annie appears like an Aryan boy, with a shiny black leather jacket, severely slicked hair and bright blue eyes. Although it's a staple pop commodity now rendered innocuous by its use in teeny pop, the black leather jacket is still a symbol of tough rebellion. Annie's leather is always tailored and sharp, a revolt that's more aesthetic than anti-social.

Mixed in with Annie's main characters are a panoply of secondary personalities, donned for the day to make a particular point. She got many of her ideas rummaging through dress hire and costume retailers such as Contemporary Wardrobe, Britain's major modern outfitters which are based in Covent Garden and service the music, film and fashion industry. It was advantageous that Annie and Contemporary Wardrobe took off at the same time, as her eclectic approach chimed with their forays into post-1930s pop fashion.

Forty-one-year-old Roger Burton started the company in 1976 when he supplied clothes for the British mod film *Quadrophenia*, and realized that there was a need for a company to hire pop fashions. A tall, quiet, neatly dressed man, Burton formulated many of his clothing retail ideas during punk.

'I had an antique shop up in Leicestershire that grew into a vintage clothes shop. I was always travelling to London, supplying stuff to places like Vivienne Westwood's Let It Rock. I sold a lot of men's period clothes, mainly with a 1940s/50s image aimed specifically at men. I'd travel up and down the country buying stock from a big network of used clothes outfits, and once punk came along I had a stall on Portobello Road where I was trying to get rid of 1960s mod things. As if by magic the art director from *Quadrophenia* walked past, and we ended up supplying clothes for the film.

'It then occurred to me that conventional costumiers like Morris Angel had lost interest around the wartime and didn't see the modern period of any importance. So much has happened in the last thirty years of pop fashion, *somebody* ought to be hanging on to it.'

Roger Burton hung onto it, and eventually became a major supplier and stylist for the music business once the video boom took off. He expanded the business from a warehouse to three Covent Garden shops. Next to Contemporary Wardrobe is Robe Noir, selling high fashion evening wear, and Chimes of Big Ben with fine period fashion and 'exotic adornment' from new designers.

The main shop is a colourful treasure trove of period clothes stacked high to the ceiling, while downstairs is a breathtakingly huge collection of platform shoes. Annie and Dave would often roam around the shop, picking out items for their videos or photo shoots. 'Annie always came with fresh ideas,' recalls Burton. 'She'd look good in anything, she's such an amazing clothes horse. She'd come and look around to get inspiration – at the time we had over ten thousand outfits.'

It was here that Annie found her ball gowns and men's suits. 'I think the suit idea was more to do with a 1960s' look than dressing like a man,' maintains Burton. 'At the time that 1960s look was fashionable, with the group Madness, etc. She was wearing it in a more anarchistic way.'

After the austerity of the butch *Sweet Dreams* look, Annie opted for something glitzy and bright for their fourth successful hit single, 'Right By Your Side'. It demanded a brash, upbeat look to accompany the celebratory soca-based carnival sound, so Annie came up with a mischievous image that represented to her 'the pinnacle of pop'. Rummaging through the shop one day she found the perfect glam glitter suit and red platform boots for the cover of the single. This was in November 1983, before pop's hip audience had rediscovered their 1970s flares, so Annie's move was a definite slap in the face of public taste.

'It's a copy of the gold suit Elvis Presley wore on one of his 1958 album covers,' says Burton. 'The original was made by a rodeo tailor called Nudie, and we did a copy – our first glitter outfit. Annie had been through the 1960s' thing; she came on to the 1970s' glitter feel and felt it was right. She interpreted the Presley suit in a Gary Glitter way with platform boots.'

Burton was so pleased with the shot, which showed Annie in the suit with her smile wide and fists clenched in a glorious glitter pose, that he requested use of the picture for promotional postcards. Ever watchful of being categorized, Annie refused. 'She feels that was then, this is now – though I feel it's really relevant now. She likes to be as many different people as possible in her work.'

The gold suit still holds a fascination for the many pop artists who visit the shop, allowing them to project a brash over-the-top image that is a humorous parody of a pop star. 'There's definitely a strong element of camp in it. So many people have worn the gold suit and interpreted it in different ways, it's really bizarre. You offer them other ones but they only want the gold one.'

Now Annie occupies the pop stratosphere, she sends her stylist Polly Cladon to pick up individual garments. Polly has worked with Annie on various videos for over six years, sorting out such costumes as the pink 'Come Dancing' ballgown, the Elvis suit in early Eurythmics' days and later items for the *Savage* album.

'No one stylist can dictate what Annie wears,' says Polly. 'You can suggest things but that's all; she has very strong ideas about what she wants herself. For performances she likes to be comfortable and she saves her more exotic looks for videos – like the lavish costumes in "King and Queen of America".'

Throughout her career, Annie has summoned up a cast of minor characters. Masked and muscle-bound on the cover of *Touch*, she represents a kind of bold female highwaywoman, while for their hit single 'Right By Your Side' she is the sophisticated lady, dressed in a Jeff Banks' creation of fake leopard skin with a pill box hat and bright lipstick. While many female artists use their career as an opportunity to model a certain designer's clothes, Annie sometimes parodies this process, looking like a kitsch or over-amplified *Vogue* fashion shoot.

Annie is the main asset to the band's image, with her face alone appearing on album covers. Each one conveys a different mood – from the live, grainy video feel of *Be Yourself Tonight* to the bleached-out 1950s cinema angst of *Savage* and the icy stillness of Mondino's *We Too Are One* cover shot, where Annie's red lips and blue eyes predominate. *Revenge* is the only sleeve where Dave is featured alongside Annie, emphasizing their status as a rock partnership.

The apex of their career as pop's most established duo came in the release in early 1990 of 'King And Queen of America'. In the video the pair of them act out an array of mocking stereotypes, from cowboy and cowgirl to football star and cheerleader, glam rockers, game show hosts and a conventional couple displaying the missionary zeal of Nancy and Ronald Reagan. The slick images pump up what is in effect a rather uninspired song, as they take their 'clever video' reputation to its logical extreme.

Annie's natural acting abilities show up on screen, so it is not surprising that she's been offered countless film parts. Her first movie role was as a flame-haired wench in Hugh Hudson's long epic *Revolution*, a gigantic film flop starring Al Pacino, Donald Sutherland and Nastassia Kinski pursuing life, liberty and happiness in 1776 America. Annie appears in the first three minutes, shouting in one of the notorious crowd scenes, and is never seen again.

In 1987 she also acted in a short film version of Harold Pinter's *The Room*, a typically Pinteresque story of implied menace in 'bedsit' Britain directed by Robert Altman. Annie's dark satanic costume, pale face and strong Scottish accent are almost gothic in their intensity. The film, however, was not an earthshattering critical success, and was quickly released on video. It seems she was more comfortable in her video role, a tight, composed medium where she can exercise control over the final product. Annie also comes over better when the shot is simple and focuses on her evocative facial expression.

In contrast to the frantically busy, peopled air of the *We Too Are One* video album, *Savage* homes in on Annie with claustrophobic effectiveness. Moving from housewife to whore starlet to ordinary woman, she goes through a cinematic catharsis, with the most striking shot reserved for the track 'You Have Placed A Chill In My Heart'. Here Annie appears as a kind of Noble Savage, barefoot with her face blanched and her eyes hollow, wearing a dark threadbare coat and screaming in the middle of a desert. She is completely alone, until a dark male figure (her husband Uri Fruchtman) wraps her in his arms and she finds 'salvation'.

It is on this level of personal, almost autobiographical intensity that Annie creates the greatest impact. When she moves away from a light look at superficial stereotypes to something as stark as the female cross-dresser or the savage screaming in the desert, she has locked into the core of her identity. That is where Annie Lennox the visual provocateur exercises her power.

6

The Savage God

'Neither of us is a song writer in that traditional sense. We like to create sound pictures, commercial music that is special but also very individual. We're always looking for something really fresh. It's a bit like mining for gold but now with the idea of loot at the end of it. I'm talking artistic terms.

'I live in a world where I feel totally alienated, and I've found a niche. If I make music with Dave that I feel is bland or pointless, I may as well cut my wrists. I'm not making music for people to tap their feet politely to or to listen to in lifts. I'm making music that people can respond to, and I feel passionately about that. Dave and I have a phenomenal sense of freedom in our work. I've learnt that I just cannot live with compromise.

'We always thought it would be exciting to make music that was accessible in terms of melody and harmony, yet contained something very dark and abstract, and I feel that the best music we've made – not in terms of record sales but of sheer musicality – was a wonderful blend of these elements, touching you in a strange, subconscious place. It's a feeling of sweet decay – most really inspired music has a kind of friction.

'Song writing is like psychic wrestling. That might sound trite, but every time we go to make an album, we both feel the challenge is to *plough* your psychic depths and articulate them the best possible way you know.

'Only in black music do the singers reach such depths of pain and heights of ecstasy, sometimes in the same song. It's elevating to watch the faces of artists like Tina Turner or Muddy Waters when they're performing because they seem lost in a trance. But a lot of black music has fairly banal lyrics: very few black lyricists write with an individual outlook. We're a white group interpreting that music in our own style.'

119

LAUREL CANYON, 1970

Hailed as the woman who 'played Yang to Bob Dylan's Yin', Roberta Joan Anderson left her native Canada in 1967 for the shores of California. Keeping her ex-husband's surname and modifying her first name, Joni Mitchell became the most famous female folk rock singer/song writer of the 1970s, influencing pop generations for decades to come.

Annie often mentions this kooky individualist as a source of inspiration. In 1970, Mitchell was beginning to expand her repertoire, moving from self-taught coffee house acoustic guitar to greater instrumentation and more imaginative melodies. Her song 'Ladies Of The Canyon' stands out for its lilting and gently comical observation of Californian life, showing Mitchell's capacity to mythologize the everyday. Throughout her later experiments with rock and avant-garde jazz, Mitchell still kept a narrative, confessional tone, referring in word play, scat and melody to her emotional reactions.

'My main interest in life is human relationships and human interraction on a one-to-one basis, or on a larger basis projecting feelings to an audience . . . I bare intimate feelings because people should know how other people feel,' she said.

Mitchell was constantly exploring the dilemma of creative independence as a woman, versus compromise in the romance and security of relationships. A free-spirited folk poet, her songs convey a landscape of possibilities outside her personal vision, in many ways articulating the rambling sense of cultural freedom experienced in the 1960s and early 1970s.

Mitchell as the lone poet carved a path for female experimentalists, stretching boundaries of song writing with her word play and eccentric phrasing. Annie, too, has applied some of those principles by taking apart the pop song, and welding it together again on her own terms.

'I think words have endless potential,' Annie says. 'Within the pop context I try to make something that's emotive and ironic. It's a challenge to redefine words that are continually being used until they're parodies of themselves. The challenge is also to find whether you yourself have still got something relevant to say, and then say it beautifully, with real depth.

'Look at Joni Mitchell, for example – she's so unique. She went where no one else had ever gone.'

It was this analytical approach to confessional song writing that prompted pop writer Dave Hill to announce in his 1985 book *Designer Boys Material Girls* (Blandford Press): 'Annie Lennox is the missing link between Joni Mitchell and The Future.'

It wasn't until the late 1980s that a new vogue for female singer/song writers took off, with the roots rhythms of Michelle Shocked and Tracy Chapman leading the way. Many female artists like Edie Brickell, Suzanne Vega and Jane Siberry worked in Mitchell's narrative or quirky tradition, writing about up-to-date themes, but with a 1970s musical feel. In contrast to this, Annie came out as a lone, haunted female voice in the early 1980s, delving into personal material, yet relaying it through the modern medium of electro pop and synthesized dance.

In the same way that Mitchell articulated her time, Annie gave voice to the urban angst and self-styled cynicism of the 1980s — baring her anxieties with a painful, almost adolescent honesty. Many hail Eurythmics as a European blend of musical sensibilities, yet Annie's lyrical view contains a strand of sardonic introspection that's peculiarly British. 'If you read the personal side of her lyrics, I think you'd get to know Annie quite well,' Dave Stewart once said.

While Annie stresses that she doesn't always write from personal experience, she needs to believe strongly in her songs. 'My thing lyrically is very internalized. If I try to write in a different way, say using a cut-and-paste technique, it doesn't work,' she says. 'I have to identify *so* strongly with what I'm writing about that I can't draw from odd outside sources — that's too plagiaristic to me.'

In their song-writing partnership, Annie writes most of the words and melodies, while Dave adds instrumentation, production arrangements and melody lines, acting as her overall editor. 'Dave is my very good external and internal barrier,' she says. 'We work together lyrically and he works like an editor. I usually say a song is rubbish, and he looks at what I've done.

'It's strange. I'm pessimistic about my own efforts — I think they're no good. It rather takes his encouragement, helping me to see what's good in a shared vision. That way I get inspired and have the guts to go away and do it quietly in a corner somewhere.'

There are several themes that Annie keeps returning to in her song writing, finding a cathartic outlet for emotions that threaten her. She touches on them with the first Eurythmics' LP, *In The Garden*, summoning up first the image of a woman loved, lost and abandoned in the sweet surf harmony of 'Belinda', then woman robotic and alienated in 'Caveman Head' with eyes closing and mouth wide. Already she is using the cold imagery of suicidal pain and revenge, referring to 'cold clean glass' and razor blades.

Although her words are strong, they lose their point when squashed in with fuzzily soft electro pop. It wasn't until *Sweet Dreams* in 1983 that the full impact of Annie's word pictures was brought out by the musical backing. *Sweet Dreams* works because every sound recorded on that diminutive eight-track can be clearly heard. From the rich bass synth to the clean dance beat, jazzy horns and Annie's clear voice, the album has an immediate, incisive pop quality that highlights the lyrics rather than buries them.

Each song has a bitter impact. The words are simple, like pieces of conversation cut, dried and spliced together, exuding a chilly sensuality. *Sweet Dreams* is starkly simple, yet, conveyed through Annie's soul clarity and Dave's synth crunch, it has become a classic. The LP is a catalogue of deceit, obsession and ambition, rendered cool and palatable by the melody and electro beat.

Annie was wise to couch her introspective terms within breezy pop. Music to match the frequent negativity of her vision would have been a doleful dirge. Her ability lies in letting hope speak through melody. As blank words on a page, her lyrics are black and sometimes flat expressions of adolescent angst, with frequent dramatic use of words like 'guilt . . . glamorous . . . jealous . . . cold . . . sleek'. Transferred to song, they take on a complex, forceful life of their own.

Annie often cites Sylvia Plath as her favourite poet, and there are many similarities in their stringently intense approach. I suggested to Annie that she felt an affinity with Plath because of the way the poet was spare with her language, stripping it down to its basics.

'Oh no, I find it very rich, you see – the actual *choice* of words and the *profundity* of that imagination blows me away. She intrigues me, making me see that words have endless potential,' says Annie.

The wife of poet laureate Ted Hughes, and a tortured personality, Sylvia Plath committed suicide after he left her in 1963. Before she died she explored in a prolific series of poems her own spiritual development and desolation, linking them to crises in the twentieth century. After the posthumous publication of the collection of her last powerful poems, *Ariel*, in 1965, she was hailed as a romantic poet, legendary victim and female martyr. The stark, self-obsessed nature of her poetry has made her an adolescent heroine. As she was still a young woman aged thirty-one when she died, much of her writing lacks emotional maturity, although it is powerful, illuminating and at times coldly beautiful. Like Annie writing songs twenty years later, Plath used words as a means of dark analysis, trying to make sense of herself and the situation around her with often brutal imagery. In 'Daddy', the famous 1962 poem dedicated to her dead German father, she summons up extreme, shocking images of Nazi Germany:

> Not God but a swastika
> So black no sky could squeak through.
> Every woman adores a Fascist,
> The boot in the face, the brute
> Brute heart of a brute like you.
>
> You stand at the blackboard, daddy,
> In the picture I have of you,
> A cleft in your chin instead of your foot
> But no less a devil for that, no not
> Any less the black man who
>
> Bit my pretty heart in two . . .

Such images are now questionable, almost gratuitous, but they convey the ferocity of female anger and her desire for cathartic shock. Annie has used similar overtones of sado-masochism throughout her lyrics, taking on every role from the stylized Dominatrix to the suffering victim. 'I always ran the risk of getting badly hurt through my experiences,' she says. 'I ran the risk of destroying myself. I think that's common to a lot of women.'

Annie's tempestuous relationship with her strict father, and later bitter disappointments in love with Dave fuelled much of her agonized soul searching. Anxiety gave her an edge, and a restless honesty. At the same time, however, in playing the consummate pop actress Annie has tended to dramatize her unresolved past, plunging into her inner depths with a determinedly serious face. There may be traces of irony in her words, but unlike Joni Mitchell's gentle laughing wit, there's not a lot of humour.

'I think it's terrible. They didn't tell me it was going to be like this when I was little. Life is the most brutal experience,' says Annie starkly.

Usually pop songs focus on lighter, more manageable emotions, but the industry has always had maverick females singing explicitly of the pain of psychological or physical violence, from Phil Spector's sweet girl group the Crystals, who in 1961 trilled rather distastefully 'He hit me and it felt like a kiss/He hit me and I knew he loved me', to singer Marianne Faithfull's hoarse paen to suffering, 'Broken English'.

'It is a kind of catharsis for me to write about pain,' says Annie. 'But it's not just *my* experience. It's a whole load, these plays that had to be re-enacted. I could choose a lover who was masochistic and I was sadistic and somehow or other it had to be that person. I had to be the one for them and they had to be the one for me . . . that's what fascinates me.'

Sometimes Annie's references to S&M are at the level of vaguely comic stereotype, as in the early 1980s publicity shot that shows Annie dressed in black with a studded belt standing menacingly over Dave. He, meanwhile, is casually sitting on the floor not looking in the least bit perturbed. At other times, Annie goes deeper, exploring emotional levels of S&M within relationships.

The connection between pain and love is unfortunately learned early on. Although her parents' marriage was solid, Annie's father was a forceful character and influence. Her friend Billy Mackenzie, 1980s star and vocalist of the Dundee band the Associates, recalls a common thread of domestic violence throughout many 1950s marriages in small town Scotland.

'There was no feminism in that era. Men were men and they were macho. Some women quite enjoyed going out to the pub with a black eye, it was attractive to them: "He hit me so he must love me" they'd say. 'I hated it. I don't like that energy, it's really destructive. But to some people conflict is sexual foreplay.'

Annie looks directly at the emotional violence in relationships, yet finds it abhorrent. While she gives vent to her feelings, she doesn't fall into the trap of the endless victim. Once she has been hurt she's fully prepared to fight back. On 'Regrets', the sparse pneumatic funk song on Eurythmics' third album *Touch*, she warns her lover about her dangerous nature, singing about fists colliding with furniture, being an electric shock inside her lover's head. Here Annie has moved from wistful self-destructive melancholy of the *Sweet Dreams* woman who smells disaster every time a lover touches her skin, to the combative androgynous creature of *Touch*.

A lover of symbolism and evocative rhyme, Annie cites another major American poet, Allen Ginsberg, as a source of inspiration. His loose street poetry reflects the tradition of US beatniks. 'Ginsberg wrote using the rhythms of speech from the American street – black speech, phrasings overheard on street corners and in bars – and the rhythms of bebop and jazz, of sports commentators and the cool DJs on the all-night jazz programmes. It had a new rhythm and used new language,' wrote Barry Miles in his 1990 biography *Ginsberg* (Viking/Penguin).

Eurythmics have been accused of being yesterday's hippies, but their musical and stylistic approach owes a great deal to the beatniks. Their favourite images are more Skid Row than Haight Ashbury, with many shots depicting Dave and Annie dressed in black 1950s leather leaning against walls or running free in derelict sections of Paris. With her stripes, beret and stream-of-consciousness lyrics, Annie exudes the air of a tense urban beatnik, while she and Dave draw on the rhythms of black dance to create a beat version of pop authenticity.

Although *Sweet Dreams* was successful on the dance floors, *Touch* is more of an extrovert dance record, with the result that in 1984 RCA released selections from the album, remixed by Jellybean Benitez and Francois Kevorkian, and retitled *Touchdance*. The uptempo sound fits Annie's more assertive mood, and in a move away from breathy tragedy she bristles with the funky shouts and decisive phrasing that have become her vocal signatures.

'Right By Your Side' was an out-and-out celebration and a Top-Ten hit. Mixing soca and carnival beats, Annie embraces the theme of a positive, protective love, saying that nothing can hurt her when she is right by her lover's side. In contrast to the tension of much of her former material the song comes as a release, breaking the cycle of pain and disappointment. Sometimes despair can be escapism rather than a source of inspiration, a negative refuge that eradicates the will to fight or create.

Touch has an international feel, incorporating patterns suggestive of Polynesia, Bali, Africa and Moorish Spain, with Annie developing a personal chant. She has been called a 'female shaman', creating moments of intense sensation rather than conventionally structured songs. Dave liked to think that they had struck a perfect commercial balance: 'the European worry that the world might end tomorrow, alongside that Afro-American exuberance and release'. He also gave an accurate summary of their musical quality as 'kids being able to sing it, old people to whistle it and intellectuals to analyse it'.

This approach was not so much in evidence on their next LP, *1984*, the soundtrack to the film of George Orwell's novel about a fantasy, future totalitarian state. Controversy flared up when *1984*'s director Michael Radford claimed live on TV at the London *Evening Standard* award for Best Film of the Year that the Eurythmics' soundtrack had been 'foisted' on him. The issue immediately hit the headlines, taking the film out of the arts pages and into the news.

'I'd planned the speech beforehand because I was so angry,' says Radford, a charismatic director with a pained expression and a pony tail, who has several acclaimed films behind him, including that tale of glossy colonial greed *White Mischief*. 'Actually during the meal that preceded the thing I'd got rather mellow and thought I'd better not say anything, but I'd told so many people I was going to do it, I had to.'

The story behind the debacle was that Virgin boss Richard Branson had put up a large sum of money for a soundtrack album to accompany the film, and was anxious to use a star name. Radford at first had discussions with David Bowie, but he proved to be too expensive for the project. The film was being made to extremely tight deadlines in order for it to be released by the end of 1984. Come August of that year no one had been commissioned to do the ambient soundtrack, so Radford went ahead and used Dominic Muldowney, who had composed the anthem tunes in the film, for the remainder of the soundtrack.

'So I'm sitting mixing the final movie,' says Radford, 'and I get a phone call to say Eurythmics are writing a soundtrack. That's the first I've heard of it, and my nerves are jangling. Anyway, I spoke to them on the phone saying "Look, I don't have any great hopes for this, but I encourage you to do your best. If it's no good then I can't use it".

'It was the first time they'd done a film soundtrack. They were working with a cut of the film that wasn't finished, and they said to me they thought the soundtrack was missing a few things – 'course it was, I was mixing them while they were writing the music! Anyway, when I got it I really didn't like it; they'd overdone it, been too crude about it. When there were scary scenes they'd put scary music, that kind of thing.'

Although Radford was reluctant to use the Eurythmics' score, Branson persuaded him to include a fifteen-second segment so he could at least get a star soundtrack album out of the deal. 'It looked like everyone would be happy,' continues Radford, 'but then the shit hit the fan. We were notified by Eurythmics' management that their music ought to be on the film. There's a fundamental principle at stake there – I object to one artist telling *another* artist what they're supposed to do. They were working for me on my film in a collaborative venture, but in the end *I'm* the director of the film. To *make* me put their music on my film, I couldn't forgive them. That spoiled rock'n'roll. If they were just about to put a record out and someone said, we don't like the record cover, it's got to be changed, they'd go apeshit. I felt they were just being spoiled children.'

With the film going over budget and rapidly approaching deadline all tempers were frayed, and concessions were quickly made. Five weeks after *1984* had opened it was taken out of the cinema and remixed with the entire Eurythmics' soundtrack. Radford was so furious that he made his controversial TV speech at the *Evening Standard* Awards. Eurythmics retorted with a very angry statement: 'We would have not even considered a request to write a soundtrack for the film if we had known someone else had also been asked to do so. Our credibility as artists has been seriously jeopardized by Michael Radford's misleading comments.'

It was the first time Eurythmics had been involved in such a project, so their high-handedness was due to a mixture of naïvety and misunderstanding. 'It wasn't entirely their fault; it was Virgin's too,' says Radford. 'And ours for going over budget and not really having the scope to change things. Time heals everything. I've seen the film since, and I actually quite like the music now – it gives it a kind of pace and intensity. At the time though it was the principle I was protesting – the director is the director of the movie.

'I'm sorry it ended in bitterness because I'm Scottish and Annie Lennox is Scottish. I've made movies in Aberdeenshire and I have a great affinity and connection with people from that area. I'd be happy to work with Annie Lennox again. I don't hold any grudges.'

Recorded at Compass Point, Nassau, in the summer of 1984, the score has a powerful atmospheric intensity, with one thoroughly commercial song, 'Sex Crime (1984)', that shot up to Number 4 in November. A bold, charged dance track, 'Sex Crime' shows off the muscular strength of Annie's multi-layered vocal style, evidence of her growing vocal confidence and versatility. The remainder of the album is atmospheric, but with less arresting experimental electro and icy synthesizer.

The film is a hard, relentlessly literal interpretation of the book, deliberately drained of colour. Starring Richard Burton and John Hurt, it accurately reflected the mood of Britain in the 1980s; it did well at the box office and was hailed in some quarters as 'a landmark in film making'. In critical terms, the record fared less well. 'Cinematic skullduggery,' said *Melody Maker* of Eurythmics' score. 'Pure atmosphere instead of pure pop, rhythmic exercises instead of exercising rhythms.' *NME* was more scathing: 'There's two moods here; take your pick, epic or plaintive, mate. David Bowie did it all on "Diamond Dogs" anyway.'

After their problematic foray into film soundtracking, Eurythmics decided to go into the studio again and record what they knew best, moving straight from the synthesized mood of *1984* to the gritty rock realism of *Be Yourself Tonight*.

This record showcases the raw edge of Annie's stage personality, with lyrics that are more declarative and extrovert than on former albums. Here she sings outrageously camp vocal gymnastics on the track 'There Must Be an Angel (Playing with My Heart)', with Stevie Wonder providing the celestial intervention of the harmonica. Not surprisingly, the song became a massive hit, reaching Number 1 in July 1985 and remaining in the chart for thirteen weeks. This was shortly followed by 'Sisters Are Doin' It for Themselves', Annie's funky feminist duet with Aretha Franklin that hit Number 9 in the chart.

By now, Eurythmics were a top world group and part of the showbiz elite, and the confidence of this ascendancy is reflected in *Be Yourself Tonight*'s casual assertiveness and the presence on the record of top-selling artists like Stevie Wonder and Elvis Costello. Gone is the pared-down bass synth, to be replaced by more robust, raunchy live instrumentation and the heavy soul inflection to Annie's voice. Musical references abound, from U2 to the Kinks, Stax and Earth Wind and Fire, prompting *NME*'s Paolo Hewitt to write: 'If not breaking new ground, Eurythmics have always managed to create the illusion of doing exactly that – no mean feat.' Coming from one of the paper's diehard dance fanatics, that was a major compliment.

The bluesy, bumptious 'It's Alright (Baby's Coming Back)' provided them with a third hit from the album, reaching Number 12 in February 1986.

Annie was still investigating the painful side to her emotions, but moving towards a bluesy interpretation, with grinding rock-out tracks like 'Would I Lie To You?' and 'I Love You Like A Ball And Chain'. Although her song writing tightened up, there was the intrusion of pat clichés and cartoon emotional detail along the lines of 'poison dart', 'winter rose' and 'tearing dreams apart'. She could still pull out a poignant image though, like that of the lover hanging on her bedroom wall, the last conclusions of her finished relationship in 'Better To Have Lost In Love (Than Never To Have Loved At All)'.

Eurythmics continued to rock out, embellishing their music stadium-style with the 1986 album *Revenge*. At that time the spectacular success of Live Aid had made stadium rock respectable again, and it allowed Dave free rein in his love of live guitar rock soul. The only problem was that *Revenge* marked a slip-away from that tricky combination of commercial success and critical acclaim that Eurythmics usually enjoyed. Although it sold in truckloads, *Revenge* was a more conventional offering.

Fred Defaye, a neat, dark and sweet sound engineer who worked in the Paris studio session for the recording of *Revenge*, remembers it as: 'Brilliant. Great crack. All the band was there with the attitude of hard work, but enjoying it at the same time. The album took three months to record and it was mixed in one month. It was really quick to make.'

Revenge emerges as a large-scale rapid rock'n'roll workout, with the graphic gospel R&B of 'Missionary Man' and the lighted-match-waving guitar balladry of tracks like 'Miracle Of Love'. The music press was disappointed. 'They're more showcase than song, designed to show off Lennox's larynx via constructs that dispense with perfunctory verses as quickly as possible to get to the high-flying fadeouts,' said *NME*. Accused of counterfeiting popular sentiment for the first time since the Tourists, Dave and Annie's creation received a severe drubbing.

Apart from the wayward indulgence of Dave's guitar solos, however, there is some elegant pop song writing and melodic simplicity, with the nervous resilience of 'A Little Of You' augmented by a Philadelphia soul lushness. Here they transcend the 'cultural thieves' tag to create their own pop epic.

Annie continues writing about the interior world of emotions, yet it has become bitter sweet rather than the incisive rudimentary scalpel of *Sweet Dreams* and *Touch*. The emblem of a red rose with blood on the thorns, featured on the inner sleeve, symbolizes a more conventional attitude towards love and hate. Their most substantial hit from the album, 'Thorn In My Side', which reached Number 5 in September 1986, has some solid soul phrasing, yet is weighed down by a ponderous rock backing.

When *Melody Maker*'s Colin Irwin suggested in an interview that they had run out of ideas, he hit on a sore point. 'Run out of ideas?' cried Annie. 'Christ, we've only just *started*! . . . Listen, we could continue like this FOREVER! We could do three albums a year if we wanted to.'

The next album appeared just a year later, but Dave and Annie seem to have taken the criticisms to heart, returning to an experimental, more personalized base for *Savage*. This was Annie's album, Annie's story – a partly autobiographical record that shows distinct maturity. 'I'd got carried away with other people making decisions for me, so *Savage* was an attempt to right the balance,' said Annie. She talked of the record's 'sense of tragedy, of brittleness, of vulnerability', a project close to her heart. 'It's a very unhappy album, since I was quite unhappy at the time. Though they may be cloaked, a lot of those lyrics are very personal statements. I don't have much of an objectifying capacity as a composer.'

Sounds hailed the record as 'A new sense of space and simplicity blending soft femininity, hardline sexual politics and upfront sexiness', while *NME* noted that the 'adult band with a dodgy rock past have suddenly seen sense, taken stock, and stepped outside their arena prison.'

Studio engineer Fred Defaye recalls how the album was recorded at a Dangu chateau in the Normandy countryside. 'Compared to *Revenge*, where we were working in a Paris studio all the time with a band, *Savage* was made in a calmer atmosphere in the middle of the countryside with just a studio and a computer. Dave had Siobhan there, and everyone was relaxing more after the *Revenge* tour.

'Professionally Annie is fantastic – she'll come in front of the mike and just do it. She goes really fast and doesn't drop a lot. Sometimes she might suddenly stop in the middle and say "take it from the start", because she knows she can do better. We wouldn't do three or four takes and try and choose – she'll concentrate on the one and do extra just for ad lib or improvisation. On *Savage* for some vocals I wasn't there because she just wanted to be alone.'

Although Dave is very influential, Annie is confident working on her own in the studio. For *Savage*, in particular, he took more of a back seat. 'Dave was away once and Annie came to the chateau by herself to do the vocal for "Brand New Day",' says Defaye. 'She knew exactly what to do with her singing. She can give you goosebumps when she sings – very few female vocalists do it like that.'

Martin Dobson, saxophonist on the *Be Yourself Tonight* album, also recalls a similar incident. 'One day Dave was holed up at the block of flats they'd rented by the Seine, suffering from a flu bug – so Annie came into the studio by herself to do "Baby's Coming Back". She had an idea for a bass line and was very enthusiastic. She enjoyed working on her own that time. When we got back she played Dave the rough mix and he said: "Oh I must get into the studio tomorrow." "Oh no Dave," she answered. "You're not really well enough, you should stay in bed!"'

Savage was Annie's personal world view, incorporating statements on her life, with the video its accompanying talking book. Opening with 'Beethoven (I Love To Listen To)', the dowdy video housewife who arranges the flowers could be the conformist side of her, the good girl who went to the Royal Academy. Speaking an interior judgemental monologue, the conventional character spies herself as another, separate girl in a café, approached by a boy 'looking for trouble'. The man in the song who awakens her wild, extreme side could be Dave.

The album is about breaking ties and learning self-reliance. Annie gradually learns to leave behind old lovers and wrangling heartache in 'I've Got A Lover (Back In Japan)', reflecting on her eloquent rage when she met her present husband.

'Do You Want To Break up?' could be about her first husband Radha Raman, the Hare Krishna monk who severely let her down and proved to be a fraud. In the video Annie sings mockingly of 'a little trouble boy', in *Sound of Music*-style from the Swiss Alps, surrounded by beerdrinkers in lederhosen. The 'car crash in my head' that she recalls could be the period she spent living in the Swiss Alps with Radha during their brief marriage.

From there, Annie moves to the sublime soul of 'You Have Placed A Chill In My Heart'. She provocatively sums up her life as a rock 'n' roll commodity, along with the disillusionment of her 'spiritual' marriage which ended up with Raman being paid off with a substantial settlement. In the video, Uri appears and embraces her as husband and saviour. Released as a single in the summer of 1988,

'You Have Placed a Chill . . .' was the most successful song from the album, reaching Number 16. 'Beethoven', 'Shame' and 'I Need A Man' meanwhile were less commercial offerings, not sliding past the Top Twenty in the UK.

At thirty-three years old, Annie had moved to simple songs that relayed her sensitivities without the self-consciousness of former albums. Where she had previously shrouded a feeling in deliberate mystery, in *Savage* each emotion is displayed visually and vocally, both bare and realistic.

'I Need A Man' is a raunchy skit on the woman who is growing older, becoming more assured and demanding in her sexuality, while 'Put The Blame On Me' is the woman taking responsibility for her destructive sense of lust. 'I Need You' harks back to the overtones of sado-masochism in her earlier songs, yet here it is so explicit in its desire for a lover's back-breaking torment it sounds like a parody.

Savage is an album of coming to terms, of meeting self-acceptance and looking to a fresh future. The song 'Wide Eyed Girl' is her most obviously autobiographical yet, looking back at her defiant adolescence, when the shy girl broke out into the rebellious teenager who liked discos and boys, much to the dismay of her parents. In the video, Annie sits in black as her thirty-three-year-old self, looking at herself first as a little girl going to school, then as a teenager. She sings ruefully that the girl and then the woman was always looking for the ultimate man – Daddy.

By the final track, 'Brand New Day', Annie faces disillusionment head on and comes up with a new sense of hope, vowing not to be sad or destroyed. In the accompanying video she's dressed in perfect white, her face radiant, surrounded by little girls dancing in dark gymslips and white tights. They are faces from her past, doing the Eurythmic dancing that she learned long ago at school in Aberdeen. It's interesting that the gentle piece is choreographed by Michael Clarke – the punk *enfant terrible* of the dance world who himself came from Aberdeen.

After the perfect cyclic structure of *Savage* there was an appropriate two-year break before Annie went back into the studio. Recording the album had been cathartic, an important project that encapsulated her musical vision at the time. In the ensuing period she took more of a back seat in Eurythmics, as Dave pursued solo production projects and she became pregnant.

The tragic still-birth of her baby son Daniel in 1988 meant that Annie returned to recording sooner than she had planned, and the next album *We Too Are One* came out in September the following year. While on one level it was a celebration of the Eurythmics' partnership, on another it was less inspired than, say, *Savage* or *Sweet Dreams*, more a case of consolidation and marking time.

Hailed by *Melody Maker* as both 'tastefully luxurious' and 'shamelessly sentimental', *We Too Are One* opens with a title track that celebrates their ten-year history together.

The rumour was that this was to be the album that would break them in America, with Arista boss Clive Davis (the mastermind behind Whitney Houston) overseeing their marketing campaign. The irony was that although Eurythmics have had respectable critical acclaim and commercial success in Britain and Europe, and the cover of the biggest US rock weekly *Rolling Stone*, they had yet to really sell records in the States. Dave was in favour of doing long, laborious college tours in order to break the band – the same way that U2 achieved their monumental success in the mid-1980s. Annie, however, has always been opposed to that slavish rock ideal, unwilling to make the concessions that a typical rock band has to make to sell vast quantities in America. She would have had to tone down her image, for instance, making it more 'feminine', and Dave would be required to insert a few more 'guitar licks'.

The music on *We Too Are One* does seem a palatable manoeuvre in the direction of American pop radio, though, with easy hooklines and thumping choruses on songs like the rousing 'King and Queen of America' and the rather perfunctory gospel R&B of 'Revival'.

Single releases from the album – 'Revival', 'Don't Ask Me Why' and 'Angel' – entered the upper reaches of the charts, but were overtaken by late 1980s disco house mania and failed to ignite. Eurythmics required a fresher sound and new versatility really to compete.

As always the songs that work best are those where Annie gives vent to deep-seated emotion, though there is less of the searing analysis. One of the strongest songs is the arrogant almost nursery-rhyme insolence of 'You Hurt Me (And I Hate You)'.

'Lyrically it's important to test new limits to what you can say. There are millions of love songs – it's time to put an extreme one about hate in there,' Annie says of the track. 'It seems to run parallel to love in so many respects — so many love affairs have fallen foul, ended up in horrendous circumstances, I'm sure everyone knows through personal experience what I'm talking about . . .'

The track 'Sylvia', a melodramatic Eleanor Rigby-type ballad about a young Amsterdam junkie, is one in a long line of songs that Annie has dedicated to women. First there was 'Belinda', a woman loved and abandoned, then 'Jennifer', the girl who drowned under the sea, followed by 'Julia', caught in the icy threat of 1984 and Big Brother. Each of these fictional women is a poetic victim, personifying areas of vulnerability that Annie can closely identify with.

The album ends on the flag-waving anthem 'When The Day Goes Down', a globally compassionate *pièce de resistance*. Although it is dauntingly sentimental, the song is also an emotive ballad for the disenfranchised.

'It has that exquisite sadness and beauty mingled together,' Dave says. 'With the voices and the snare drum rolling, it's almost like turning over pages to the next decade. Annie and I have been together for thirteen years now; it's hard for us not to work with each other. Whether we like it or not, we seem to be musically and creatively tied.'

His words marked the end of a particular phase of their togetherness, as Dave went on to make his solo *Spiritual Cowboys* LP and Annie left pop to try for another baby. By 1990, the savage god that had acted as her muse was beginning to mellow. What she had left behind was her mark on pop's legacy of lyrical pain.

7

You've Stepped on My Karma

'I had to be very protective about my marriage to Radha because it was a very quick decision to get married, and the person I was marrying has particular religious beliefs that I suppose to some people are rather unusual. I knew that it would make brilliant copy for the gutter press.

'Radha wasn't particularly attractive, but I thought I had found someone who was genuinely on a kind of spiritual path. I felt that with him I was going to give up everything that's ordinary in life to achieve something that is much higher. I went to Bhaktivedanta Manor, the house where George Harrison has Krishna Consciousness meetings. The thing that really struck me, even though I was very much "I don't know about this, it's all a bit strange", I felt refreshed to be around people who weren't motivating their lives around purely material gain. I drove away from that place feeling just a little refreshed.

'I was very tired and unhappy in my personal life, and a bit confused about how to figure out my life away from the Eurythmics. The whole marriage was just a mistake, though, a total mistake, and now I want to forget about it and live the rest of my life. I'm totally divorced now – free.

'I never had a religious upbringing, so that was helpful to me, because if I had it would have been a lot of conditioning that would have been difficult for me. I probably would have baulked against it. I've never been able to embrace one particular faith, though the philosophies religion have to offer really do interest me . . . There's so much more to life than what people do and own, and because my life hasn't been tied down to all the details of a job, home, family, I've been free to explore much more deeply than most people. It's terribly important to me. I wouldn't say I'm devout – I'm just trying to develop my spiritual life.'

BANGOR, 1967

On 24 August 1967, the same week that their orchestral hippy anthem 'All You Need Is Love' was at Number 1 in the American charts, the Beatles caught the train to Bangor to meet the Maharishi Mahesh Yogi. In the rush of photographers and fans at Euston Station, Cynthia Lennon was held back and missed the train; although she was in tears, John symbolically and literally left her behind in his desire to meet the new guru and a new dawn. From that moment the link between Eastern religion and pop music was firmly established.

As the late 1960s' generation engaged in student protest, meditating to levitate the Pentagon, and searching for alternative political cultures, there was a corresponding interest in non-Western philosophies. Thousands of young people followed the hippy trail to the far reaches of India, while religions such as Buddhism and Sufism preached a spiritual enlightenment that had been obscured or ignored in the materialistic West.

When they went to visit the Maharishi, the Beatles popularized Transcendental Meditation, turning on thousands of fans to Eastern mysticism. They became involved by chance one day in August 1967, when Patti Harrison persuaded her husband George and the rest of the Beatles to attend a lecture given by the Maharishi at the Park Lane Hilton Hotel in London. With his white dhoti, long greying hair, thick beard and hypnotic gaze, the Maharishi was a persuasive, charismatic speaker. A Hindu guru from North India well-versed in the PR machinations of the Western world, he pioneered Transcendental Meditation (TM), a technique whereby any ordinary person could reach a new dimension of consciousness, a state of being and tranquillity apart from the chatter of everyday existence. Adapted to the demands of modern society as an accessible approach to nirvana, TM became *the* buzz philosphy of the 1970s. By the 1990s, TM's associations with merchant banking rather than meditation had brought it into disrepute.

In 1967 $50 would buy you a mantra. For one week's wages a person could purchase a mantra selected according to age, sex and other variables, after a short initiation ceremony which consisted of offerings of flowers and fruit to the Maharishi's guru predecessors. The customer would then learn the mantra (one word from a historically ancient stock) and repeat it twice a day for twenty minutes at a time, thus bringing him or herself in touch with a deeper creative awareness unsullied by everyday stress and tension.

After the lecture the Beatles sent a note to the guru requesting a private audience. He accepted, and within hours, the band offered themselves to him as his disciples. Two days later they went to a 'Spiritual Regeneration' course he was holding in Bangor University, North Wales, accompanied by Rolling Stone Mick Jagger and his girlfriend Marianne Faithfull. John Lennon said afterwards that the experience was like 'going somewhere without your trousers'.

As journalists swarmed over the university in search of a quote, the Maharishi and the Beatles held a press conference at which Paul McCartney announced that they had given up drugs. 'We don't need it any more. We're finding different ways to get there.' The euphoria of their spiritual redemption was broken by the news that their manager Brian Epstein had been found dead in his London flat, after an overdose of sleeping pills. Shocked at the news of the tragedy, the Beatles were told by the Maharishi that Epstein's death, being in the realm of the physical world, was 'not important'.

Six months later the group were still disciples, yet wavering. In February 1968, just as their soundtrack album *Magical Mystery Tour* topped the charts, the Beatles, their wives and Mia Farrow and Donovan flew to Rishikesh in India for two months of Transcendental Meditation study with the Maharishi. After two weeks Ringo and Maureen Starr returned to England, complaining about the spicy food. The others stayed a little longer, Paul taking the opportunity to write 'Back In The USSR' with another famous Maharishi pop disciple, Beach Boy Mike Love. The meditation course was scheduled to end on 27 April, but no Beatle finished it.

Although the group later declared their dalliance with the Maharishi was 'a public mistake', George Harrison (and to some extent, John Lennon) remained interested in Eastern philosophy, and by the end of the 1960s Harrison became an ardent supporter of the Hare Krishna consciousness movement. His move into Eastern religion had been enhanced in 1965 by meeting Ravi Shankar, a composer/player of Indian classical music and a best-selling artist in India, who taught Harrison how to play sitar for the track 'Norwegian Wood'. The sitar then became a psychedelic rock fad, prominent in much of Harrison's solo material.

He recorded his first solo LP, the soundtrack to the film *Wonderwall*, in Bombay in 1968, and the following year produced the recordings by the Hare Krishna Temple, entitled *Hare Krishna Mantra*. After the Beatles split up at the beginning of the 1970s Harrison was big news, spreading the Krishna message via the pop industry with the release of his Phil Spector-produced album *All Things Must Pass*. His single 'My Sweet Lord' reached Number 1 and went gold on both sides of the Atlantic in 1970, which was very advantageous for the Krishna movement at the time, considering the Krishna mantra echoing at the end of the song. The only fly in the ointment was the song's similarity to an old Chiffons' hit, 'She's So Fine', causing a lawsuit that eventually cost Harrison $5 million.

Harrison was the centre of publicity again in 1971, when he organized large-scale summer concerts for Bangladesh at New York's Madison Square Gardens. The two shows were put together to raise money for the starving of Bangladesh, an issue brought to his attention by his then mentor Ravi Shankar. Presaging the huge charity rock concerts of the 1980s, the star-studded bill included Eric Clapton, Bob Dylan, Ringo Starr and Leon Russell, and the album of the show (with proceeds earmarked for Bangladesh aid) went gold. In 1973 Harrison channelled some of his personal fortune into the Krishna movement by purchasing for them Bhaktivedanta Manor, the huge mock-Tudor mansion in the Hertfordshire countryside that is the base of the British Krishna shrine.

Harrison did much to publicize Krishna consciousness, bringing it into the pop mainstream while at the same time giving it a mystical aura that was beguiling and attractive. By the early 1970s, assorted Hindu gurus had attained a quasi-pop star status, like the Beatles' Maharishi and later the flamboyant Marharaj Ji who travels in a Rolls Royce and preaches the Divine Light American-style, saying, 'Don't meditate for me, you meditate for yourselves. *You* should get high. I am high. I am high enough.'

In contrast to this show-business spirituality, Krishna devotees see their religion as the pure form of Hinduism. The movement was founded by Bhaktivedanta Swami Prabhupada, a guru who arrived in New York in 1966 with, as legend has it, a few rupees, a couple of books and a pair of sandals. He preached a philosophy and culture of ancient India derived from the epic poem *Bhagavad Gita*, naming Krishna as the true incarnation of God. In Hindu mythology there are over 300 million gods of India, but there is only one divine Absolute, that is Vishnu, who says, 'I come down to earth and take human shape.' There is controversy over the correct number of his 'descendants' or avatars, but it is said that Krishna is the only complete avatar.

A dancing, playful deity, Krishna had a sensually sublime aspect that appealed to the young, alienated 1960s generation. Prabhupada's interpretation of the Vedic scriptures preached a pure anti-materialism with the promise of divine revelation, a philosophy that was made accessible by the patronage of an ex-Beatle.

For Hindus the inward search is considered the only one that reveals what is important, for awareness of the external world shows only a superficial vision. Meditation, austerity and even sacrifice are necessary before one can reach this level of tranquil purity, with an almost complete eradication of 'earthly' desires.

The spiritually enlightened are endowed with an aura of heroism, hence the attraction of such a philosophy for pop stars, accustomed as they are to being treated as singular human beings. There is also the fact that, after amassing vast amounts of money in record sales, what else is there once you have material gain? Spiritual enlightenment seems the logical next step.

By the late 1970s many ex-punks were joining the Krishna movement, following the path of the hippies ten years before. Although punks maintained that hippies were their sworn enemy, there was an ironic similarity in their embrace of an alternative disaffected culture. 'Krishna attracts people who're disillusioned with the status quo, looking for something meaningful. Punk is rejecting everything, and if someone is sincerely looking for something deeper, then that rejection doesn't satisfy,' says Krishna devotee Jagannathesvari Pasi, now a resident at Bhaktivedanta Manor. Ironically, with their shaved heads and pony tails, many of the Krishna men look similar to the anarcho punks that sauntered down Britain's streets in the late 1980s.

After the day-glo punk band X-Ray Spex disbanded in 1979, two of its members became wholehearted followers of Krishna – the quirky half-English, half-Somalian lead vocalist Poly Styrene, and the sax player Laura Logic. Their raucous feminist anthem, 'Oh Bondage, Up Yours!', was a punk classic, with Poly Styrene presenting a raw 'anti-singing' stance. She also ran a small boutique in the King's Road, selling bright, wackily plastic clothes as a deliberate antidote to the dark, dreary bondage wear on offer at the other end of the punk spectrum.

These days she has toned down her act, singing with sweeter, swirling melodies, aiming to create an idealistic fusion of Eastern and Western music. A regular visitor to Bhaktivedanta Manor, she first became interested in Krishna consciousness when she was fifteen, travelling round festivals at the tail end of the hippy scene. 'I met devotees who were so clean and tidy, and they also seemed very intelligent.'

It was this cleanliness that initially attracted her ('cleanliness is next to godliness!' she quips), and informed her vision for X-Ray Spex, with the song 'Germ Free Adolescence' a paen to teenage purity. Punk provided a temporary diversion, before Poly Styrene was back in the fold, liberally dousing pop interviews with eulogies on the Krishna godhead. She also takes the message to victims of 'post-punk fall-out' on the streets. 'I see young people begging, and as I don't have that much money I just give them sanctified food that's been cooked by the priests. If you give them money they'll just go and buy a hamburger or a syringe, or stuff it up their nose. I don't want to get involved in that karma.'

Using ecstatic phrases like 'phantasmagoria of illusion', she pinpoints punk alienation as a sad result of Western 'civilization'. 'People were frustrated because they had an abundance of material facilities but they weren't really happy. Something spiritual was lacking.' The body is rather charmingly summed up as 'no more than blood, puss, mucus and stool', a mere vehicle for the soul which is separate and eternal.

This message of sublimation was one that appealed to the pristine side of Annie's nature. A lover of mystical understanding, she was drawn to Hare Krishna at a time in her life when she felt unfulfilled and unhappy. Eurythmics were at the peak of their first wave of success – *Sweet Dreams* had broken them into the mainstream, the *Touch* album was a highly successful follow-up, and the band played to sold-out venues wherever they went. The promotional grind, however, meant that Annie was drifting from hotel room to hotel room, constantly unsettled and isolated. She was yearning for something stable, and an antidote to the materialism of the music industry that was draining her.

By 1984 when she met the German Krishna monk Radha Raman, Krishna connections to the rock world were firmly established, with devotees attracting many of the young and disenfranchised from within music industry ranks.

INSTANT KARMA

The story of Annie's marriage to a Krishna monk seemed to bring out the worst in everyone. Her father wouldn't speak to her, her friends were plotting against him, Radha was coasting on her coat-tails, while her video producer Jon Roseman sold the story to the tabloid the *News of the World*. Despite the Krishna promise of sweetness and light, no one emerged smelling of roses.

'I eternally regret what I did,' says Roseman, on his decision to talk to the tabloid two years after the event. Annie's story was told in lurid detail under the headline 'MAD MONK TRIED TO BLACKMAIL NAKED ANNIE'. 'I didn't take a penny for it – all the money went to AIDS research,' Roseman maintains. His action was motivated by disillusionment and anger, an inability to comprehend the inevitable distance that pop stars put between themselves and former friends.

'I knew Dave and Annie when they were penniless. I worked with them in the Tourists and did the first three Eurythmics' clips for no mark-up, just to help them. There was every reason to have a good relationship, and we were close friends. Then they became rock'n'roll millionaires and it all changed. One year Annie and her then boyfriend Billy were due to go to Bali for the Christmas vacation and wanted me to come too. I couldn't because I was busy – so suddenly I was persona non grata. I couldn't get through to Eurythmics, I tried on numerous occasions, left messages – they never got back to me.

'Annie phoned me from Australia after the *News of the World* article, crying "How could you do this?" What they're saying is, "We can do what we want – befriend you or not, do whatever we like, but you, punter, can only be firm, loyal and true." I thought that was so wrong.'

The truth was that Roseman hit Annie where she was most vulnerable – her emotional life. Her marriage to Radha was something she bitterly regretted, in the same way Roseman regretted betraying her.

It was late in February 1984, in the middle of a gruelling world tour promoting the *Touch* album, that Annie met Radha Raman after a concert in Stuttgart. An avid fan of hers, he singled her out, tried to contact her and couldn't get through. 'He arranged for his followers (he was quite high up in this mafioso operation) to leave all those vegetarian dishes outside her hotel room. In the end she was impressed by that. She agreed to meet him and he stayed. They were in Germany for a while, and he'd sleep in her room, but on the floor. They weren't allowed to have sex unless they were going to marry,' says Roseman.

Within weeks of meeting each other, Annie and Radha were secretly married on 14 March at a Wood Green registry office in North London. In order to distract the press from the event, Dave announced his engagement to former Labelle singer Nona Hendryx. 'It was just a joke,' she says. 'A bit of fun. We did it for Annie. I like her very much . . . she's kinda whimsical.'

Shortly after Annie acted on her whimsical, whirlwind decision, she and Raman moved to Switzerland to a tiny mountain village near the sunny Italian border, and close to a Krishna farm community and temple.

For the first few months Annie was in complete bliss, taking time out from touring as often as she could to be near Radha and the Krishna community. At the time she met him she had a deep need of emotional solace and peace of mind, with the grind of touring and being publicly accountable as a pop star wearing down her defences. On one level she yearned for a spiritual fulfillment that was missing from her world of bleak hotel rooms, record company units and pragmatic business cynicism; on another she was just looking for love and a supportive relationship.

At first Raman 'love-bombed' Annie, making her the centre of his world, creating a sphere of scented bliss for them both. Annie took an active interest in the Krishna faith, never quite becoming a devotee, but extracting comfort from its philosophy. At the time she was asked on the BBC programme 'Earsay' how her marriage had changed her life. Annie smiled benignly and said, almost coyly:

'Quite a bit actually – in a very positive way. For a long time I've thought it's easier for me to be married than to never quite have a stable relationship. It's a very solid thing for me. I know it's a reverse role, I'm the breadwinner going out and doing my thing.'

When asked how her husband felt about being Mr Lennox, she laughed and said: 'A lot of people don't know him, because I've protected my marriage. He's very supportive of me and very nice.' She didn't seem to know a great deal about him. When asked whether he was a musician, she had to think, not sounding too sure or interested when she said: 'He played bass guitar, I think . . .'

Her friend Laurence Stevens wasn't too impressed with Raman. 'He was slightly slimey, slightly aggressive,' he recalls. 'He didn't seem to be interested in Eurythmics' music or anything – just Annie as a person. "I want to make her a vegetarian, I want to pull her away from all of this, she doesn't need the pop thing," he said. I didn't see what he was going on about.' Pete Phipps, drummer on part of their 1984 *Touch* tour, remembers Raman as 'a mysterious shadowy figure who always wore a long coat'.

Although many of her close friends voiced similar reservations, Annie was in a rebellious mood, determined to follow her heart in a totally new direction. She was marrying the spirit of his philosophy rather than just the man. Her eyes misted over when she spoke about visiting Krishna consciousness meetings at Bhaktivedanta Manor.

The first question I ever asked my mother and father was "where do I come from?". I think everyone in their heart of hearts has to have that question.'

Annie became a strong vegetarian, giving a long interview to the *Vegetarian Times*. She was very interested in the Krishna view of karma, 'the law of action and reaction', seeing compassion as the ultimate route to redemption. 'Compassion is a very valuable part of our existence. I feel now that one cannot be fully compassionate unless one has become a vegetarian, because then one ceases to have involvement with killing.'

Although she spent many hours in discussion with the devotees, Annie refused to take the final step and become initiated. With one eye on her career credibility and pop star status, moving totally into the spiritual world was an impractical step to take. At the same time, she was aware of how she could integrate the Krishna principles into her life, finding it relatively easy to keep away from meat, drugs, alcohol, cigarettes and gambling – the Western toxins and vices that corrupt the soul. Annie has always been someone who's attracted to the idea of purity.

'Krishna consciousness isn't something where one has to go into a temple, disappear and become a recluse, which would have been of no interest to me because I feel that my function as a musician is a very valid one. It really started to interest me when I saw that I could integrate it with my activities.'

The accepted viewpoint was that Annie was looking for something spiritual after her material existence. 'She was certainly looking for *something*,' claims Jon Roseman. 'At that time the material existence hadn't come to fruition. It took a while for the royalties to soak through, by the time the advances were taken. And RCA were still trying to get back £100,000 of Tourists' money.'

Other clues to Annie's interest in the religion can be seen in Poly Styrene's interpretation of Krishna. The former punk star makes repeated references to 'cleanliness', while Annie herself has often said when she is in love or has peace of mind that she feels 'happy, clear and *clean*'. There is a promise of inner purity about Krishna consciousness that, to someone disrupted by emotional demons, can seem refreshingly uncomplicated. It deliberately turns away from the ugliness of life to contemplate 'higher planes'. There is also an emphasis on asexuality or celibacy, an assertion among Krishna women that they are not 'the object of some man's lust'. According to Poly Styrene, 'wearing saris and sitting in the background in the temple gives us more respect, because they [men] are not wanting to see our body.'

To Annie, who was still unsure about exploiting or revealing her sexuality in the pop business, this attitude offered security. In the same way, the religion could offer her a solid base, with Krishna her traditional protecting angel. 'He protects me and the worth of what I'm trying to say,' says Poly Styrene. There is also the influence of the Hindu belief in reincarnation, that in seeing yourself as a free spirit soul the power of your parents automatically diminishes. 'Spiritually I know I'm attached to God. I've always felt some detachment from my parents. In my more immature days I've said it to my mum and really upset her,' says Poly Styrene.

Annie, too, has felt a certain detachment from her family, a factor that was exacerbated with her marriage to Radha. Sensing that he was losing his daughter, Tom Lennox vehemently disapproved of her marriage, and the two didn't speak to each other until shortly before his death two years later. In 1984, however, Annie was in her thirtieth year, longing for emotional comfort and peace of mind, and finding solace for a while in the Krishna faith.

Bhaktivedanta Manor is a very soothing place. Tucked away off the M1 motorway in the small Hertfordshire village of Letchmore Heath, it is a huge, polished mock-Tudor mansion with a temple and residential college for devotees. On the sunny early summer day I went there, it was as if I had died and gone to heaven. The place is peaceful and contemplative, with young monks wafting to and fro in saffron robes, shaven-headed children playing on the lawn and eating vegetarian pizza, and women, Western as well as Asian, all wearing saris.

We were required to take our shoes off before entering the manor, our bare feet sinking into the deep pile carpets. The decor is very sensual, almost suffocatingly beautiful with light blues and pinks, gold chandeliers and rich Krishna pictures. We were shown into a room that was a decorative, pulsating shrine to the deity and the movement's founder, with a rather disconcerting wax dummy at the centre. 'That's the founder Prabhupada, he passed away in 1977,' said our guide, Jagannathesvari Pasi, a young Western woman in a sari. She had left Essex University in the 1970s, then a hotbed of student radicalism, to follow the hippy trail in India and become a fairly conventional convert to the Krishna faith.

'It's very fashionable nowadays to have a guru. Anyone can pose himself as a guru, come out and *invent* some philosophy that sounds good. How is he really helping people?' remonstrates Pasi. 'A lot of people are motivated just for some material reason. The pure devotee is the person who can give people the real thing, the secrets by which they become eternally liberated.

'We chant the Hare Krishna mantra everyday to purify ourselves. Of course it doesn't happen overnight, not like an automatic thing – chant a certain number of mantras and you'll get enlightenment. One has to wait for the mercy of the spiritual master, Krishna.'

Pasi admitted she had 'a long way to go' before reaching purity, even though she had been a devotee for thirteen years. Like many of the devotees, she spoke slowly and drowsily, as if she was literally on another planet. Bhaktivedanta is a very beguiling place, somewhere you could make endless daisy chains on the lawn in the sun talking of spiritual enlightenment, but it is also a passive escapism, a denial of desire, anger, aggression and awkwardness – the more undignified human emotions.

By March 1990, however, the real world was unpleasantly beginning to intrude, with a local council pressure group urging the government to close down the temple. Worried at the effect that the Krishna manor would have on property prices in the village, local councillors petitioned the Department of the Environment, claiming that the Krishna community was a nuisance. The Secretary of State Chris Patten gave them two years to find an alternative site.

'We've had pretty shabby treatment all the way along,' said the manor's president Martin Fleming, who prefers to be known under his religious name Akhandadhi das. 'We've had no assistance with planning permission or finding alternative sites. Sites can be given away all over the place, but if it's a religion that's not considered mainstream, it just doesn't count. I've had letters from people saying "We're prepared to lose our blood rather than lose our temple." Imagine if Lourdes was shut down!'

When it comes to outside politics, pop's Krishna supporters seem less in evidence. Individual spiritual enlightenment is one thing, but the implications of day-to-day politics are less appealing. 'George Harrison is not doing very much,' said Akhandadhi das. 'He's hard to contact and he's in and out of the country. He felt he'd done his little bit and doesn't like to be too public. We don't have many high-level celebrities.'

Keeping up the chaste spiritual connection while remaining fully enmeshed in a pop career is difficult and demanding. And despite the majority of devotees who chant to become pure, there are bound to be a few bad apples. Jagannathesvari Pasi was understandably reticent about the subject of Radha Raman and his marriage to Annie. 'I don't think he's got much to do with us any more,' she says. 'We do have a lot of people who join the movement and then leave again. They can't quite meet the standard and find after some time they have some other desire that becomes stronger. It's not easy to *stay* in the spiritual life, you've got to be really committed, you've got to have had enough of the BS (bullshit).'

It didn't take long for Annie to become fed up with Krishna consciousness. Within months she was estranged from her husband, by February 1985 they were separated, and in April she had started divorce proceedings. The problems between them began to surface early on. Although women are protected within the movement (marriage is the conventional solution to sexual attraction, with the man expected to provide fully for his wife), their spiritual enlightenment doesn't extend to feminism, with women's liberation considered something that has been invented by men to exploit women more easily.

Once he had won Annie, Raman became very demanding. 'All he wants is sex,' Annie was to complain. 'He's broken all his religious promises.' Roseman recalls that her Krishna husband was a very controlling influence.

'Mr Loopy. He had no sense of humour and he was a religious maniac. No doubt he was a gold digger. Once we were shooting the "Sex Crime: 1984" video at some place in Wandsworth, and everything was going great until he turned up. When he came along the atmosphere went clonk! de-*press*-ing. She changed completely when he was around – very quiet and non-communicative, I think she was scared of him, a real nasty piece of work.'

Roseman also remembers an incident when they were recording the *1984* album at Compass Point in the Bahamas. 'Because of the wind or something, there's always power cuts. Anyway, one night there was a power cut so Dave and I decided to go down the road to Radha's and get some candles. Annie was still in the studio. We got there and saw candlelight everywhere and all these people in white robes. It was fucking freaky. To me it didn't matter whether there was power or no power, these people would've *always* had candles.

'Annie liked her drink, she loved her red wine. Course, being with old Radha, there was none of that. One day I turned up at the studio and Annie whispered: "Let's go out for a drink, quick!" 'cos he wasn't around. She got her red wine and we sat for a long time talking in the car, she cried and told me all her problems. Suddenly she saw Radha and said, "Quick, get out, he mustn't see me in the car with you!"

'He was apparently very possessive. I felt really sorry for her over that period.'

Roseman and Dave spent many a drunken evening trying to work out ways to get rid of Radha, but in the end it was Annie's instinct for self-survival that enabled her to separate herself from him. She couldn't leave him without a price, though, a strange karma for someone who entered the spiritual life yet had to buy her way out of it.

Once she initiated divorce proceedings, speaking to Raman only through lawyers, he reputedly attempted to blackmail her, threatening to publish intimate photos of him and Annie unless she paid him £100,000.

'They weren't pornographic, but intimate pictures that couples take. We're not talking animals here,' Roseman says. Raman apparently threatened violence unless he got his way, saying rather distastefully that he would have Annie 'cut up'. She eventually settled for a sum in the region of £20,000, with Raman signing an agreement to return the photographs and not talk about their relationship.

'Annie was burned before, that's why she entered into the relationship. She had a lot of problems with her father, they found it difficult to understand each other. She's a very sensitive old soul.' Annie at first relied on Raman for a great deal of emotional support. When she was asked whether her marriage to a Krishna devotee had given her stability, she answered: 'No . . . you'll have to ask my husband. I'm still a very unstable person.' Leaving him was particularly upsetting, because she grew to be more afraid than fond of him.

An official spokesman for Raman said: 'They both came from very different backgrounds – Annie from one of opulence, wealth and fame, and Radha from one of austere poverty. He had abandoned material possessions as part of his spiritual pursuits. It was one of the issues which brought them into conflict.'

Not surprisingly, Raman denies that he ever tried to blackmail her. In an interview with *Rolling Stone* shortly after the divorce, he said: 'All I want is for her to be happy. I said to her, I don't want to talk about money and that sort of thing. All I want to do is straighten us out. I don't mind leaving the house, but I don't want to leave a mess.'

For someone who'd just suffered divorce, the balding thirty-two-year-old devotee didn't sound too perturbed. 'I wasn't interested in her body or her fame or her credit card. The relationship didn't get physical for a long time. I lived celibate in the temple. But we were together twenty-four hours a day. Oh, it was very beautiful. To me it was like a film, it wasn't real.'

He went on to say that Annie became 'strange' around the time they broke up. She was tired of the press focusing on her unconventional marriage, and in an effort to prove that she wasn't crazy or weird, she distanced herself from Raman. 'Annie gets pessimistic at times. She draws premature conclusions. Sometimes I think she expected a miracle or something, and I couldn't hold up with it. But I helped her with all sorts of things. You all see Annie Lennox the pop star, but she's a small-town girl – very deep and very beautiful, but a small-town girl. She didn't drop from heaven. She's like anybody else. Sometimes you need somebody to pep you up – it took a lot out of me to give so much strength to somebody else.'

Embarking on a new career as a photographer after his marriage, Raman was obviously struck with the pop world. 'Boy George is the nicest person I've met so far. I might get married to him next,' he quipped. It's rumoured that his vows of celibacy didn't stay intact: once he and Annie split up he was apparently trawling around Los Angeles drinking and 'pulling every chick in sight'. As their marriage went on he became an increasingly forlorn figure. Annie never introduced him to her parents, and as she distanced herself, he found it more and more difficult to maintain Krishna discipline.

Annie was, according to him, 'a girl with moral standards, not a quick food girl'. It was important to her to keep a polite, private profile, so despite her anger with Raman she issued a statement, protesting: 'The split between Radha and myself is personal. The decision is amicable and mutual and something we feel is the best thing. There is absolutely no animosity between us and no truth in the suggestion that we're communicating only through our solicitors.'

After the divorce with Raman, Annie threw herself back into work, banking less on spiritual sustenance. She never stayed too long at her house in Switzerland for fear of 'getting bored'. Now she had a restless urge to negotiate the world again, a factor that became abundantly obvious when at the 1985 Montreux Pop Festival she appeared in a crisply chic black leather jacket, announcing 'We're moving into leather, and getting away from vegetarianism.' The fall-out from her marriage left her for a while with an even greater nervous cynicism, claiming in 1986 that she 'didn't believe in anything'. She said impatiently, 'I'm not a religious person, I'm a spiritual person. The way certain people were writing it was as if I'd shaved my head, was chanting and rattling beads. All I ever said was I was interested in his religion.

'I go through phases where I read every book there is on spiritual subjects, but I'm the sort of person who wants it *now*. I want to realize it and if I don't, I get very fraught.'

Now she is wary about putting her name or face to any organized religion. 'I'm a bounder, I go from place to place,' she told *NME* in August 1989. 'Sometimes when I'm very afraid, I think there's a possibility there might be something more to it than it seems, but I can't put a name on it – I can't put a religion to it.'

When someone suggested that in the late 1980s political pop performers were fulfilling the role that the church had once performed, Annie reacted very strongly. 'I hope they haven't become moralizers!' she said. 'I feel a particular disregard for the morality of the church. I'd hate that false sense of morality to come spouting out of musicians' mouths!'

A different strand of spirituality that she has felt comfortable about exploring is that of telepathy or ESP, making a great deal of the telepathic feelings that exist between her and Dave. She speaks of life after death and a collective soul – 'Even though the physical body dies, it's those grander, nobler qualities in human nature that endure.' Her vague feelings about a psychic force are addressed more specifically in the video for 'Angel', from the 1989 album *We Too Are One*, where Annie is at the centre of an old-fashioned seance. Spiritualism became more attractive with the advent of 1990s New Age ideals, and it fits in with Annie's unfocused yearning for a transcendent philosophy. Buddhism is a religion she also flirted with, looking at a form that is more rooted in everyday materialism.

NAM-MYOHO-RENGE-KYO

Hare Krishna is not a faith that fits easily into modern-day Western life. The odd chanting procession of saffron devotees that snakes its way down London's Oxford Street every week simply emphasizes their life lived at one remove from everyday reality. By contrast, Nichiren Shoshu Buddhism, the most popular Eastern religion of the 1980s, is much more industry-friendly, preaching complete integration of faith with a materialistic society. It became increasingly popular throughout the entertainment world, with top London PR agent Lynne Franks working hard to spread the word through her clients.

Annie has also been interested in Buddhism, since Jeff Banks, her clothes designer in the early 1980s, taught her the Nichiren Shoshu mantra *Nam-myoho-renge-kyo* in order to calm her nerves before a show. This mystical phrase is considered the summation and essence of Buddhist teaching, and chanting it will bring the believer in tune with 'the rhythm of the universe'. Distinct from the more intellectual, contemplative Zen form that was widely popularized in the 1970s through books like *Zen And The Art of Motorcycle Maintenance* and stars such as David Bowie, Nichiren Shoshu offers the more straightforward technique of chanting for enlightenment, material as well as spiritual.

Founded by the fiery-spirited monk Nichiren Daishonin in twelfth-century Japan, this Buddhist sect preaches that Nirvana or transcendent wisdom is available to all, that 'earthly desires are enlightenment'. Anyone can set up a Gohonzon or shrine in their front room. Anyone can set their problems before the incense and evergreen and chant for a resolution. The first aim is for personal fulfillment, while the ultimate goal (in tune with the standard Buddhist code of taking collective responsibility) is for world peace.

The

many looks

of Annie

Lennox...

The growth in popularity of Nichiren Shoshu in the media world coincided with the monetarist rise of the Thatcherite 'me' generation in the 1980s. Not surprisingly, the religion has its critics. A former follower says: 'Orthodox Buddhists, if you can use that phrase, are slightly worried about Nichiren Shoshu, which is very *me*-orientated, very now. It centres around this mantra so that if you chant long enough you'll get your heart's desire. Critics see it as the perfect Thatcherite spirituality. In the very high-stress media-pop world, chanting has the benefits of a quick meditation. Focusing on one mantra is a form of self-hypnosis. It's a way of giving yourself prime time, which is something we very rarely do . . . it's also a no-guilt religion – you can bonk groupies, take the drugs and take all the money without worrying.'

The problem is that the ego can become its own spiritual adviser, creating a kind of spiritual materialism. Although there's a danger that pop star chanters can get fixated on their own success, some high-profile Nichiren followers are also effective political campaigners, working on a genuinely humanitarian level. Sixties star Sandie Shaw, former wife of Jeff Banks, feels she resurrected her own career in the 1980s through chanting. 'If you're an artist you need to go back to yourself to rejuvenate,' she says. Having gone back to herself and achieved success, she felt confident about championing wider causes she believed in, performing countless charity benefits for AIDS, gay rights and CND.

'I think we're in the age of consciousness, we're just getting past the materialist time. I think people actually regard the material side with a cynicism now,' she says. 'Like if people look at the results in Africa and the Third World, and the divisions it causes between East and West, they realize that materialism isn't the god they thought it was. People will now start looking into themselves. Then after that they'll see how to merge the two, both the spiritual and the material. They'll see they have to go hand in hand, that you have to purify both sides to get the right perspective.'

At first Shaw fought shy of talking about Buddhism, 'because it always comes out like born-again-pop-star and all that crap', but now expounds it without embarrassment. It is easy to become unbalanced in the pop world; religion provides a context and a structure outside the vagaries of the music business. Tina Turner found Nichiren Shoshu empowering, first on a tentative everyday level, then as a way of getting the confidence to leave her abusive husband Ike.

After I would say the Lord's Prayer, I'd do five repetitions of the chant – nam-myo-ho-renge-kyo . . . I was really excited about it. The first little thing that happened . . . well, I had a problem with the make-up I was using. I was allergic to it, breaking out in a rash. I needed to get this other brand of make-up, and had been looking all over for it, but I couldn't find it. Then, right after I started chanting I got a phone call from a girl I knew. She was at Bloomingdale's. She said, "You know that make-up you were looking for? Well, they have it here." And it was on sale! Now, this sounds kind of silly, but I knew it was the chant – that it was helping me to rearrange my place in the universe. Make-up – I know: a small thing. But it was a start.

As her confidence grew, she became less frightened of Ike.

I knew at last that he wasn't all-powerful, that he wasn't God, that there was a little piece of God inside each of us – inside of me, too – and that I could find it, and it could set me free. That's when I *really* started chanting.

Tina Turner is one of the key figures in the music and fashion world who practises Buddhism, along with Herbie Hancock, Sandie Shaw, Boy George who dabbled a little, and designer Katharine Hamnett who has dabbled a lot. Her famous slogan T-shirts included one enscribed with the Buddhist mantra 'CHOOSE LIFE'. A prime mover in the promotion of this brand of Buddhism has been Hamnett's PR, Lynne Franks.

A briskly effervescent woman who worked on the teen magazine *Petticoat* in the 1960s, Franks set up her own PR company in the late 1970s, winning accounts for Gloria Vanderbilt designer jeans and Raleigh bikes. Throughout the 1980s she ran high-profile campaigns for Swatch watches, Brylcreem and the Labour Party, eventually becoming so successful that the company was bought by top financial PR outfit Broad Street for £2.65 million. She and her husband (and company director) Peter Howie attribute their success to Nichiren chanting. 'It energizes us,' she says. 'It teaches that the individual can change things through effort. Life is not unfair. But if you do business by lying and nasty games and tricks, that gets a karmic retribution for sure, in this life, never mind the next. I'm responsible for my own life.'

While it may have unleashed her creativity, one former employee jokes that after a good hour's chant she would get on the phone and aggressively bawl out a difficult client.

On a lighter level, Mark Moore, the cult London DJ turned disco star, paid tribute to his Buddhist friends with S-Express's 1989 hit 'Mantra For A State Of Mind'. A revolving House track, it combines hypnotic dance with transient pop. 'The record's for my friends who chant and meditate,' he said. 'It has fluctuating rhythms and repetitive lyrics – it's made to lull you and calm you down with certain select phrases like "Feeling good, feeling better, feeling good, doggone winner", so you feel good within yourself.' The link between Buddhism and the acid disco craze of the late 1980s was a strong one, to the extent that one prominent London gay club, Kyo, derived its name from the Buddhist chant.

Although it is construed by some as 'the curse of the 1980s' and 'designer yuppie Buddhism', many people gain inspiration from Nichiren Shoshu. A bright, enthusiastic follower and an avid fan of Annie Lennox, dress-hire assistant Chrissie Carr interprets her faith with a down-to-earth belief in personal responsibility. 'It's not an easy religion to practise because instead of running away from your problems you go *to* them,' she says. 'You're not forced to do anything. You take responsibility for your own life.

'I think it would be great if Annie chanted. She's not got brilliant karma. A lot of her life has been very unhappy. You need to be strong within yourself, though, you can't grab everyone to you, because when they've gone you have nothing. The paradox is that underneath that powerful image is someone easily hurt and vulnerable, because she does rely so much on other people for support. She says she's atheist now, that she's not interested in any religion.

'I always chant for her happiness. I always thought I'd be the best person to tell her about Buddhism.'

Annie has always been spiritually vulnerable, her energies easily depleted by the frenetic pop star lifestyle, so it is not surprising that at times in her emotional life she clutched hold of spiritual security in religion. 'That awful German trauma I think was on the rebound from Dave,' says her former friend and photographer Joe Bangay. 'If she hadn't been so vulnerable that would never have happened – she wouldn't have been that stupid.'

That 'awful German trauma' was Annie's marriage to Radha Raman. When she met him outside her hotel room on the exhaustive

Touch tour, she was searching for a form of solid spirituality he promised to provide. His religion forbade sex before marriage, so against the advice of her friends, family and her father in particular, she married him. Annie wanted to prove to her strict father that she was a mature, successful woman and if she wanted to marry this guy, she was going to marry him.

The disastrous end to her marriage taught her that trust in the music business is hard to come by, especially for a rich woman uncertain whether a man is interested in her for herself or her money and fame. Someone close to her once speculated that 'she needs a forty-three-year-old businessman who owns a company that produces aircraft – completely nothing to do with music.'

Some former lovers complained that they were required to be 'Mr Lennox', and most men's egos wouldn't take that kind of life. A female pop star's husband has to stay out of the limelight but still be strong enough to command her respect. The answer for a lot of women has been to make sure their husbands work with them. Alison Moyet chatted up her future husband when he decorated her house, and promptly appointed him manager when she married him, Sinead O'Connor's husband was in her band, blues singer Elkie Brookes married her lighting man, while Suzie Quatro's husband is her guitarist. It is very difficult to sustain a relationship with someone who works outside the business.

'What I do as a rock star is so time-consuming that if I meet anyone at all it is so briefly,' Annie told radio presenter Anne Nightingale in 1985. 'I might get on with a new friend on a certain level, but usually that person is into their own thing full time. I am then off around the world and never get the chance to meet him again.'

Peter Ashworth, the Eurythmics' photographer who had an 'on-off' relationship with her for several years from the time he shot her musclebound image on the cover of the *Touch* LP, told the *Sunday Mirror* in 1986: 'She often feels trapped. She is menaced by self-doubt in her own ability and constantly needs to be reassured. She can be schizophrenic and melodramatic, but at the base of her emotions is a genuine fear of being rejected. When we were together she would talk a lot about her past. I always had the feeling she was trying to escape from it.'

Their relationship was a troubled one. Both are strong, proud personalities, and Ashworth still feels some bitterness towards Annie. Laurence Stevens recalls an incident in Los Angeles when Ashworth met Annie to discuss work on the 1985 *Be Yourself Tonight* album. 'It was a bit hostile. I remember Peter saying: "I don't know whether they brought me here to calm Annie down or get us back together", and Annie was saying, "Don't bring Peter into the meeting because he's got quite a temper and he'll explode. Go and calm him down."

'They had a meeting in the hotel and at one point Peter stormed out, slammed the door, and there was an enormous crash and splash. He'd chucked himself in the pool and drenched everyone around him. He did two lengths really quickly and strode out. All the guests sitting there paying X amount of dollars a day were thinking, "Who the bloody hell was that?"

'He had a chip on his shoulder because he felt Annie wasn't really treating him properly – he felt that because of their relationship she was treating him just as a photographer, rather than a photographer/friend.'

Annie wanted to be the centre of her lover's life, but found it difficult when they became dependent on her. Soon after the break-up of her marriage to Raman, she went out with Billy Poveda, a tall, athletic dancer whom she met while shooting the 'Would I Lie To You?' video. At first they were very close, but after living with him for nearly two years she began distancing herself. He is a warm, kind man who was maybe reluctant to stand up to Annie.

'Annie liked to go out, and she loved arguing and discussing,' recalls her former friend and video producer Jon Roseman. 'One night we all went to the Hippodrome in London, and she argued late into the night with me about capital punishment, Irangate, etc., etc. Billy would say "I want to go home now", and she'd say "Shut up! Listen Roseman . . ."

'Something was never quite right there. He got dumped. He was a choreographer, she fancied him, one thing led to another. Then he found himself in the terrible situation of looking after her life and living off her. He was a lovely guy: if the boot had been on the other foot – she a man, he the woman – it would've been more acceptable somehow. She was travelling all over the place. He could hardly get work if he didn't know where he'd be from one day to the next. He became an unofficial manager-type figure. I saw it begin to degenerate. There's a thin dividing line between using someone *per se*, and using them because you think there's a reason for using them . . . it was very sad.'

Annie claimed afterwards that the split with Billy affected her deeply, fuelling much of the material for the *Savage* album. 'Breaking up with the man who I had been living with for two years left me reeling,' she says. 'I wasn't prepared for it and felt as if my world was caving in around me. I'd been living in hotel rooms for so long I just didn't know what I was doing or who I was. It was as if I was all alone on a mountain top . . . an isolation that was quite dangerous.'

Although Annie left Billy, she was very confused about what she wanted. After they split up, he carried on working for Annie, and now takes care of her Oil Factory video business in Los Angeles. He bears no animosity, and still feels very affectionate towards her.

Annie needed to strike the right balance between someone who would care for her unconditionally, yet also regularly challenge her. Dave had fulfilled this role for a long time, but by 1987 he was less and less part of her personal life. His marriage to Siobhan Fahey from the best-selling British girl group Bananarama was a highly meditated and highly emotive event. 'It came as a shock to us all,' says Keren from Bananarama.

Joe Bangay recalls how he first heard about the marriage. 'Dave was always phoning up saying, "I've got a new girlfriend, come and photograph her with me at the airport". He was very much into the publicity style. Anyway, he and Siobhan decided to get married one night, and he rang asking me to do his engagement pictures. We did them in a dirty, tacky studio at the back of Wandsworth somewhere, but she looked really glamorous in this fluffy can-can outfit. Siobhan was definitely going to leave the band because she's very ambitious, the most ambitious woman I know.'

The wedding was a high-profile affair, with hundreds of celebrity guests being flown in a chartered jet from Heathrow to Normandy's Chateau de Dangu in August 1987. It was a £500,000 Hollywood-style bash, as vulgar and loud as Annie's registry office wedding to Raman had been secret and quiet. 'I was invited to go to the wedding, but I didn't got, out of loyalty to Annie,' says Bangay. 'I thought Annie put herself under a lot of pressure in going. It was tough for her to have to do that, and she left the wedding pretty sharpish.'

Although Annie has an easy-going relationship with Siobhan, the two have had to work at it – both assiduously deflecting media speculation that they are arch rivals. 'I was terrified when I met Annie. She always seemed so strong, so sure of herself,' said Siobhan, who learned a lot from Annie about poise and autonomy when she moved from straight commercial pop to cult pop in launching her own band Shakespear's Sister. 'I was afraid she wouldn't like me. But Annie's always been really friendly and supportive.'

Annie made a clear, conscientious statement about Siobhan in return, saying: 'She's a great girl. She's made Dave very happy — when I first met her I thought, here was somebody who would provide him with the sincerity that was missing before. In the past his affairs were all so frantic, as if he was looking for something he'd lost. Now he's found it.'

The wedding made Annie come to terms with the fact that she really did have to live her life without Dave, and she wanted something good for herself. In the early stages of Dave's honeymoon, Annie was making a commitment too, this time to a dark, doe-eyed Israeli film maker called Uri Fruchtman.

The one word that Annie has used over and over again to describe the main men in her life is 'supportive'. She speaks less about loving them, more about the rock-like influence each one has had in her life. This seems strange when in her career she has done so much to define herself as a separate entity. Although she seeks a spiritual self-sufficiency, she has often thrown her insecurities in with a relationship, relying on the chosen man to sort them out. For a long time she still spoke of Dave as 'the one'. They were no longer together as lovers, but their relationship was important to her: as long as Dave was 'the one', another man would simply be 'the other', acting as an emotional prop. By the time she met Uri, though, she had grown through a lot of these anxieties towards a more philosophical outlook. 'Something happened to me on my thirtieth birthday,' Annie said. 'I felt more positive than I'd ever done before.'

She referred to Uri as 'my refuge and my rock', but said this without the desperation she'd felt regarding former lovers. When she met him Annie had come through the emotional catharsis of the *Savage* LP, and recognized the precarious nature of her own pop existence. Eurythmics were world-famous, but yet again she seemed to be pacing hotel rooms without a home base and a family to call her own. Meeting Uri opened up possibilities away from the music business, offering Annie a new kind of domestic security.

A quietly intense man, Uri provides Annie with the support she needs, but has intelligence and independence enough to hold his own in the volatile rock world. He benefits through being connected to it, yet at one remove. A documentary film maker, Uri met Annie in 1987 when his crew were shooting *Brand New Day*, a video of the Eurythmics' tour of Japan (which incidentally never got released – ironically Dave and Annie felt it portrayed them too much as typical rock stars). With his dark good looks, Uri was immediately attractive to Annie, and before long they were involved in a serious relationship, moving into a Paris flat together above a baker's shop in Montparnesse.

Early in 1988 they were married. Uri was an altogether more secure proposition than Radha Raman. He was thirty-six when they met, she was only three years younger, and both were ready for commitment. Born in 1951 in Tel Aviv, Uri also has a German passport. His father Bruno Fruchtman, an ambitious, intellectual Jew, changed his name to Benno and left his hometown Meuselwitz in Germany with his four brothers and sisters just before the Second World War, to escape the Nazi Holocaust. Having married and settled in Israel, Benno had no wish to return, and worked for many years as a commercial artist. Literature was his first love, though, and he started writing books in 1970. He is now one of Israel's most popular authors.

'His work is dominated by the conflict he has with himself,' says a friend of the family, Jana Chantelau, now living in Bremen, West Germany. 'He writes in German language, but it's the German that was used fifty years ago! He's very literary, and in one of his books, *Masquerade*, some of the sentences ran into six lines. He's difficult and complicated to read, but in person he is so charming you can't say anything against him.'

Uri carried on the artistic family tradition, directing his creativity into film making. He was inspired by his uncle Karl, a maverick Fruchtman who left Israel to work as a manager for El Al Airlines in London before returning to Germany and establishing himself as a committed independent documentary film maker. Karl and Uri have collaborated on several TV films, including the award-winning *Witnesses*, a German production shot in Israel which featured interviews with survivors of the Nazi concentration camps. Made in 1980, *Witnesses* was Uri's first film, winning the Gold category in Germany's prestigious Adolf Grinne Prize.

Serious-minded and a one-time National Service conscientious objector, Uri was a comfortable choice for Annie. 'It's about time I had a relationship that works,' she said. 'It's marvellous that I've actually found somebody I love. I feel very happy, clear and clean.'

After embracing his family and finding some solid peace of mind, she felt settled enough to become pregnant. Siobhan had given birth to

Samuel Joseph Hurricane in November 1987, and within four months Annie admitted she was desperate to have a baby. 'At thirty-three, it's about time physically,' she said. 'And I know a baby will enrich my life. Friends are getting pregnant all around me, but I don't want just to be part of the fashion. It is all a question of who you're with – you can't just buy a bag of kids in the shop!'

Shortly after she gave that interview to *Sunday* magazine, Annie announced she was pregnant. She appeared three months into term at the Mandela birthday concert at Wembley looking radiant, and then took time out of pop music before the birth. Although she was careful about her diet and exercise, attending daily yoga classes and eating high-protein foods, something went tragically wrong.

On 4 December 1988, she entered a west London hospital, two days before the baby was officially due. She felt contractions, but movements were slowing down considerably. Doctors tried to monitor the baby's heartbeat, but couldn't find it. They walked with her to another part of the hospital to take a scan. Annie suddenly realized that she no longer felt any physical pain, and the scan showed that the baby's heart had stopped beating. Within an hour of expecting to go into labour, she found that the baby had died.

She was given an epidural injection, and after a long, sad night, gave birth to a stillborn baby son. They called him Daniel, and in accordance with the counselling of the Stillbirth and Neo-natal Death Society (SANDS), asked for the baby to be washed and wrapped in a shawl. When Annie and Uri were ready, they held the dead baby and took pictures of it, to create real memories to help their grieving process. 'At first I thought doing that might be a disturbing experience,' she said later. 'But that's what the experts advised. It was a great comfort for Uri and myself.' Annie searched in her mind for reasons for Daniel's death, aware that she had taken every precaution to make sure the pregnancy would be healthy. In giving birth, though, there are no guarantees. Annie had hidden away and refused show-business invitations six months before the birth. She'd even moved from Paris to London during that time to get the best possible treatment. She'd taken continual scans right up to the week before she went into labour, and the baby's heart had been beating, so when her 'last ambition' died it was all the more shocking.

In her determination to avoid sinking into depression, she came to terms with the trauma by grieving openly and talking to the press about her plight in an effort to help thousands of other mothers who'd had stillbirths. The press had a field day, presenting another facet to the 'Tragedy Annie' story and filling their pages with 'human interest' headlines like 'BRAVE ANNIE WINS'. Although it sensationalized the topic, the coverage gave a boost to the stillbirth campaign for more medical research on the subject.

One out of every hundred couples in Britain share this disaster each year: over half the babies involved are stillborn, while the others die during their first week of life. 'Women find it hard nowadays to accept that they have lost their baby,' said Dr Donald Gibb, senior consultant in obstetrics and gynaecology at London's King's College Hospital. 'Technology does help. It is the reason why babies shouldn't die in labour, and the rate of stillbirths has fallen dramatically over the last thirty years. But in many cases the cause cannot be explained.'

It was as if, despite her careful preparation, Annie was not ready to have a baby. Someone close to her has suggested that she was not really 'the mothering type. She liked kids, but when she wanted to work she didn't want to be disturbed. She seemed more interested in her career.'

It's true that soon after the tragedy, Annie was busy back in the limelight. She won Best Female Singer of the Year at the BRITS awards the following February, and was then back in the studio with Dave to record the *We Too Are One* LP. By plunging back into frantic work, Annie avoided brooding on her loss. It is common for mothers of stillborn children suddenly to become very active in their lives. 'When the baby dies, you're totally unprepared for it, and something in you dies with it,' says one mother who lost her son after a seven-month pregnancy. 'But when you see that dead baby it changes your life forever – you realize that life's too short, that you can't procrastinate or wait for things to happen anymore. *You've got to make things happen.*'

Although Annie emerged hollow-eyed and strained after her experience, she was determined to try for another baby and made plans to conceive after the promotion and *We Too Are One* revival tour which ended just before Christmas 1989. 'It takes six months to a year before the body has physically recovered and the emotions are starting to settle,' said Alison Melville, SANDS information officer. 'The vast majority of parents eventually do have other babies.'

After she won the Best Female Singer BRITS award for the second year running, in February 1990 Annie bowed out of the pop world, ostensibly to work for the homeless charity Shelter. She was also making plans to start a family, away from the media glare, as she felt superstitious about the press attention and speculation that had surrounded Daniel's birth. Four months later Annie triumphantly announced that at thirty-five she was pregnant again. 'I am feeling on top of the world,' she said. 'It took me weeks to get over losing my baby, in fact you never really get over it. And everybody knowing and talking about your heartache is not exactly the best medication in the world.'

Annie's search for spiritual fulfilment reflected as much her urgent emotional need to be loved in a secure environment. Now she has found some familial peace with Uri, the religious question is less an ideal for her to grasp at, more an issue that she approaches with a realistic understanding. Like many pop stars before her who lack emotional ballast in their lives and relationships, she turned to religion at a time when she felt most vulnerable.

Having conceived another baby, Annie was happy to spend more time with her family, away from the strenuous demands of a pop career. Like many pop mothers, she reached her mid-thirties with the kind of serenity she thought she would never experience. From the age of fourteen to thirty, when she reached a new level of maturity, Annie had often been dogged by black days of depression. Marriage to Uri mellowed her, gave her new hope and a sense that her darkest anxieties had been left behind.

8

Stage Fright

'There's nothing worse for me than going onstage and being slightly off-sync with myself, not being able to give 100 per cent. I use the fear I have to focus in on songs. I get really panic-stricken up there; not stage fright but a real fear of – myself, I suppose. Sometimes my intensity gets so strong that I hallucinate onstage.

'At first I liked to make a transition that was very important because the clothes represented almost a ritualistic thing – these are my stage clothes, this is what I wear when I want to communicate our ideas to people. . . .

'The only time I get *stadium syndrome* is if the stage is so high I can't see the audience. I like to be able to *touch* people, to see that they're okay at the front because sometimes they can get crushed . . . On tour my personal objective is to leave that stage feeling that the people who have just witnessed that concert have just had an incredible time. I find it very therapeutic getting up on stage. I bare my soul.

'I think it's important to talk to fans. People see too little of you really. I try to defuse my fame, to show that there is a funny person underneath the star, who is quite accessible. Fame is like winning the donkey derby. For a couple of days you think, God, I'm on the cover of *Rolling Stone*. Wow. Then . . . you forget about it.'

STAGE TACTICS

Annie has a very industrious relationship with her audience. She approaches stage performance the way she would any contract that she has signed: with her full commitment. If an audience does not respond, she feels as if she has personally failed, that her music has not been forceful enough. Every Eurythmics tour has been a careful projection of each album they're promoting; never slapdash, always rigorously rehearsed with a careful variety in the tone and presentation.

'Pop music and pop culture is fascinating, with endless possibilities. You can make it any way you *want* it to be. It depends on your invention and your abilities,' says Annie. 'It's not about being a fantastic singer or a fantastic technician. It's more about a certain sort of energy and strength of character coming through – either not saying anything in charismatic silences or exuding lots and lots of energy. Each successful pop performer has their own enigmatic quality that just shines. It's an elusive, indefinable thing – magical.'

Does Annie feel she has that?

'I'd hate to think I'd missed the mark.'

In her desire to hit the target Annie assesses the mood of each crowd every time she goes on stage, and slants her act accordingly. When members of the 20,000-strong audience hurled abuse at Eurythmics during a 1983 concert at Dublin's Phoenix Park, throwing firecrackers and calling the group 'English bastards', she retorted by speaking directly to them. 'It's hot and people have hot temperaments. Be kind to each other,' she pleaded. 'Remember that we're all human beings. I'm doing this because I believe in the human spirit . . . I can't play to faces full of hatred.'

Her lip quivered. There was an uncertain silence, and then the crowd cheered. 'Let's just play,' whispered Dave.

Instead of ignoring it, Annie confronts hostility head-on. 'Quite often I've had something like a girl at the front staring me out, curling her lip and sneering,' she told *The Face*'s Max Bell in 1983. 'It's a way of taking attention away from an entire audience and turning it onto them, a perversion of the proceedings. If that happens I go and whisper in their ear and ask them to leave. I used to shout but that's a mistake. There's something about a quiet power which is stronger than losing your temper; something James Brown has. When he steps up he commands attention by his presence. He knows his power and he functions properly. That is reassuring.'

During the *We Too Are One* Revival tour in 1989, Annie would sing with the full strength of the band behind her before leaving the stage for a number to change her clothes. Returning in a pristine grey suit to do a quiet acoustic set with Dave, she would stand stock still and stare calmly at the audience. Waiting almost like a friendly schoolteacher to see that she had them in her command, she then broke the silence with one swift body movement, launching with Dave into the duet 'I Need You'.

'I found it difficult to concentrate on my keyboards sometimes, she was such a stunning, spellbinding performer,' says Vic Martin, a wry, down-to-earth musician who toured extensively with Eurythmics in the early days, and has since worked with the Bee Gees, Boy George and Curiosity Killed The Cat. 'Annie would become absolutely lost in it, and incredibly focused.'

If she is not assured of the audience's attention, Annie gets petulant and frustrated. Pete Phipps, the drummer on Eurythmics' international *Touch* tour in 1983, recalls an incident when they were touring the States and they played a beach club in New Jersey.

'The Night of the Mustard, it was called. We were in a real out-in-the-sticks place full of surfers, beach boys. What we were doing there I just do not know. Just before I went on stage I had cheese on rye, I put mustard on it and the top came off the mustard pot, so I had all this mustard dolloped on my sandwich. I forgot to screw it back on properly.

'Anyway we only did a quarter of a set before coming off stage. We went down abysmally . . . like a . . . like a calm sea. It was a waste of time: they didn't want it and we didn't want it. Annie was annoyed we'd been put in there, it was hard enough being in America anyway. She picked up the mustard pot and threw it across the room. Unfortunately at that point Dave walked in wearing a pure white suit. The mustard went all over him, covering him from head to toe. He said, deadpan: "Can you go easy on the mustard Annie?"

'Annie burst out laughing and broke the tension. After that we had a party. Dave has a lovely sense of humour – nothing fazes him at all.'

A tall, gently humoured man, Pete Phipps joined Eurythmics on tour after ten years playing with the Glitterband, glam rock superstar Gary Glitter's backing group. 'They were knocked out that I'd worked with Gary Glitter. At that time Annie had worn the gold lamé suit for the promotion of 'Right By Your Side'. I was sick of the sight of gold suits to be honest. I thought, oh no, from one gold suit into another. I thought, as long as she doesn't ask me to wear one!'

Annie had very definite ideas about stage presentation, something she had learned early on from those days in Aberdeen with Bill Spittle's danceband, and she would often advise the band on stage wear or choreography. Martin Dobson, saxophonist on the *Touch* tour and the *Be Yourself Tonight* album recalls an episode when 'Would I Lie To You' was moving up the charts, so he was required to accompany Eurythmics on a TV 'Top Of The Pops' appearance. Annie was anxious for a slick stage show to accompany this raunchy pop-blues number.

'She asked us to move a bit. We moved a bit. "Well that's not really what I had in mind," she said. She got her choreographer to teach us a few steps, so he took a cassette machine into the dressing room and he was doing all these steps. Dave [a fellow horn player] and I were trying to follow, saying "Oh God, we're not dancers, we're musicians, we'll never get this."

'We weren't feeling confident about the dance steps. We went up to the bar and had several large ones; then ten minutes before transmission I said to Dave, "Let's go over to make up and get them to do a job on our hair." They did a real job, so we got on stage to do a take with our hair really silly and spikey. Annie turned round and said "you *bastards*!". Trouble was, what with the dancing steps and the miming to what we'd played, we were moving at times where the brass was going but the sax was out of my mouth. It didn't look too good. When Annie saw "Top Of The Pops" the next day she went bloody mad!'

Although an excellent sax player, Dobson is more avuncular and self-effacing, without the sleek image required for a perfect pop presentation. 'For the "Would I Lie To You" video, they used half a dozen black guys playing or miming instruments. That pissed us off because Dave and I had done it and should take credit for the brass section, not have a so-called brass section that doesn't exist.'

He is aware of Annie's meticulous attention to detail, seeing it as a quality that was sometimes more abrasive and over-attentive than effective. 'She's a perfectionist, like many artists. Anyone who's good in music tends to be that way. You can overdo that perfectionist thing. It's not always important to get everything exactly right. Sometimes there's a feel or bit that's more important – other people can see it from a different perspective, whereas you have it under a microscope because *you* know what you were doing at the time. She got on the pianist's nerves a bit. She'd get on the piano and say, "This is how it's done." He wasn't too keen on that.'

Vic Martin, a keyboardist who toured with Eurythmics on both the *Sweet Dreams* and *Touch* tours, recalls Annie as a very complicated person. 'She has great and horrible sides to her. She could be terribly abrasive and insensitive, but that wouldn't be a problem because Dave was a spectacularly good foil for her and he could defuse any potential situation. He's a pretty handy interface to have around, a really sweet bloke, always buying people little presents and calming things down. She's quite tactless – there are ways of handling people in order to get the best out of them. Stewart Levine, for example, is a master psychologist in the studio – but Annie didn't have that ability.'

There are tales of Annie getting through three sound engineers a day. 'She'd give the engineers a really hard time, especially before live performances,' says a former engineer. 'She'd freak out, be all emotional and take it out on people who were doing their jobs perfectly well. The general feeling was that she could sing her songs all right, but she couldn't talk to you.'

Pete Phipps, too, noted that Annie was intent on keeping the band to certain intense standards. 'She's short-tempered at times, but who wouldn't be when you have that bunch behind you? She knew how to get what she wanted. She'd quite rightly express an opinion.'

Dave and Annie were different from many rock artists who are content to go out on the road and build up audiences gradually. 'With Dave and Annie it was always perfectionist – "we've got to get this right, *more* right, now",' remembers their PR Sheila Sedgwick. 'Annie had very high standards, she was very hard on herself, sometimes ridiculously hard. She has high standards for herself and other people, and can be quite aloof if she feels someone's not behaving right. She doesn't suffer fools, which perhaps gave her the 'difficult' tag. She felt many people she came across were idiots with no understanding at all – that comes out of her own high ideals for herself in work and relationships. Annie appears to have calmed down now, which is good.'

From the very start, Annie had a strong confidence in her live performance. Logo Records boss Geoff Hannington remembers the time after a Tourists' gig at London's famed rock venue the Marquee club, when Annie darted into the dressing room, her fists clenched in triumph. 'She had a very forceful presence,' he says. 'She came backstage really confident saying "that was great!". And she knew it was great. She knew how to get a response from the crowd, how to control and move them. She had it. She's not like a lot of artists I've seen who after a gig feel down or insecure about their talent. She was on a real high.'

Annie is a magnetic focal point on stage. Sometimes during the

Revenge tour she would go backstage while the band got on with rocking out, Dave wielding his guitar wild-style. The presentation would seem flat though, until Annie came on stage again and livened up the show immediately. Although her movements are a little stiff and she is not a fluid dancer, she has a peculiar icy energy that adds colour and light to the spectacle. She *commands* that stage.

'On stage she has a singular rapport with the audience,' says drummer Pete Phipps. 'She doesn't have to speak with them but they're all there; she has a charisma that sparks something with them. She has it naturally in a room full of people. If she walked in to a room everyone would gravitate towards her. She also knows how to project her voice, even off stage. Peter Gabriel's a bit like that — he has a charisma that really makes you want to talk to him.'

Eurythmics are a stage industry as much as they are a video band, religiously going out on tour to promote each album. Their first major tour was for *Sweet Dreams*, undertaken in 1983 on a shoestring record company loan of £70,000. 'It was a big gamble on everybody's part,' recalls Jack Steven, the band's A&R at the time. 'Before the tour they were completely unknown – but because of their success on the dance floor it made sense to have them out on tour. It began really poorly and, I thought, this is probably the end of my career in the music industry.

'However, as they went into a town, the twelve-inches had happened before them and there was already a buzz. The buzz spilt into the press, the press started convincing media people and by the time they reached their final gig at the Lyceum Ballroom in London, which holds a few hundred people, over 3,000 turned up and there were actually forged tickets for a Eurythmics gig! The thing was so big by that time – it had just snowballed.'

Although it was big, the occasion was tense. '*Sweet Dreams* had just hit, the place was full of sheep all waiting for that one number, and Dave and Annie were so aggressive, so desperate to clinch success, that they overdid it,' wrote Paul Strange in *Melody Maker*.

When they returned to the venue nine months later on their second major tour, promoting the *Touch* album, the prognosis was more encouraging. 'More confident, more assured and with an audience who were better acquainted with their terrific material . . . the performance proved that Eurythmics have become one of Britain's most intriguing . . . and most important new groups.'

The *Touch* tour took off with a full-scale ten-piece band, including three backing singers known as the Croquettes. Singer/song writer Maggie Ryder, who was one of the original three Croquettes, remembers Annie as 'very talented, a very discerning musician. She was precise about what she wanted, but she had an unfortunate manner when trying to explain things.'

Annie would sometimes let her backing singers ad lib, but she was careful that they kept to her vocal arrangements. 'There was one bit where I opened "Who's That Girl" while she did a costume-change,' says Maggie. 'And she made me sing it *exactly* as she would do it, with her pronunciation and everything.'

Such a meticulous approach paid off. 'As everyone must know by now, the Eurythmics are more than just another synthesizer band,' announced one Birmingham journalist after their Odeon New Street gig. Aside from the hectic pacing of hits like 'Right By Your Side', covering every musical style from calypso to rock, there were flute and bagpipes thrown in at the end of the show to underline the band's Scottish connection.

By the time the band made it to New York to play their showcase gig at the Ritz, there was a lot of American interest. 'That gig stands out in my mind – it was obviously setting us up for greater things,' says Pete Phipps. 'Everybody was there to see us. Lots of guys turned up, including Robbie Robertson.'

As they became bigger, Dave and Annie's experiment of keeping themselves as the Eurythmics' commanding nucleus with a changing line-up of musicians was resolutely put into effect. Although it gave Dave and Annie greater versatility, their musicians received some pretty offhand treatment. Just before the *Touch* tour began its European leg, Pete Phipps, keyboardist Vic Martin and horn player Dick Cuthell were sacked and replaced. 'I was told they couldn't afford me,' said Cuthell at the time. 'It really is a blow. I feel upset that they left it so long to tell us while secretly rehearsing new guys.'

With his wife expecting a second child, he was worried about the immediate financial future: 'I'd already cancelled work because I thought my time would be taken up with Dave and Annie.'

Vic Martin was disappointed because he had been with Eurythmics on their very early 'Only Fools And Horses' tour of seaside towns, and recalls with affection the *Sweet Dreams* tour that followed. 'I was such a fan then, I thought the *Sweet Dreams* LP was so innovative and it was good to see them develop. I didn't enjoy the *Touch* tour so much. I found the music superficial and less interesting, and I'd had a bellyful of it. I'd been on the road with them for a year, and that's an awful long time. You lose a lot of the session time. The thing is, Eurythmics are very self-sufficient, and you're used very much as an auxiliary musician – that's your place.'

Pete Phipps, too, felt left in the lurch, though he takes a more philosophical attitude now. 'I was upset about it, but within days XTC rang up asking me to work on their album, so that took my mind off it. I was pissed off at not doing the world tour with them – but then that's how the business is. It's not like a marriage. We were a band, we definitely had a year together, and there were no different limos – we all travelled together – no separate hotels. Bands have problems, people have differences, and everybody changes their line-up.'

Eurythmics' response to this situation did not allow room for discussion, as they issued a statement saying: 'Eurythmics are essentially Annie Lennox and Dave Stewart, and it is their decision to keep the rest of the line-up flexible.'

Eddie Reader, a backing vocalist with them in the early days who went on to front her own successful band, Fairground Attraction, also came in for some high-handed treatment. Having bought a new outfit for a tour, she was then dropped at short notice. Although greatly disappointed, she had to chalk up that incident to music business experience.

Jack Steven feels that Eurythmics had problems coping with their success, and in trying to find people they could trust the band would often distance themselves without warning from people they had been close to. 'My communication with the band was being taken away from me internally within the company,' he says. 'No one wanted me to deal with the band. They were bigger than anything RCA had had for years. So all of a sudden after being so close to them my ties were being severed left, right and centre. I was very young so I felt hurt by it. Now I realize that's just the norm of the business; somebody becomes hugely successful so all the heavyweights jump in.'

Although Eurythmics might have set out to do things differently, they fell into the usual business procedure of shedding people as they moved upwards without apology or contact. Their video producer Jon Roseman was aggrieved when after five years working with them, he was unable to get Dave on the phone. 'I always said to Dave, you've used me for so many videos, there's bound to come a time when you'll want someone else. But you tell me first. They never mentioned it. It wasn't till later that Dave said to me, "I heard you had trouble with one of your companies at the time." I thought, here's my mate saying – I heard you had business troubles, so that's why we used someone else.

'When you have a friend in trouble you stick by them. But they were just rock'n'rollers. I'm not saying they're any better or any worse than the others – they're just the same.'

Once Eurythmics were surrounded by countless people and a barrage of management, it was easy for them to lose touch with old friends or deal less directly with employees. The strain of touring exerted its own restless pressure; never staying long in one place, it became difficult to retain continuity in personal relationships.

The *Touch* tour became a marathon, with Eurythmics out on the road for the best part of 1984, playing over 175 dates. It became known as the Homewrecker Tour, as it was during this time that Annie's first marriage broke up, and relationships among band members foundered. There was also the curse of Annie losing her voice. Halfway through the *Touch* tour she was becoming weary, living with a constant sore throat and having to communicate in sign language during the day in order to rest her vocal chords.

Her voice coach Tona de Brett remarked to the *Daily Mirror* in 1983 that the problem was fashion. 'Men sing at the tops of their voices, and women at the lower end of the scale – quite unnaturally. If your voice gets strained, most ordinary people can stop, but with today's singers there's too much time and money at stake. The troubles are far more common in the pop world because the singers don't get any basic training at all. Classical singers are trained to cope far better.'

Annie's classical training hadn't extended to her voice, and she had constant problems adapting to the forceful requirements of a rock set. The strain of over-singing resulted in her developing nodules, or small growths on her vocal chords, a common affliction among pop stars from Paul Young to Frank Sinatra. She went to see many doctors, including a top throat specialist in Vienna, and in later years she would learn to pace herself more. 'I've got such a big responsibility *not* to lose my voice, and to give the best vocal performance I can. So it can curtail my social life,' she said.

For the Eurythmics' 1985 album *Be Yourself Tonight*, the band decided not to risk another tour so soon. 'The songs are so demanding I'm really scared I'll make my throat worse by just steaming into another tour,' said Annie. 'I'm going to go to singing lessons and strengthen my voice so next time we go out on the road my voice is really solid.' Instead of touring, Dave and Annie made a stack of promotional videos for the album, conserving their energy for the next on-the-road extravaganza – the world *Revenge* tour, which started in November 1986, eighteen months after their last live date.

Revenge was a clean orchestrated rock dream of white space and black leather. Although they avoided dry ice, the stage show included long boring guitar solos and grand hand gestures. 'Everything I do is very consciously done, so it's partly music hall as well,' Annie said. Dubbed 'a professional entertainment machine', they used the traditions and pacing of rock'n'roll in a performance that was smooth and slickly rehearsed. Built loosely around the themes of evangelical religion the stage was a huge white cross, with the performers dressed in missionary black.

It was a sell-out stadium tour, hailed in the press as the most important show of 1986, yet despite its success a few journalists remained sceptical. Lesley-Ann Jones of the *Daily Express* wrote that: 'far from coming over as the Scottish sexpot . . . Lennox appeared as an aggressive under-fed greyhound . . . she is a stiff and awkward performer who dances like a computer salesman on a night out with the boys.'

In a move to counteract the accusations that she just wanted to 'be a man', Annie threw off her bra at the end of the set in Birmingham, much to the consternation of the world's press. The chaste Annie! Flinging off her bra! Whatever next!

The gesture came over as a final ironic flaunting of her sexuality after keeping it so carefully guarded all these years. As a shock tactic, though, the move was somewhat mis-timed, rather like Julie Andrews in the film *10*, trying to reinvent her goody-goody reputation with some down-to-earth sex. As Andrews frolicked with Dudley Moore, all we could think of was Mary Poppins. For someone who has been as determinedly asexual as Annie, exposing herself was just bemusing to fans and critics alike.

Former boyfriend Peter Ashworth was not impressed. 'She needs to know she is in control of an audience. It doesn't work for her if they don't respond,' he told the *Sunday Mirror* in 1986. 'Personally I don't know why she has taken to stripping down to her bra on stage. It's so unnecessary. Maybe she thought it was all becoming like a circus and took the bra off because it was the unpredictable thing to do.'

Many fans, too, were disappointed with this provocative move, as Debbie Pierce from West London recalls: 'When I saw her at Lyons she had soft gorgeous black leather trousers and an ivory coloured silk shirt. You couldn't see her shape underneath. Then she took her shirt off. I didn't think there was any need for that. She's not a sex goddess like Madonna and I don't think she needs to start taking her clothes off or trying to portray that sexy image. Her music is far better than Madonna's music will ever be.'

Annie maintained at the time: 'Now I'm able to let my feminine sexuality come through much more, but I still feel my mannish sexuality as a performer coming through on stage.'

This mid-1980s' version of gender confusion was subtler than the out-and-out male disguises of *Sweet Dreams*, with the combination of sexual opposites neatly summed up in her butch black leather trousers and bright red feminine bra. Annie sometimes laces her act with ambiguous contempt as a distancing device, a cool 'look but don't touch' pose that consolidates her role as an inaccessible enigma, the reluctant star.

After the *Revenge* tour, Eurythmics began to slow down their output. They went back into the studio to record *Savage*, the video album that marked a return to their more innovative roots, while Annie withdrew a little from the pop scene, living in Paris and planning to start a family with her husband Uri.

It was the loss of her baby at the end of 1988 that spurred Annie back into the business full time. From the moment she received a BRITS award for Best Female Vocalist of the Year the following February, Annie was high profile once more. Major label Arista took over Eurythmics' affairs in America in an effort to push the band in the States, an area where, despite their established reputation, the band had yet to make substantial inroads.

The *Revival* tour, a 64-date spectacle running from September to Christmas, was their most organized yet. With the gargantuan Swede Ollo Romo on drums, Joniece Jameson and the Gap Band's Charlie Wilson on backing vocals, Pat Seymour playing keyboards and bass virtuoso Chucho Merchan, it was also the most professional. As if she had spent the previous two years preparing herself, Annie undertook everything with precision – the promotion, the photographs and the performance itself. A former RCA press officer recalls the palaver when she was summoned to Paris to sort out promo shots and T-shirts for the tour. 'There was great angst, especially over the

T-shirts. Dave and Annie wanted them more designer-y . . . they were only tour T-shirts for God's sake!'

All this was part of the careful preparation for a tour which pleasantly startled everyone. Dressed first in a flowing red silk dress and then cool grey suit, Annie ripped through numbers from the *We Too Are One* album with an ease and self-assurance she hadn't exhibited before. For the *Revenge* tour she came across as chaste and tense despite the sexy bra, whereas her *Revival* dates exuded a fluid maturity and a new sensuality.

Having returned to the limelight, Annie ducked her head back again once the tour was over, spending 1990 making sporadic appearances, concentrating on charity work and starting a family. This reflects her complicated relationship with fame, a status that she both ardently desires and actively shuns.

In the early struggling days of Eurythmics after the demise of the Tourists, Annie felt defeated by obscurity. Lack of recognition meant she was uncertain and unconfident about her place in the pop world – but once the band struck gold with *Sweet Dreams* Annie achieved not only musical recognition, but the kind of fame that meant she was pointed at in shops, jostled by fans and, according to the press, her private life was fair game. This wasn't quite how she had intended to play it.

'She had to come to terms with the fact of being a pop star,' says Jack Steven. 'I found her a bit peculiar because she had this burning ambition to express herself, yet when *Sweet Dreams* was at Number 2 something happened that freaked out the record company. Annie was suddenly all over the place – I think a relationship was going down the tubes – and she *flew* into the record company saying she was going to give up, retire, go back to waitressing. Meanwhile Dave was sitting there tutting, saying "Christ, I wanna go the whole way, shut up."

'She was a little bit angst. I don't know why, because she didn't compromise her musical talent on that album at all. They had struggled in the doldrums for so many years to express themselves that when it all happened fast and furious I don't think they could accept the change of pace. She didn't understand why one minute people were saying effectively you're a pile of shit, and next minute the greatest thing since sliced bread. The ambition suddenly coming to fruition freaked her out.'

Annie has had periodic escapes from the goldfish mentality of the rock world, the most spectacular being her marriage to a Hare Krishna monk – though that desire for peace and quiet ironically backfired on her. She is acutely self-conscious of her fame, often talking about the subject in her interviews.

She likened fame to having an extra leg: 'You can't forget about it because other people don't let you – there's always an extra thing around you.' She admired someone like Boy George who at first seemed to be able to play fame at its own game, comfortable with living his life in the tabloids. Unfortunately when his career started going awry through heroin addiction, the papers were not so accommodating.

'His private moments, his public life and his private life blend together somehow,' Annie remarked. 'There's not much of a separation between the two. But for me, I'm such a different person to what I am onstage.'

Anxious for people not to think that fame has made her stuck-up or blasé, Annie constantly draws attention to it by saying things like, 'It looks incredibly flash, but everything is like that for comfort. I thank God I can travel in a limousine and stretch out, not hunched up in a little car, so that when I get to the concert I am able to *do it*.' She and Dave have at times slipped into the pop star trap of self-justification, reiterating clichés like: 'Fame and success is not all it's cracked up to be', or 'it's boring . . . just something that gets you into clubs and parties', or 'success isn't always such a wonderful gift'. Annie is very worried about how she appears to the public in handling her fame, rather than just living with it, enjoying and accepting it.

'Entertainers are seen as people who are adored by their public. But as you're lauded, you're condemned and loathed,' she told *The Observer* in 1989, resurrecting ghosts from the Tourists' past, when the press didn't spare the criticism. 'No matter how used to it you are, there's no way you don't spend the next day wishing you were dead.'

One press article that affected her deeply was a Julie Burchill diatribe in the London magazine *Time Out*. Burchill has made a good living out of decimating popular personalities, and early in 1986 Annie came under her scrutiny. Calling her a 'female eunuch', Burchill criticized Annie's 'much-flaunted instability', comparing it unfavourably with Madonna's cartoon toughness. 'A genuinely interesting person doesn't mind being seen as a cartoon character; a frigging bore, on the other hand, will have nineteen nervous breakdowns in order to prove to the world how uniquely intricate and complex they are,' she wrote.

Burchill then laid waste the concept of Eurythmics, accusing them of that heinous crime – being 'hippies with haircuts who stepped into the breach after punk', making a safe consensus sound where 'everything they touched turned to treading water'. The line that outraged Annie the most, however, was 'Please, let the Eurythmics die painlessly in a plane crash.'

After the article came out Annie was deeply depressed and wouldn't talk to anyone for days. 'She said she wanted us to *die*, in a *plane crash*,' moaned Annie. The piece had hit home. Rather than treating it as the joke rantings of an ex-punk, Annie took it seriously and for a long time after Burchill was Number 1 on her hit-list. The irony is that such an attack was a perverted compliment – it was a sign of Annie's public success that Burchill deigned even to single her out.

The effect of her piece, though, was for Annie to strengthen the barriers that she had already erected between herself and the hostilities of the outside world. She rejected the high visibility lifestyle of clubs and parties in favour of one-to-one engagements, discreet dinners and get-togethers with a few friends. Having a husband also became an important retreat, someone who would always be there to return to, like a safe base.

'You will never find me in the company of people with illusions of grandeur,' she maintains. 'I try to defuse my fame, to show that there is a funny person underneath the star who is quite accessible, that people shouldn't be too afraid or impressed.'

This self-effacement extends into her personal life. Shortly after she married Uri Fruchtman, she was having dinner with his sister-in-law Janet. A friend of Janet's didn't know who Annie Lennox was and asked 'What is your job?'

'Oh, I just compose a bit,' was Annie's overly modest reply.

She tries to avoid drawing attention to herself, yet at the same time relishes the recognition of her status in pop. Although she is at pains to come across in interviews as down-to-earth and accessible, she is wary of meeting fans and participating in that area of media idolatry. 'I think it's important to talk to fans,' she told *Melody Maker* in 1983. 'People see too little of you really, in interviews, videos and onstage, and they don't see that behind all that there really is somebody that's just as real and human and sweats and gets upset and farts and has bad breath.'

Since Eurythmics' phenomenal success in the mid-1980s, Annie has not let fans near enough to see whether she has bad breath. Ruth Kirk, a twenty-year-old Eurythmics' devotee from Birmingham, has chatted to Dave on the phone, but Annie is altogether more inaccessible.

'I would love to meet Annie, but she's hard to get to speak to. She shies away from it a bit. I remember her saying once in an interview she didn't like the responsibility of all these people following her. I can understand that to a certain extent, I just wish she'd make an exception sometimes.

'Once I went with a group of fans to the BPI awards to try and see her. We waited for about five hours. We saw her go in, and waited ages afterwards for her to come out. "She's coming out the back", we were told, so we all raced round the back, and she nipped out the front. We got to meet Phil Collins instead – which wasn't quite as good.'

Another fan, Kristina Heikkinen from Karlskrona in Sweden, recalls how she and some friends got backstage passes after a concert in Rome, and met everyone except Annie. 'We were very disappointed. We felt that she could have stopped for a minute, it wouldn't have cost her anything. But then I thought about it afterwards – she definitely doesn't owe *us* anything after having given a great concert – why should we ask for more? Sometimes I feel strongly that I'd like to talk to Annie, to get to know her, but I know she has to be "inaccessible" in order to protect herself. We're selfish when we ask her to pay attention to each of us, it would be impossible for her even if she wanted to. After all she's communicating with us through the music, isn't she?'

The more Annie distances herself from her fans, the more she remains an enigma. To her, though, unwarranted attention makes her panic, press paparazzi seem 'freakish and ugly', and she has difficulty comprehending the obsessive nature of fandom. Fan worship has always been a psychological phenomenon, but the 1980s saw a huge growth in the heroes' industry with the sell-through of video classics, satellite stations buying old films and TV series, and the marketing of CDs spawning an orgy of pop nostalgia as record companies delved into their back catalogues.

The status of the fan in pop has moved from one of unquestioning adulation to a much more challenging commercial media force. The proliferation of TV, videos, touring and promotion ensures that the star's presence is never kept far from the public eye, and fans know that rather than being powerless followers, it is partly their cash and support that keeps the star in the media. Annie's response to that tricky contract has been more dutiful than eager.

On the *Revenge* live video album there is a taut second when a sweaty and intense young man bounds onto the stage, grabs Annie from behind and smacks a huge kiss on her cheek, before being bundled away by the bouncers. At the moment of his kiss, her eyes are wide with a mixture of surprise and indignation. As he is moved off she looks at him and, once he's at a safe distance, smiles with relief. For her it was not a pleasurable exercise.

'If the famous are called upon to act and hide behind a mask, it is hardly surprising that so many appear ambivalent about being famous at all,' psychologist Dr Anthony Clare said in the Sunday *Correspondent* in 1990. 'Stars regularly abuse their fans, fans frequently decry their idols' ingratitude.'

When the *Revenge* tour went on to Australia, a woman came backstage at each show, hysterically screaming that Annie was her long-lost daughter. This mental fixation amounted to star-stalking, that terrifying process by which the fan becomes so obsessed with the object of their fascination that there is a desire to consume or kill that object. By shooting John Lennon, for instance, Mark Chapman drastically claimed the object of his obsession, and achieved a close association with one of the most famous pop stars in the world. Through this connection a social misfit and destructive fantasist obtained a peculiar kind of fame for himself.

That is the ugly side of fandom that makes Annie wary. Although most fans are simply enthusiastic admirers, she is slightly repelled by their idolatry. On the 1990 video album *We Two Are One Too* there is a telling sequence that plays in with the line from 'Love Is A Stranger' – 'I want you so, it's an obsession'. Dave is talking to Eurythmics' devotee Danny E. Chi, a gangly boy with long black hair and haunted eyes who asserts: 'It's not an obsession, it's love. I've been following you for eight years. I didn't know how to get to you . . . I don't just love you as a video band, I love you both as human beings. I love your ideas, your philosophy, a lot of what you're about. I get it. Out there they don't get it. They think Eurythmics are a *trendy* band, a video band. They don't understand. I understand you.'

Annie looks on with reserved horror as Danny lays out his Eurythmics' record collection and paraphernalia from all over the world. He admits that a good part of his supermarket salary goes into chasing and collecting these items. He has devoted his life and most of his spare time to following a band and forming a relationship with a fantasy. He feels party to their imaginary intimate world. 'When you were on stage the other night,' he says to Annie, 'you stumbled a bit on "You Have Placed A Chill" in the acoustic section. You lost the lyrics just for a second and Dave looked at you with *so much* concern. And I caught it, I *saw* it.'

Staring back at the fan in fascination, Annie says: 'This kind of stuff is unbelievable. But this isn't about Eurythmics. Eurythmics is about music.'

The fan and the star are at cross-purposes – in asserting that pop is just about music, Annie is ignoring the complex impact of image, presentation and individual desire, while Danny reads her whole life into a fantasy aura around the Eurythmics – a pop vision of which music is only one part.

There are many fans who find that excerpt distasteful. Danny E. Chi is expressing a sense of powerlessness and frustrated dreaming that is present in any fan who has idolized and yearned for contact with Annie. David Daglish, an articulate young student from London's Goldsmith's College who has been following the band since the early 1980s, recalls Danny's presence in the video with discomfort.

'I felt really uncomfortable for them, because he's showing them their career in front of their faces, awkwardly, and he wants gratitude from them. He's collected them. There's a good couple of lines where the fan says, "This is your life", and Annie says, "No, the music is our life". The fan doesn't register this, which is not surprising.'

The stockpiling of records, cassettes and books gives the fan a concrete identity and purpose. Following a distant idol, however, is a recipe for insecurity and dissatisfaction, and a peculiar sort of 'I love them more than thou' competitiveness. Daglish testifies that Eurythmics' fans, on the whole, display a balanced view.

'We're all together on the fact of how good they are. When I've met people it's always been a friendly conversation and not a competitive one. It's nice that some fans want to collect and collect and collect, because as a fan it's quite satisfying to collect records.'

Some Eurythmics' fans worry about their own obsession. 'It's hard to be a fan because you always feel frustrated,' says Muriel Vieu from Mauguio in France. 'Something is missing when you always want to reach your dream. My everyday life is influenced by the band and I have a lot of respect for them, but I want to keep my own personality. I don't want the passion to turn into an obsession.' Kristina Heikkinen, too, is concerned about the effect the group has on her: 'There's been times when I've been almost scared when I think about how I depend on them.'

Eurythmics' fans are saner than most, tending to be analytical about their feelings, articulate and welded to the music. 'I think you have to be really, to get that much out of the music,' says Daglish. 'It's easy enough to play a New Kids On The Block record or something, and just enjoy it, but if you want something challenging or rewarding it's the perfect thing. You can actually *talk* about Eurythmics, not just on a very simple level. It's nice to swap your ideas with people.'

Daglish feels that Eurythmics' records work on many different levels, particularly the fans' favourite album *Savage*, with its 'deep, dark, emotional' quality, while he sees Annie herself as 'immaculate. She's a very strong person, visually and emotionally. I think she's had to be to exist through the 1980s and still survive now. She doesn't really compromise herself in photos or interviews.'

This sense of honesty or integrity is a strong attraction for Eurythmics' fans; her frankness about depression and emotional vulnerability taps into a core of sensitivity in the fans themselves. Mark McAuley, an isolated fan from Belfast, Northern Ireland, appreciates the complexity of her personality. 'From various books and interviews she seems to alternate from one extreme of being an extroverted, sociable person, yet from the other a very introverted, anti-social and easily depressed person,' he says.

'These extremes are very much apparent in Eurythmics' music – particularly in *Savage* which I think is a magnificent record. I have always found Annie appealing because I can identify to an extent with her diverse razor-sharp personality, although I'm a man.'

Some of the fans are amateur rock critics, taking apart the music to such a degree that one remarked: 'each song is a mini-movement of a symphony, almost Wagnerian in degree.' Annie's stark lyrical imagery creates vivid sound pictures for them, an articulation of emotions they feel unable to express.

'"I Could Give You A Mirror" is probably my favourite song,' says Ruth Kirk. 'The line "I could give you a mirror to show you disappointment". It's so simple but really clever.'

Jana Chantelau from Bremen, West Germany cites lines from *Sweet Dreams* as both very powerful and depressing. 'It doesn't happen very often that someone you don't even know and to whom you never talked manages to touch your emotions so deeply. I have to admit that Eurythmics are my best English teacher. In 1986 I translated a whole book about Eurythmics within two weeks. So thanks Annie Lennox for your great lyrics!'

With their Euro-synth pop appeal, Eurythmics have succeeded in projecting themselves as a European rather than just a British group, with dedicated fans stretching from Scandinavia to Eastern Europe. French fan Muriel Vieu has started with the French fan club a complete translation of Eurythmics' lyrics in all European languages, including Turkish and Greek. The European effect is compounded by Annie's willingness to speak other languages, particularly French, the language of her adopted country, and she has also spent periods living in Switzerland and Germany. Although Scottish, she has always striven for a culturally cosmopolitan style, along with music that's a glossy mixture of continental influences. 'I see myself as British rather than Scottish,' she says. 'The more you travel, the less the differences are. They just shrink.' It is the chic androgynous twist to her image that has been most successful in crossing boundaries and attracting fans.

'I got interested at the beginning when I wasn't quite sure . . . boy or girl?' says Kristina from Sweden. German fan Jana Chantelau also recalls her cross-dressing power. 'I especially like the political idea behind "Sisters Are Doin' It For Themselves", even though political attitudes are not often to be found in Eurythmics' work. Her idea to be a gender bender confused me quite a lot, but on the other hand I felt it was just her way to try to be different from all the other female pop singers. Annie managed to avoid becoming a media-whore and one has to pay respect to her for making it her way.'

Whether she likes it or not, Annie is a standard-bearer for a certain kind of visually assertive femininity. In a 1989 poll of 1,000 young Londoners conducted by *Time Out*, respondents were asked to state who they would be if offered the chance to be someone else. The highest number of women's votes (15 per cent) went to Annie Lennox.

Female fans mention time and time again their admiration for Annie's androgynous image. 'I went through a phase a couple of years ago where I bleached my hair, had it white and quite short, and lost weight because I wanted to be really angular in the face. I'd love to look like Annie Lennox,' says London fan Debbie Pierce. A massage practitioner in a gymnasium, Debbie has spent hours analysing Annie's physique, trying to work out what is so attractive for her.

'You read articles about androgynous women like Brigitte Nielsen and Princess Stephanie, who are very fitness-orientated with broad shoulders and narrow hips. They include Annie in that category, even though her physique isn't actually suited to it. She's very skinny, not at all muscular and quite pear-shaped in a way, and in the early days when she had those narrow tight-fitting trousers with braces or a bra top it didn't look right. Now she wears clothes that suit her more, like floppy jackets with subtle padded shoulders that give her some shape, make her look more angular.'

The real power of Annie's image is concentrated in her face, her startling features framed by immaculately cropped hair. 'Personally I find her very attractive, she has the most beautiful face,' says Debbie. 'I once went through a phase of watching her on video every single night before I went to bed, looking at every detail and freeze-framing. Her eyes are so expressive. If you slice a model's face down the middle, it should be exactly the same on both sides, and she's got that to a tee.'

Women remain fascinated by Annie because she presents possibilities of gender and image that are quite separate from the run-of-the-mill, often male-defined, presentation of female sexuality in pop video. Although she is not always a fluid performer or a hot dancer, it's Annie's very awkwardness that gives the edge to her charisma, a cerebral command that both intrigues and inspires female fans. It is her achievement that she's loved by women and men in equal measure.

'She's got control over what she does,' says Chrissie Clarke, an arch, ebullient West London fan who has followed Annie since the days of the Tourists and is completely focused on her idol. 'She seems to do her own styling and is responsible for her own image. She writes 50 per cent of the songs, unlike such singers as Tina Turner, who doesn't write her own material. It's that control really.

'I think about her so much – the music just relates to my life so much. Shortly before the *Revenge* album came out a boyfriend had completely done the dirty on me. It had been a dreadful relationship, very unhappy and sad, but also angry. I was a nervous wreck basically. I bought *Revenge* and the complete album was exactly my story – especially "Thorn in My Side".

'There seems to be a link there. Before I met her I thought she'd be a bosom pal, she was just right for me. I then met her after a gig. and it was really good for me, really healthy, because it brought me down to earth. The woman is actually human. But I do feel as if I'm tied to her – I still adore her, but don't see us becoming bosom pals. She would if she'd known me before she was famous. Definitely.'

Many fans profess to an instant love affair with Eurythmics, mainly from the moment of *Sweet Dreams*, though Chrissie remembers the first time she saw her at Wolverhampton Poly, fronting the Tourists. 'I just happened to go down to the Poly that night with my friends, and this small band was playing. I saw this woman singer in a sequin top and black leggings. I thought, she's brilliant, who is it? Then years later *Sweet Dreams* came out and I thought, oh God, it's that woman again. She's just wonderful.'

Chrissie professes to being a little in love with Annie, yet the stronger feeling is that Annie has something she wants. 'I realize now that it's the voice. I wanted to become a singer, that's why I was so mad on her.'

Our heroes are often a source of inspiration, a realization of an ambition that may have been buried deep. Annie's talent made Chrissie Clark realize she wanted to sing, while Ruth Kirk, an engineering student at London University, was interested in a career as a sound engineer after visiting the Eurythmics' studio at The Church. 'They always seem to be having such a brilliant time,' she says. 'I also play the guitar . . . very badly, and I'd love to sing in a band. I sing my head off in my bedroom.'

For David Daglish, the inspiration was more nebulous. 'I get a very positive attitude from the band. All through their career they've shown you can achieve what you want even though it might be depressing at times. If you want something you *can* do it. Whatever it takes.'

Dr Obhozer, a consultant at London's Tavistock Clinic of Psychotherapy, argues that people still think heroes are necessary. 'It's partly to do with the human make-up – an idealized aspect of the self that you haven't been able to realize,' he says. 'If you're a young, spotty unsure adolescent you can move *outside* yourself by identifying with a demi-god adored by other people. You get out of an impotent state of mind.'

As well as symbolizing an individual motivating force, following pop heroes allows fans to get together in a social situation. 'It's a great way to meet others,' says Bill Harry, a bearded Merseyside entrepreneur who in 1987 launched *Idols*, a glossy magazine that runs stories on twentieth-century stars and acts as a contact point for most fan clubs in Britain.

'A lot of readers are in out-of-the-way places, little villages where they don't get to the big concerts. Through idols, people they admire, they get in touch with like-minded people,' he says from his offices in Paddington's appropriately-named Star Street. 'There are Marc Bolan discos, Elvis Nights Out, Mario Lanzo Society AGMs. *Star Trek* fans have over fifty clubs. We heard about the Elvis Presley Impersonators' Society in the US – they reckon there are about 3,500 Elvis impersonators in America, and the club has 85 on its books.'

The Eurythmics' fan club activities are more low-key. Established in 1983, it was initially run on a small scale by Dave's brother's girlfriend Dinah Marmery, who left to have a baby. Karen Ciccone then streamlined the operation after answering an ad in the summer of 1983 for a fan club secretary, organizing the traditional club fare of newsletters, competitions, tour dates and merchandising. By 1985, membership had grown to such an extent that Kim Hilton was drafted in to help process the fees and sell promotional sweat shirts, posters or signed photos.

Unlike many clubs, the Eurythmics' organization did not develop the razzmatazz of yearly conventions, opting instead for a more low-key personal, 'family-style' approach. Even when the three separate units of the club – International, UK and American – were amalgamated in one office on Hollywood's Sunset Boulevard in late 1985, the club still answered fans' letters individually. Dave's ex-wife Pam Stewart ran the club for five years from this Los Angeles base.

A friendly chatty woman who co-wrote with Dave an early Long-dancer song, 'Sweet Leaves' ('I wish I'd written "Sweet Dreams"'), Pam managed to galvanize many fans throughout the world to do a spot of unpaid work on the Eurythmics' *Revenge* tour. 'Enrolling booths' were set up at the entrance to each concert, and volunteer fans were given a pile of fan club flyers to distribute to the crowds. 'The Fan Club is relying on your EURYTHMIC spirit and conscientiousness,' she wrote in a rare flash of Eurythmanic evangelism. Ruth Kirk went on one of these enrolling expeditions: 'We handed flyers out to people queuing for tickets outside Birmingham NEC at four in the morning. I managed to get fifty people to join.' Needless to say, she was unpaid.

Although the initiative was effective, by 1989 the running of a club in the States became too unwieldy, especially as the bulk of the Eurythmics' fan base is in Britain, and by 1990 the club was operating again from North London.

The fact that the fan club is more of a news and merchandising base than a social extravaganza reflects Annie's personal attitude towards fandom. By keeping it low-profile, she will not be required to come too close to the fans. In the same way she treats those who want too much of her personally or professionally, the message to her admirers is a polite, appreciative, yet firm 'keep your distance'. For Annie the boundaries between the star and the fan, the crowd and the stage, will always remain intact.

9

Gimme Shelter

'I've never voted because there has never been a party or an individual I felt I could endorse. It's too naïve an idea to believe that the pop world can be a platform for change. I was very touched by "Shipbuilding", but there it stops. I don't think I have anything interesting to say. I *do* have opinions in life, but what difference does it make to anyone else? It makes *no* difference.

'When my father died and I saw cancer and what it does to people, I thought about my own fragility and the fragility of the human race and how we can so easily take it all for granted. We have to say, what next? Chernobyl?

'There are certain movements that I would like to become part of. I'm very much against animals being exploited and I'm planning to get involved with that . . . I find something intrinsically ugly about the mass consumerism of animals. There's a terrible brutal butchery which is governed by commercial greed. I always feel for the underdog and identify with those who are suffering.

'Live Aid made me question the solutions in the Third World. The issues are really immense: corruption in government, climate, agriculture and so on. Some of those issues crop up when we look at what's happening to the eco-system.

'Once I got involved in charity benefits, the letters arrived in their hundreds, and I asked myself what I could do without seeming like Joan of Arc. Shouldn't we be more anarchic, rather than turning into these mealy-mouthed, pompous, self-congratulatory, 'We Are the World' type diplomats. I think we should be more dangerous, take more risks . . . I haven't figured it all out, but it's the direction I'm heading in.'

LONDON, 1988

The 11 June 1988 Eurythmics played the Mandela Birthday Tribute, with Dave and Annie cavorting on stage in black leather and silver rock studs. Although artists taking part were told not to be 'political', Annie reminded the crowd why they were there. Not normally seen as a political pop star, this concert marked an important stage in Annie's 'coming out' as a campaigning performer.

She appeared with a communion of international stars at Wembley Stadium in celebration of Nelson Mandela's seventieth birthday. With the leader of the ANC still imprisoned, it was an emotional, high-profile event watched by 72,000 people in the stadium and beamed live by satellite to 63 countries. Stars on the bill like Whitney Houston, Dire Straits and Stevie Wonder ensured that the eleven-hour charity extravaganza gained maximum publicity. While many questioned the efficacy of the concert at the time, within two years many of the artists were back at Wembley, with the released Nelson Mandela giving a proud speech to the stadium crowd and a TV audience of millions.

Just before his release, when Annie won the category of Best Female Vocalist in the February 1990 BRITS Awards, her speech was more than a mere thank-you to her management.

'I just want to say that playing on stage at the Mandela concert was the proudest moment of my life; and I want people to remember why we were there, that the fight's not over yet,' she said quietly but firmly, clutching her statuette of Queen Bodiccea. It was a surprisingly candid speech for an awards gathering that usually consisted of mutual music industry back-slapping. In the same way that Vanessa Redgrave once disrupted the Oscar procedures with her 'politicking', Annie had picked an opportune moment to speak out.

The awards ceremony also marked her bowing-out of a full-time music career. The next day the papers were full of her announcement that she would be taking a two-year break to concentrate on working for the homeless charity Shelter. 'I feel very strongly about the plight of the young people on the streets,' she said. 'All those poor kids who leave home to come down to London and end up walking the streets.

'Money is a great privilege in life but I couldn't bear the responsibility of keeping it all to myself.'

Annie had come a long way politically from when she first started out in the business. Her political education was a gradual process of coming to terms with the PR power of her position as a pop star.

Whereas in the early days of the Tourists she fought shy of any direct political statement, by the time she stood on the stage at London's Dominion Theatre for the 1990 BRITS Awards, she felt comfortable using her position as 'Queen of Pop' to raise awareness.

'I don't like political expression in pop,' Annie told *Melody Maker* back in 1983. 'It's too naïve an idea to believe that the pop world can be a platform for change.'

Some suggest that the fact her father was a card-carrying member of the Communist party meant she rejected party politics early on, in her rebellion against parental values. Everyday socialism and a sense of civic responsibility were strong traditions within the Lennox family – personified publicly in the second most-famous Lennox, Alderman Robert of Aberdeen, Annie's great-uncle.

Annie respected those traditions, but was intent on finding her own way, refusing for years to vote for any one particular party. 'People are no longer concerned with issues but personalities,' she once complained. In the Tourists, she and Dave were keen to distance themselves from the political impetus of punk, wary of energetic and upfront initiatives like Rock Against Racism or the Anti-Nazi League.

'We're not about cults, and we're not about elitism, and we're not about minority groups particularly,' Annie said in 1980. 'We sing about emotions and personal politics as opposed to "on the surface" politics.' Dave later was even more unspecific in his description of Eurythmics' music: 'It's about people's alienation from other people and their surroundings.'

The band could have been accused of wafting culpable naïvety. Although many punk outfits from the Clash downwards exhibited an unclear but generally 'revolutionary' rock posturing, there were just as many bands with a focused set of political goals. In Britain in the late 1970s racist ideas were gaining hard currency with the rise of the National Front, and the work of RAR and the Anti-Nazi League did a great deal to check and highlight this issue. The Tourists' reluctance to take part in any overt political activity was due more to wariness and lack of real interest than clear alternative reasoning.

Until the mid-1980s, mainstream pop was almost aggressively apolitical. There has always been the view that 'politics should be kept out of music', but pop is an everyday cultural form, and like literature, theatre or TV, it reflects life. It is naïve to expect pop artists to suspend any political or moral judgement when they're writing songs and confine themselves to cars, girls and romance.

Each form of music from American soul to Irish folk has its own political momentum, and late 1970s punk was just another kind of music rooted in the youth debates of the time. What was different was the directness with which it assaulted the mainstream. Annie was clearly turned off by the aggression of songs like the Clash's 'White Riot' or Stiff Little Fingers' 'Alternative Ulster'. There was an incident when the Tourists were on tour and happened to stay one night at the same hotel as the Stiff Little Fingers.

'They were acting like stars in their eyes by smashing up a hotel room, getting pissed first thing in the morning,' Annie said. 'If that's being a star I'm not really interested . . . sort of Ulster boy star, voice of the youth movement in Ulster – I think it was a bit despicable actually.'

Dave pointed out that a member of the band had accused the Tourists of 'ripping off' their audience by selling programmes, 'then the next thing he's talking about screwing some chick while his mate tosses beer on her. Let's meet the next voice of Ireland. We're talking about human politics. We wouldn't go on like that. We respect people.'

The fusion of punk, pop and politics was rife with contradiction, but the movements that it spawned, such as Two Tone, went a long way towards a realistic representation of the difficulties and triumphs of a multi-cultural society. Dave and Annie were less motivated by outward issues such as racism or youth unemployment, choosing instead to focus on the inner world of personal relationships. 'We're covering more basic issues than the politics of Ireland,' claimed Dave, ignoring the fact that the conflict of Ireland is pretty fundamental in itself.

Dave and Annie were both in their late twenties by the time they launched Eurythmics, with a political awareness influenced by the 1960s hippy counter-culture ethos of 'live and let live', a humanitarian bent that was vaguely anti-establishment, but never too specific in its analysis. Although Annie cut a striking figure during her cross-dressing period, she was wary of calling herself a feminist. She diluted the impact of 'Sisters Are Doin' It For Themselves' by saying in interviews: 'We aren't gonna take anything over, because a man still loves a woman and a woman still loves a man. "Sisters . . ." is simply a song about women. I don't have to say "I bleed!" or "I won't have anything to do with men". Some of my best friends are men!' This apologist note muddled what could have been a very direct message. The record was released with four different picture sleeves; one showing an early woman racing driver, and the others a gang of laughing teenage girls, a woman in the army and a 1940s secretary. On its own it was a bold release, without Aretha's ('I like men to open doors for me') and Annie's ('Some of my best friends are men') rather mystifying comments. If they felt that way, why did they bother to record it?

Dave once explained how, because Annie was looked up to by feminists and gay rights activists, she had to 'carefully sidestep things'.

'I don't want to be the head of a movement. I'm singing purely out of my satisfaction, my good feeling about women. And men as well, for *allowing women to do that*,' she said after recording the duet with Aretha Franklin. Falling over herself to avoid any kind of feminist or 'political' label, Annie would compromise the strength of what she was trying to say, sometimes making statements that were either coy or downright gauche. Wary of being seen to have an unequivocal political commitment on a given issue, she had an infuriating tendency to 'bland out' in interviews, a habit she can still fall into today.

Apart from the brief burst of punk, politics during early 1980s designer pop was decidedly unfashionable. Bands like Duran Duran, Wham! and Spandau Ballet advocated the Good Time, while on a global level, mega-outfits such as Dire Straits kept their message politics-free. The success of Band Aid and Live Aid totally changed the context within which the top pop acts operated, ushering in a new sense of responsibility and establishing a platform that made political pop respectable again.

Prompted by a harrowing TV news report on the Ethiopean famine, Bob Geldof brought together in late 1984 most of Britain's top pop talent to record the Band Aid charity single 'Do They Know It's Christmas?' With sales of over £7 million, it became the best-selling British single of all time, and spurred a similar initiative in America with the 'We Are The World' single.

This encouraged Geldof to launch the grandiose Live Aid, a mammoth rock spectacle consisting of two simultaneous star-studded concerts in Philadelphia and London. On 13 July 1985 the world's biggest names, including Queen, Madonna, U2 and Phil Collins (who flew Concorde coast-to-coast in a stunt that enabled him to play both concerts), were beamed to a TV audience of one and a half billion. The first big charity event since George Harrison's concert for Bangladesh in 1971, it reaped over £50 million from telethon donations and television sales.

Despite reports of backstage bickering and petty power struggles, all the artists taking part greatly benefited in terms of album sales and raised profiles. Suddenly politics in pop was no longer the great turn-off. Stars now had a chance to air their consciences without being penalized, and coming out in support of causes post-Live Aid, from Farm Aid to CND and Amnesty International, was positively hip. 'Live Aid was very healthy behaviour,' says rock artist Nona Hendryx. 'The old order said "you're entertainment, you shouldn't have anything to do with reality. I come to lose myself in what you're presenting." Well those kind of fantasies are for children. That said, I'd like to've seen Live Aid benefiting people more than feeding them today, forgetting them tomorrow.'

Eurythmics were offered a place on the British Live Aid bill, but they declined, as Annie was still having problems with her throat. When the show was being transmitted, however, on that fateful day in July, Annie purportedly sat slumped in an armchair in front of the TV, glumly regretting her decision not to take part. Some say it was because Annie realized she should have acted on her conscience, while others come up with the more uncharitable view that she wished Eurythmics had been there for the prestige.

'The reason they hadn't done it I believe was because they thought, we're Eurythmics, we're too big for this. Then they saw what an event it was,' says their former video producer Jon Roseman. 'Annie's always been confused as to what she is into and *isn't* into. She and Billy were staying at my house that weekend, and the morning after Live Aid she was so depressed she wouldn't get out of bed. My daughter who was four then camped outside her bedroom waiting for her. "When's Annie coming out?" she asked. She ain't coming out.'

Roseman denies that Annie felt guilty – 'Guilt presupposes you care about it beforehand. Geldof told me a lot of artists were doing it for their careers. They'd put in nothing but time. I've spoken to a lot of people in the business about this, and if all those artists in America and England had made substantial donations, they'd have raised a lot more money than they did.'

There is controversy within the industry about the fact that the fans who had made the artists multi-millionaires in the first place were forking out for Live Aid, while many of the stars themselves contributed little more than their career-boosting presence on stage. Such giant pop extravaganzas inevitably have their cynical side, but cash considerations apart, Live Aid created a climate in which issue-based charity pop, however flawed, could thrive.

It was this context of developing awareness that gave Annie the confidence to state her views more definitely and come out publicly in support of certain issues. She had begun the process a year earlier when, ironically, her marriage to the Hare Krishna Radha Raman consolidated her views on vegetarianism.

'My ex-husband was a very strict vegetarian and influenced me greatly towards a different lifestyle,' she says. 'Part of my family are farmers, so I grew up aware of animals. Granny would go into the yard and kill a chicken to eat for dinner. Grandfather was a gamekeeper. This seemed fair enough at the time and was the way of things. My uncle fattens beef cows for a living. It's all he knows, so discussing vegetarianism wouldn't make any sense to him.'

One of the largest industries in Aberdeen is in cattle, with frequent bull sales of prized Aberdeen Angus drawing buyers worldwide, from Argentinian farmers to Texan ranchers. For the Lennox family, meat eating was a business as well as a staple of their diet, so Annie's decision to become a vegetarian went against strong family tradition. The qualms she felt about eating meat were brought to a head when she met Radha Raman and became involved in the Hare Krishna movement. It was because of his Krishna vegetarian food that Raman found a way into her heart, as the night after he left an introductory selection of dishes outside her hotel room she invited him along on their tour as a cook.

In an interview with the *Vegetarian Times* in 1984, she recalls how it was a documentary about animal slaughter that first made her identify with their suffering. 'We were horrified by the holocaust,' she says, 'but for some reason it hasn't dawned on the general public that the animals are suffering at our hands in an almost holocaustic way.' Meeting Raman opened up a whole new area for discussion on the subject, prompting Annie to take that final logical step and give up eating meat.

The connection in Krishna consciousness between killing animals and war then made a deep impression on her, the karmic notion propounded by the Krishna founder Prabhupada that 'war is a direct

191

effect of our meat eating . . . when men stop slaughtering animals, then we will stop having to send our sons to war.'

She was a strict vegetarian for a few years, advocating 'a kind of austerity, a self-discipline' in not eating meat, but after leaving Raman she went back to eating fish and clammed up if asked about her vegetarianism. 'I'd rather keep the fact that I don't eat meat just as a point of conversation right now, because I think that all it does is turn a lot of people off,' she firmly told a *Rolling Stone* reporter shortly after her divorce.

Her viewpoint has since become more assured and sophisticated, incorporating practical knowledge about diet and a healthy lifestyle. Her father's death from cancer at the age of sixty-one shook her profoundly. 'During his illness I drew my parents' attention to diet. Even though this represented difficulties, mum has now virtually cut all meat from her diet and has been surprised that the rheumatism in her hands has definitely improved. Her friends have also cut their meat consumption considerably. This is quite a shift for people brought up on a meat-based diet, but it shows that people are interested in their health.'

While Annie came out strongly in favour of vegetarianism, it was a long while before she attached her name to other 'causes'. In 1986, traumatized by her father's death and the break-up of her marriage, Annie declared: 'I don't believe in *anything*. At this point I don't have any faith. But that doesn't mean I'm a cynic. I just don't want to put my thinking into a belief system.'

She made her first high-profile entry into charity pop post-Live Aid when she sang with Chrissie Hynde at the Columbian Volcano Benefit in February 1986 at London's Albert Hall. Twenty-five thousand people had died at Nevado Del Ruiz three months before, and aid was urgently needed. Columbian bassist and Eurythmics' stalwart Chucho Merchan organized the star-packed concert that made music history with a finale that featured Annie, Chrissie and Pete Townshend in a performance of KC & the Sunshine Band's old hit 'Give It Up'; £20,000 went to survivors of the volcano disaster, finally convincing Annie that pop could provide a useful platform for raising funds while raising consciousness.

Her next foray onto pop's by now prestigious political stage came at Nelson Mandela's birthday concert in 1988. Although Eurythmics appeared there as a successful unit, Annie has tended to take part in pop campaigning and fund-raising independently of Dave. While he has branched off into producing other people and creating solo musical efforts, she has moved further and further into the more political end of pop compassion.

In April 1989 Annie really came to the fore when she promoted the Greenpeace charity LP *Breakthrough*, a double-album compilation of twenty-six British, American and Australian acts which was released by RCA under the title *Rainbow Warriors*, to coincide with the opening of a Greenpeace office in Moscow. Dave had been to Russia the year before to produce Boris Grebenshikov, the cult lead singer of the country's top-selling band Aquarium. His trip was strictly to do with music, however, whereas Annie was on a diplomatic mission.

She was surrounded by friends Chrissie Hynde, Peter Gabriel, U2's guitarist The Edge, Aswad's Brinsley Ford and David Byrne from Talking Heads, all there to help promote the album, and one of the most ebullient moments of the trip was when Annie stood for a photo call with the Soviet army in Red Square.

'She really came out of herself in Russia. She was so excited and I saw such a change in her there. If people really knew what she thought politically they'd be very surprised,' said her friend and former RCA press officer, Neil Storey, who now works for Arista. Another member of the party had a different view: 'She was like a bloody mother hen, shepherding the boys around and continually saying "Come on, come on!",' he remarked.

Whatever her approach, Annie was uncharacteristically outgoing. Usually careful not to pin her deep-seated opinions to the mast, at the launch of the Greenpeace album Annie spoke up strongly about the negligence of political leaders. 'Obviously it's useful for both Mikhail Gorbachev and Margaret Thatcher to be seen to be Green. But then Margaret Thatcher keeps promoting nuclear power, which in our country is one of the main ecological issues,' she said. 'One could be very cynical about the Russians inviting us here to put a human face on things, but what do you do, just pack up and go home?'

Widely quoted in the British and Soviet press, Annie created the most impact in this unusual Greenpeace delegation. So much so that in Russia now she is as popular as the Beatles. 'Most of us were Russia-virgins – we'd never been to the USSR before, and she was in that category. Because it was a big strong experience everybody loved it to bits,' recalls Neil Spencer, an *Observer* journalist who went as part of the media entourage. Usually a sceptical pop commentator, he was very impressed with Annie.

'What struck me about it was how exceedingly nice she was, which I hadn't expected. She's neurotic but she also has a very acute sensibility. She was highly natural and vivacious, and the Russians were completely crazy for her – everywhere we went she was the Number One attraction. I thought she had a Northern ice maiden look to her. That blonde, pale, blue-eyed look appealed to some tundra archetype. The Russians also love any Westerner who gives a shit. She was well informed and committed to the cause.'

Surrounded by members of Greenpeace, Annie was well briefed and on confident ground. Eastern Europe was an ecological disaster area, with the fall-out from Chernobyl and pervasive industrial pollution. The problems were tangible and urgent, demanding co-operation on an international scale, and the confluence of pop stars and the world's press did a great deal to publicize the issue.

For a long time the closest that Annie had got to overt political commentary was wearing a Katherine Hamnett 'Save The World' T-shirt, but her opinions at the Moscow bash were openly expressed and rooted in the realism of everyday politics. She grasped each fact with emotional fervour, often unable to distance herself from the enormity of the material.

'Somewhere in the back of my mind for years I had the feeling that things were not quite right. I never voted; I was completely cynical and disillusioned with all political parties, having a sincere mistrust of all politicians. Finally, after all these years it turns out that groups like Greenpeace have been quietly working away without much exposure, and now it's just clicked, everything's gone into place. Through a union of the media and people like myself, we're sounding a clarion call. The advent of the Greens is as significant as the advent of socialism at the turn of the century. No question about that.

'I'm a very passionate person,' she went on to say. 'Not just about Greenpeace, it's far wider than that. Something like Live Aid raised many questions, because although it generated a great deal of money, one doesn't know exactly what it did for the people of Ethiopia. Perhaps in the short term someone got a bowl of rice, but it was like a finger in the dyke. It made me think about the nitty gritty of Third World problems.'

Talking firmly about government corruption, economics and the eco-system Annie placed the blame at the door of 'big corporations'. Unlike her friend Chrissie Hynde, who urged all young people to 'firebomb MacDonalds', Annie neglected to mention which specific corporations were destroying the ozone layer, but at least she was coming closer to a critique of capitalism.

With her forthright tongue and wholehearted espousal of 'Green' issues, Chrissie Hynde has been a strong and influential friend for Annie. Chrissie admits that pop campaigning doesn't always have its advantages. 'It's to the sacrifice of your career, up to a point,' she says. 'It doesn't aid your career because as soon as you get behind a cause you alienate certain people. In the business you're supposed to sit on the fence and keep your yap shut, because that's what gives you the highest profile. You don't piss anyone off. Personally, I think that's dead boring.' She doesn't stop herself from speaking out, loud. 'I have a pretty black sense of humour,' she explains.

Impressed by the incredible personal risks that were taken by many Greenpeace activists, Annie had taken small but sensible steps in her domestic life. 'I recycle our bottles, paper, etc. The very least we could have is an intelligent recycling system,' she said. 'In Switzerland and Germany you have bins for bottles everywhere, even in little villages. You don't think twice about it. I'd hoped to see that happening in England. I hate the fact that the word "recycling" has such an "alternative" ring about it.

'It will become part of the accepted norm. Not that long ago people were turning up their noses at health food. Now supermarket chains stock it because they discovered it was profitable.'

Being in Russia, too, was a revelation. She had gone expecting to find it restrictive, rigid and bureaucratic, but found it was not that dissimilar to Western society. Her hosts, of course, were the epitome of hospitality and friendliness.

'The differences are far less dramatic than I'd expected. I've been exposed to a wide variety of cultures so I'd probably find this place too drab. The other night we asked ourselves, if we'd been born here would we be straining to get out? Well I was straining to get away from Aberdeen at seventeen, so I'd definitely have been straining to get out of here!

'But things aren't worse because you don't have a wide range of deodorants. When I go to America, which is the seat of all capitalism, I notice people who warp their whole sense of dignity to try and become an idealized version of what they see in the media. When I walk into a hotel in LA and someone says "Hi Annie, welcome home!" I'm feeling very strange about that.'

Annie's frankness earned her the dubious compliment of being included on a rumoured CIA blacklist of 'nuisance' activist rock acts. In the same way that 1960s' hippies had galvanized public opinion against the Vietnam War, government authorities began to worry about the vote-carrying impact of political pop stars in the 1980s. Just before the first Mandela concert in 1988, at the height of South Africa's State of Emergency, Conservative politicians complained loud and long about the TV airtime that was being given to a 'political organization'. Theirs was a paranoia fuelled on old notions of divisive political systems that were gradually restructured throughout the 1990s.

When the Greenpeace *Breakthrough* album was launched in the days before the collapse of Eastern Europe, the most penetrating idea that mainstream pop had about Russia was in the song 'Rasputin', the worldwide hit by the tacky late 1970s disco group Boney M. Apart from well-publicized tours in Russia by the likes of Paul McCartney and Elton John, one of the few superstars to tackle the political implications of the Soviet system was Sting, with his 1985 hit 'Russians'. Although he wrote a song on his first solo LP about the 1984 miners' strike in Britain and was actively involved in Amnesty International, he stressed then that his stance was simply humanitarian.

'I'm not in the political arena,' he said when the LP *Dream of the Blue Turtles* came out. 'I'm making personal statements. Instead of beating people over the head with an idea, I think it's better to get people comfortable . . . Then you start beating them with the message. If we're going to save the world, we have to do it from the inside. Save yourself first, be happy, then you can save the world.'

This rather indulgent view, typical of a Western rock star, began to modify when he became involved in the fight to save the Amazonian Indian tribes in the Brazilian rainforest. Setting up the Rainforest Foundation in late 1988, he and his partner Trudie Styler took on the role of international observers for the Kayapo and Yanomami tribes, campaigning for government protection for Indian land. In the equivalent of the 1868 gold rush in North America, when the indigenous Sioux were nearly wiped out, the invasion of 50,000 miners into the rainforest hunting for gold meant that Yanomami people were dying from white man's malaria and syphilis. 'Unless their territory is protected, the legalized genocide of the Brazilian Indians will soon be complete,' said Styler in 1990.

Looking harassed, sweaty and tired, Sting and his partner spent long, frustrating days negotiating between the Indians and the obdurate Brazilian government. 'We're a conduit between these people and the media,' he said of his position. 'Fame is like a commodity – you can use it to purchase certain things. In this instance we're using it to transfer an idea. We're a fly in the ointment.'

There is a big difference between standing on stage for fifteen minutes in support of a cause, and actually getting involved at ground level for a prolonged period of time. Concentrating less on lofty song writing, and more on the Indians' harrowing everyday problems, Sting had become resignedly pragmatic. 'I'd rather be singing now but I'm into this up to my neck, so I have to keep going,' he said. 'I feel this weight on my shoulders. I'm only an individual.'

Fame may be a commodity, but for an individual it only has limited status that works most effectively when there are limited goals. Rather than solve all the problems in the aftermath of post-Ceaucescu's Roumania, ex-Beatle George Harrison and his wife set themselves the task of getting fixtures and fittings for the horrifically dilapidated children's orphanages. 'Plumbers can go down there and plumb in toilets,' he said after the release of his Travelling Wilburys charity single 'Nobody's Child' in July 1990. 'While I can pick up a guitar and make a song.'

Sting, meanwhile, was taking on the entire Brazilian government, and his frustrated petitions would have carried much more weight if he had been part of a high-profile coalition. 'When you go to Brazil you realize corruption is the system of the day,' says Annie. 'Inflation rates change daily with the black market and currency is devalued by half in the space of a week. It's all very well going to save the rainforest, but how the hell are they going to get round the corruption?'

The power of Sting's rock star status would have multiplied tenfold if linked to a political pressure group or party. When Annie, Chrissie and the rest of the 1980s pop elite gathered in Red Square to promote Greenpeace, they formed a powerful lobby, conveying a message that had force in numbers. There are many similarities between pop stars and politicians. Both promote themselves and take on the media, both perform for the camera, both have a constituency and both want to win fans or votes. Pop stars, however, can be more direct and easily populist in their message, plugging into a ready market with an ability to combine politics and show business that politicians can only envy. At the same time there is the necessarily trivial side of pop that can diminish the serious nature of what an artist is trying to say. Many pop performers start young and with fame they have little experience of the world in which the rest of us live.

'I suspect that part of Annie feels she's worthless,' says Neil Spencer. 'A lot of musicians carry that guilt because ultimately what they do is very frivolous. Even if you go on stage you're basically just showing off.'

Annie remains aware of that dichotomy, advocating a role that fits somewhere between conventional politics and the situationism of showbiz. 'I think we should be more dangerous, should take more risks,' she told herself frankly, four months after the momentous Russian trip.

To be or not to be a modern-day Joan of Arc became a vexed question, and Annie spent a lot of time pontificating about the political potential of her position: 'On the one hand I would like to do something anonymously and wouldn't want to take the credit, but on the other hand it would be foolish not to use the influences I do have. Pop stars doing things for charity is a positive thing. But sometimes the concepts of sainthood and pop stardom are at odds with each other. I think society and politics have a lot to answer for, and pop stars have done more than politicians in the last few years to highlight the terrible mess we're in.

'I find that ironic. Am I being more effective being a politician or a pop star? And should I shut up? Should I continue?'

She enjoys the discussion, but debate itself can become a form of procrastination, a substitute for concerted action. For months she went over the same difficult theoretical questions: 'Why doesn't the government do something, and why do we have to have charity? Can't our society wake up to the fact that Greenpeace shouldn't be a charity, that cancer affects everybody. There are millions of causes. I know about them, because they write to us.

'Yes, you can be an effective mouthpiece and get some money going, but that's not the solution. Live Aid wasn't the solution to Ethiopia. It was a fantastic thing, but why expect Bob Geldof and Live Aid to be a *solution* for Ethiopia? Sting, Chrissie, Peter Gabriel – we're all frustrated individuals who are sick of society being the way it is, and have discovered we have access to the media.'

She was also conscious of the fact that her songs contained emotional detail rather than *issues*. 'I wish I could be more crafted,' she says. '*Bring in a viewpoint*, you know, like Sting does. With me it's all too wrought and fraught.'

Annie's former press officer and friend Sheila Sedgwick notes Annie's garrulous nature, but has every faith in her ability to convince others politically: 'She's come to terms with herself. She knows she's an able person and has found her way in the world. I could see her taking on the mantle of bringing people's attention to certain issues. With her there's no doubt about her sincerity.

'A possible problem is that people will see her as too serious. She'll have to be careful about that. Geldof is terribly laid-back and laconic about it all, but Annie couldn't be *that* easy-going. If something really matters to her, she'll tell you. She's not a jabbery girly female – but she can talk the hind legs off a donkey, Annie can seriously *talk*! If she can tell five million people, she'll tell five million people. There'd be staggering amounts of money coming in if she said "You have *got* to do something about this".'

By mid-1989 Annie was becoming preoccupied with an issue that would take centre-stage in 1990. The day after the start of Eurythmics' *Revival* tour in Cannes, Annie sat looking out across the sumptuous hotel grounds, lamenting the state of France's most famous playground. 'It's the trashcan of the Western world,' she said poetically. 'I've never seen so much display of money and bad taste. We were in New York for a while – I found it a very challenging city. I couldn't step outside the door without falling over some terrible victim of the streets. After a while I found that unbearable. It would drive me insane living in New York because I'd feel unable to do anything about that.'

Bitten by this experience, she wrote the anthemic ballad 'When The Day Goes Down' on the *We Too Are One* album, as a hymn to the homeless. The sentiment is a little biblical, viewing the homeless purely as victims or objects of pity, but it still has a compassionate power: 'the lonely & the weak/And the lost & the degraded/& the too dumb to speak'.

By early 1990, Annie had moved from a position of impotent outrage to constructive action. It was in February of that year that she made the surprise announcement that she was taking two years out of the business to work for Shelter, a gritty, politicized organization founded in 1966, with solid roots in the community. It had a practical down-to-earth spirit that would chime with her sense of accountability. 'I'm going to be taking a little break from singing and performing,' she told Radio One DJ Simon Bates. 'I'll not be giving up music for good, but I'm having a very long rest. I just need to refuel my batteries, relax with my family and get involved with the causes I feel very strongly about, particularly Shelter.'

The announcement caused a media stir, with the sober Sunday newspaper *The Observer* devoting a page to Annie in a profile section normally reserved for top politicians. Written under the slightly mocking headline, 'POP'S QUEEN GOES AMONG THE PEOPLE', it was a remarkably sympathetic piece, hailing Annie's 'quiet fluting against all-conquering Greed Inc . . . as representative of the spirit of our new decade.'

Annie had touched on a nerve in the aftermath of the hard, monetarist 1980s, where the fall-out from big business expansion left many disadvantaged and living on the streets. The issue of homelessness affects pop artists perhaps more than any other, because the contradictions are clear and immediate. While someone like Dave Stewart has personal wealth of an estimated £20 million, with a luxury house in Los Angeles, a flat in Paris, a studio in Cannes, a Maida Vale town mansion and the Crouch End Church, thousands of people affected by stringent cuts in government subsidy sleep on the streets of London and New York. For millionaire pop stars, this can present a stark dilemma.

Man of conscience and professional 'Diamond Geezer' Phil Collins was clearly troubled by this inequity, and along with Annie he was one of the first of the 'rock aristocracy' to draw media attention to the plight of homeless people in the 1990s. His agonized ballad 'Another Day in Paradise' told the story of a homeless old woman ignored by City yuppies on their way to work, and despite the unsexy subject matter, it became a massive hit.

Ironically the day he finished recording the song, a man outside the studio begged him for some money, and paralysed by guilt and confusion, Collins walked off. 'It was weird,' he said later. 'I didn't know what to do.' He later resolved this on his next tour by placing collection buckets at concert exits, and offering alongside his record company Virgin to match whatever was raised. This noble move was offset by his complaint that if a Labour government was returned, he would have to become a tax exile – ignoring the fact that it was tax cuts and the concommitant slash in public spending that landed many people on the streets in the first place.

For pop not to become an extension of Victorian philanthropy, artists have to take a tougher stance. In America, the homelessness movement had become steadily more organized throughout the 1980s, with its own high-profile campaigners. Having glided from the folk protest scene into the musical mainstream via the first Wembley Mandela concert, the dreadlocked songwriter Tracy Chapman cut to the emotional heart of current issues. Her song 'Behind The Wall' highlights the vulnerability of battered wives, one of the largest constituents of the homeless population, while 'Subcity' places blame squarely on the government for the burgeoning problem of homelessness. Folk Roots heroine Michelle Shocked has also been a long-term campaigner for the homeless and the global squatters' rights movement. She left America when Reagan was re-elected, determined never to go back, but in 1989 she returned to fight for her country's homeless, helping to organize a march on Washington.

'My solution is, once you're there to squat on the White House lawn, like in the 1930s Depression when they built some cardboard shanties there known as Hooverville,' she said. 'An encouraging sign for me is the mobilization in the homelessness movement. It's great that money's donated and charity is established, but now much of the initiative is gonna come from the homeless themselves. Like the anti-nuclear campaigns of the 1970s, it'll become a major movement.'

This issue was at the centre of one of the biggest pop events of 1990, the Big Day in Glasgow, on 3 June. Already enjoying its position as 1990's European City of Culture, Glasgow played host to a day-long musical extravaganza presented by Liveshot, a tripartite Scottish media organization. A cross between a street-party, a carnival and a massive open-air concert with such stars as Sheena Easton and Deacon Blue, the Big Day pulled in crowds of 250,000 throughout the city, was screened live on Channel Four television and then shown worldwide. Funds raised during the day went straight to the city's main campaigning body on homelessness, the Glasgow Council for Single Homeless.

Annie didn't take part and indeed has never explicitly identified with Scottish politics. In the late 1980s when most major Scottish pop groups, including Simple Minds, Deacon Blue and Hue And Cry, rallied together against the poll tax and in favour of an independent Scotland, Annie was conspicuously absent. Although in her teenage years she was disturbed by a TV dramatization of Culloden, showing the historic massacring of the Scots, and although she has worn tartan shawls and Highland regalia, national identity has always been a problem for Annie. She is more a product of international pop culture, and rarely engages in the politics of her homeland.

After the flurry of her intial announcement about working for Shelter to tone up its image, there seemed to be little in the way of concrete developments. There was some speculation that Annie's interest was waning, that her statement about Shelter had been thrown out to deflect the press so that she could start a family in peace and privacy.

Jessica Morris, Shelter's press officer, disputes this view, saying that on the contrary, the star was heavily involved in campaign plans for the launch of their twenty-fifth anniversary celebration in 1991. 'Annie Lennox has been talking to us for a few years,' she said from the Shelter office in London's Old Street. 'We were delighted that she decided to come on board – she's really committed. What attracted her to Shelter in the first place was the way it combines direct action to people in housing need to some high-profile campaigning. And it addresses the root causes of homelessness. She's been coming to our aid primarily through publicity, helping us attract more members and supporters.'

Enlisting the support of such a well-known pop star was a new departure for Shelter. Unlike other charities, like Amnesty International and AIDS organization the Terrence Higgins Trust, Shelter had not attracted high-profile fashionable rock star support until Annie walked through the door. Before that they had run several successful initiatives with TV soap stars, but the endorsement of the Queen of Pop meant they could step up their campaign.

Her support has tended to be behind the scenes rather than through high-profile benefit concerts. Although it hasn't been as public as some anticipated, ('She'd just come into the office every once in a while with her husband and then piss off,' grumbled one Shelter supporter), lending her name to the homelessness cause has encouraged other pop stars to support Shelter fundraising events for Shelter. A week before the 2 December anniversary celebrations, an array of pop memorabilia was auctioned for the charity at Sotheby's. Included in the star-studded haul was Annie's famous leather coat and jodpurs, the gold basque Madonna wore on her 'Blonde Ambition' tour (must have been a little sweaty), Bono's suede jacket, a suit from Phil Collins and a jacket from George Harrison decorated with Hare Krishna motifs. The initiative attracted media interest with the *Daily Mirror* reserving some memorabilia for competition prizes.

For Annie, her commitment to Shelter and Greenpeace shows that she *does* feel sincerely about particular political issues, and it was lack of confidence that kept her from politically 'coming out' sooner. The minute Annie bowed out of the mainstream music industry, she was besieged with requests to support other charity events. Invited to perform in the second Mandela concert where the freed ANC leader was welcomed home to Wembley, Annie agreed at first but then declined, nervous about appearing on her own without the full Eurythmics' band behind her.

At this time Dave was busy saving the world in his way by recording an item for the 'One World, One Voice' TV spectacular, a kind of amorphous chain pop video that featured 292 musicians from all over the world in a technological raising of consciousness. Broadcast by the BBC on 26 May 1990, and liberally bounced off the satellites, it marked another development in the global charity jamboree. Some criticized the programme as being little better than a Coke commercial.

Britain's Green Party were excited at this TV environmental concern, but unlike the practical results of a Shelter or Amnesty campaign, it was difficult to see the concrete result of a televised musical jam. Campaigning and raising consciousness by video, however, became an established media device, and before long Annie had signed up to take part in Red Hot & Blue, another global TV spectacular that focused this time on AIDS research and relief.

Organized by Chrysalis Records, Initial Film & TV and BMG video, this niney-minute programme was transmitted on World AIDS Day 1990, featuring top artists interpreting the music of Cole Porter, with a message that combined safe sex with having fun. Each act, from U2 to Iggy Pop, Neneh Cherry, Sinead O'Connor and David Byrne, was teamed up with a particular name director to make a video to accompany their particular cover version. Annie sang a sensitive rendition of 'Everytime We Say Goodbye', and was originally going to have Derek Jarman to direct the video. When it came to the scheduled video shoot in early August, Jarman was unable to work. An AIDS sufferer himself, he had undergone a relapse and was in hospital. The video was eventually directed at Palace Pictures by Ed Lachman, incorporating an emotional tribute to Jarman. It has a shivery, stylized quality, with Annie standing dressed in pure white in front of a projection screen, the home movies of Jarman's idyllic childhood super-imposed over her face. With her bright red lips and contemplative pose, Annie gave a breathy, intensely poignant edge to Cole Porter's words: 'How strange the change from major to minor'. Considering the aim of Red Hot & Blue, the layered meaning of this video was particularly powerful.

A veteran pop video-director as well as film maker, Jarman enjoyed bringing avant-garde film technique to the bright, blunted world of the pop promo. His dark, surreal video for Marianne Faithfull's 'Broken English' came out before video was even an established form in the music industry, while his work with the Smiths and the Pet Shop Boys presented a passionate and exotic view of their musical Englishness.

'As a film maker you want *not* to put the musicians in as performers. I've always tried to make my videos a suggestive combination of music and image – not simply performers flying here, there and everywhere,' he said. He was a fan of Andy Warhol's 'home-movie attitude to cinema', shooting videos in Super 8 to get that grainy, evocative quality.

Both sensitive innovators in the field of pop imagery, Annie Lennox and Derek Jarman (via Ed Lachman) were the perfect video combination, while her version of 'Everytime We Say Goodbye' was crystallized with sweetness on the inevitable *Red Hot & Blue* compilation LP. Released two months before the TV spectacle, the LP was hailed as an unusually tasteful and effective compilation ('The most consistently listenable and endearing compilation ever', according to *Select* magazine). In the publicity surrounding the release, Annie refused to send out pictures from the video shoot that showed Jarman superimposed on her features. Some contributed this to egotism, but another factor was Annie's concern to distance herself from sensationalism, wanting to keep the message focused on political issues rather than personalities.

'I'm delighted to be able to contribute to this project,' she said at the time. 'However, we should all be aware that the problem of AIDS is international and direct action by governments is certainly insufficient up to this point. Let's hope we highlight this fact.'

As the 1990s took off, Annie's life changed dramatically with the successful birth of her second child. After her little girl Lola was born just before Christmas 1990, Annie was said to have been 'ecstatically happy', and flowers and cards from wellwishers arrived by the sackload. Taking a two-year sabbatical from Eurythmics, she initially devoted her time to her family, living quietly in Paris 'just being a housewife'. Spotted several times since with her baby, having put on a little weight, dressing casually and adopting a nonchalant, almost anti-pop-star pose, it seemed that Annie had turned her back on the business.

Music has exerted its unavoidable pull, though, and ever since rumours surfaced early in 1991 that Annie was recording a solo album, there have been questions poised over the future of Eurythmics. By October '91 Dave Stewart had released two solo albums; the first, *Spiritual Cowboys*, was an ambitious collection of contemplative rock'n'roll songs in the spirit of Dylan and John Lennon, while *Honest* was a more experimentally wayward mix of steel guitar and samples. Neither was hugely successful, but they showed a Dave Stewart content to remain in the thick of the music business, socializing, creating and producing new records.

Taking time with charity projects and with her family has consolidated for Annie a new sense of self and purpose. It also means that she and Dave are no longer a creative musical team. As long as they are distanced from each other, living separate lives in different countries, there is no musical communion of ideas and, hence, no band.

For a few years before their break, Dave had been itching to record his own solo project, and some say he was irked by all the attention that was inevitably focused on Annie. 'I think I've always been perceived as this semi-comic character who's in the shadows of the thing that's really happening,' he said shortly before the release of his first album in July 1990. 'But if you ask Annie it's not really like that at all. I have very strong opinions about the creativity, the words, every aspect. I'm a song writer, basically.'

His assertion seems a tad defensive, especially without Annie's vocals and sharp lyrics, his music lacks the focus of Eurythmics. Even if a star has been in a famous band, building up a solo identity is not as easy as it might seem. The style of female spiritual cowboys in his later videos bore a suspiciously close resemblance to Annie.

At the time of going to press in early '92, Annie herself is facing a similar challenge in going solo. She has just finished recording a solo LP, with guests on the album including ELO's Jeff Lynne and Scotland's premier cult band Blue Nile, a bunch of illusive individuals who are famed for their lush musical soundscapes. Nervous about how her new offering will be received, rehearsals with her live band

and recording sessions at Charlotte Street Studios in London and studios in Los Angeles, have been shrouded in strict secrecy. Both the album and the tour coinciding with its release in late spring, have had to be true to her standards of perfection. With its commercial sound of 'intelligent' pop, ranging from soft melancholy ballads to uptempo New York dance, Annie's solo project is not a million miles from Eurythmics. She didn't take the introverted acoustic path many expected.

Whether or not Dave and Annie get back together as musicians, the potential for renewal always remains. As their 1989 *We Too Are One* album sounded more like a pastiche of Eurythmics than Eurythmics themselves, it will probably benefit both Dave and Annie to spend some time working apart, gaining fresh input from unfamiliar quarters.

Despite a dilution of ideas by 1989, Eurythmics, their synthesized 1980s creation, has reached classic status. The release of their *Greatest Hits* LP early in 1991 confirmed this when it shot to the top of the album charts. Confident of the band's selling power, BMG included that collection in the first small batch of their much-trumpeted Laser Disc releases. The Eurythmics' sound is so instantly recognizable that it is regularly sampled on other records – indie-techno band the Utah Saints, for instance, had a huge hit in 1991 with 'What Can You Do For Me', a track that liberally sampled Annie's 'There Must Be An Angel' vocals. She was reputedly very flattered with the result.

Annie and Dave may now be working separately, but they take pride in the fact they managed to stay together so long as a professional outfit. 'She's an amazing person, Annie. She's very strong, very tough,' said Dave. 'They should give Annie and me the award for successfully maintaining a working relationship having formerly been a couple.'

The interesting question is whether she will return to the business on her own or with Dave: either way, their relationship will be newly defined. At the time of going to press in late 1990, there were already rumours that Annie was looking for new management, with plans to record a solo album.

Annie's upfront support for certain issues combined with her constant commitment to a personal musical integrity has transformed our expectations about pop's royalty. She has always challenged what it is to be a female star, embodying the dark, honest heart of con-fusion at the centre of that role. In 1991 she has come a long way from the woman who once stressed, in a torment of unconfidence: 'I don't have anything interesting to say.' Annie has always veered towards a complex degree of difficulty, while others choose the easier option of instant pop caricature.

'I don't believe in preaching any sort of "doctrine" about life,' she says. 'But if you're positive about your life and are yourself, this is more likely to inspire people around you towards change. That's why I'm here.'

Annie Lennox: A Discography
1977–1991

This disc and videography includes all of Annie Lennox's releases as part of The Catch, The Tourists and Eurythmics.

Many thanks to Ruth Kirk for her help in compiling this discography.

THE CATCH

SINGLES

'Borderline' / *'Black Blood'*
(October 1977)

THE TOURISTS

SINGLES 7″

'Blind Among The Flowers' / *'He Who Laughs Last'*
(May 1979)

'Blind Among The Flowers' / *'He Who Laughs Last'* / *'Golden Lamp'* / *'Wrecked'*
(May 1979)
'Loneliest Man In The World' / *'Don't Get Left Behind'*
(July 1979)
'I Only Want To Be With You' / *'Summer's Night'*
(October 1979)
'So Good To Be Back Home Again' / *'Circular Fever'*
(January 1980)
'Don't Say I Told You So' / *'Strange Sky'*
(September 1980)

ALBUMS

The Tourists (June 1979)

'Blind Among The Flowers' / *'Save Me'* / *'Fools Paradise'* / *'Can't Stop Laughing'* / *'Don't Get Left Behind'* / *'Another English Day'* / *'Deadly Kiss'* / *'Ain't No Room'* / *'The Loneliest Man In The World'* / *'Useless Duration Of Time'* / *'He Who Laughs Last Laughs Longest'* / *'Just Like You'*

Reality Effect (October 1979)

'It Doesn't Have To Be This Way' / *'I Only Want To Be With You'* / *'In The Morning (When The Madness Has Faded)'* / *'All Life's Tragedies'* / *'Everywhere You Look'* / *'So Good To Be*

Back Home Again' / 'Nothing To Do' / 'Circular Fever' / 'In My Mind' / 'Something In The Air Tonight' / 'Summer's Night'

Luminous Basement (October 1980)

'Walls And Foundations' / 'Don't Say I Told You So' / 'Week Days' / 'So You Want To Go Away Now' / 'One Step Nearer The Edge' / 'Angels and Demons' / 'Talk To Me' / 'Round Round Blues' / 'Let's Take A Walk' / 'Time Drags So Slow' / 'I'm Going To Change My Mind'
Plus free 7" 'From The Middle Room' / 'Into The Future'

EURYTHMICS

SINGLES 7"

'Never Gonna Cry Again' / 'Le Sinistre'
(May 1981)

'Belinda' / 'Heartbeat, Heartbeat'
(August 1981)

'This Is The House' / 'Home Is Where The Heart Is'
(March 1982)

'The Walk' / 'Step On The Beast' / 'The Walk Part II'
(June 1982)

'Love Is A Stranger' / 'Monkey Monkey'
(September 1982)

'Sweet Dreams Are Made Of This' / 'I Could Give You A Mirror'
(January 1983)

'Who's That Girl?' / 'You Take Some Lentils And You Take Some Rice'
(June 1983)

'Right By Your Side' / 'Right By Your Side' (Party Mix)
(October 1983)

'Here Comes The Rain Again' / 'Paint A Rumour'
(January 1984)

'Sexcrime 1984' / 'I Did It Just The Same'
(November 1984)

'Julia' / 'Ministry Of Love'
(January 1985)

'Would I Lie To You' / 'Here Comes That Sinking Feeling'
(April 1985)

'There Must Be An Angel' / 'Grown Up Girls'
(June 1985)

'Sisters Are Doin' It For Themselves' / 'I Love You Like A Ball And Chain'
(October 1985)

It's Alright (Baby's Coming Back)' / 'Conditioned Soul'
(December 1985)

'When Tomorrow Comes' / 'Take Your Pain Away'
(May 1986)

'Thorn In My Side' / 'In This Town'
(August 1986)

'The Miracle Of Love' / 'When Tomorrow Comes' (Live Version)
(November 1986)

'Missionary Man' / 'The Last Time' (Live Version)
(February 1987)

'Beethoven (I Love To Listen To)' / 'Heaven'
(October 1987)

'Shame' / 'I've Got A Lover (Back In Japan)'
(December 1987)

'I Need A Man' / 'I Need You'
(March 1987)

'You Have Placed A Chill In My Heart' / 'Chill' (Acoustic Version)
(May 1988)

'Revival' / 'Precious'
(August 1989)

'Don't Ask Me Why' / 'Rich Girl'
(October 1989)

'The King And Queen Of America' / 'See No Evil'
(January 1990)

'Angel' / 'Angel' (Choir version)
(April 1990)

SINGLES 12"

'Never Gonna Cry Again' / 'Le Sinistre'
(May 1981)

'This Is The House' (Extended Version) / 'Your Time Will Come' (Live) / 'Never Gonna Cry Again' (Live) / '4 / 4 In Leather' (Live) / 'Take Me To Your Heart' (Live)
(March 1982)

'The Walk' / 'Invisible Hands' / 'Dr Trash' / 'The Walk Part II'
(June 1982)

'Love Is A Stranger' / 'Let's Just Close Our Eyes' / 'Monkey, Monkey'
(September 1982)

'Sweet Dreams Are Made Of This' (Extended Version) / 'I Could Give You A Mirror' / 'Baby's Gone Blue'
(January 1983)

'Who's That Girl?' (Extended Version) / 'You Take Some Lentils And You Take Some Rice' / 'ABC Freeform'
(June 1983)

'Right By Your Side' (Extended Mix) / 'Right By Your Side' (Special Mix) / 'Plus Something Else'
(October 1983)

'Here Comes The Rain Again' / 'This City Never Sleeps' (Live) / 'Paint A Rumour'
(January 1984)

'Sexcrime 1984' (Extended Mix) / 'Sexcrime 1984' (Single Mix) / 'I Did It Just The Same'
(November 1984)

'Julia' (Extended Version) / 'Ministry of Love' (Extended Version)
(January 1985)

'Would I Lie To You' (Eric 'ET' Thorngren Mix) / 'Would I Lie To You' (Extended Version) / 'Here Comes That Sinking Feeling'
(April 1985)

'There Must Be An Angel' / 'Grown Up Girls'
(June 1985)

'Sisters Are Doin' It For Themselves' / 'Sisters' (ET Mix) / 'I Love You Like A Ball And Chain'
(October 1985)

'It's Alright (Baby's Coming Back)' / 'Conditioned Soul' / 'Tous Les Garcons Et Les Filles'
(December 1985)

'When Tomorrow Comes' (Extended Version) / 'Take Your Pain Away' / 'When Tomorrow Comes' (Orchestral Version) (May 1986)

'Thorn In My Side' (Extended Version) / 'Thorn In My Side' (Album Version) / 'In This Town'
(August 1986)

'The Miracle Of Love' / 'When Tomorrow Comes' (Live) / 'Who's That Girl?' (Live)
(November 1986)

'Beethoven' (Dance Mix) / 'Heaven' / 'Beethoven' (Extended Mix)
(October 1987)

'Shame' (Dance Mix) / 'I've Got A Lover (Back In Japan)' / 'Shame'
(December 1987)

'I Need A Man' (Macho Mix) / 'I Need A Man' / 'I Need You'
(March 1987)

'You Have Placed A Chill In My Heart' (Dance Mix) / 'Do You Want To Break Up?' (Dance Mix) / 'You Have Placed A Chill In My Heart' (Acoustic Mix)
(May 1988)

'Revival' (Extended Dance Mix) (ET Mix) / 'Revival' (7" Version) / 'Precious'
(August 1989)

'Don't Ask Me Why' / 'Sylvia' / 'Rich Girl'
(October 1989)

'The King And Queen Of America' / 'See No Evil' / 'There Must Be An Angel' / 'I Love You Like A Ball And Chain'
(January 1990)

Annie Lennox

'Angel' / 'Missionary Man' (Acoustic Version) / 'Angel' (Choir Version)
(April 1990)

ALBUMS

In The Garden (October 1981)
'English Summer' / 'Belinda' / 'Take Me To Your Heart' / 'She's Invisible Now' / 'Your Time Will Come' / 'Caveman Head' / 'Never Gonna Cry Again' / 'All The Young (People Of Today)' / 'Sing Sing' / 'Revenge'

Sweet Dreams Are Made Of This (January 1983)

'Love Is A Stranger' / 'I've Got An Angel' / 'Wrap It Up' / 'I Could Give You (A Mirror)' / 'The Walk' / 'Sweet Dreams (Are Made Of This)' / 'Jennifer' / 'This Is The House' / 'Somebody Told Me' / 'This City Never Sleeps'

Touch (November 1983)

'Here Comes The Rain Again' / 'Regrets' / 'Right By Your Side' / 'Cool Blue' / 'Who's That Girl?' / 'The First Cut' / 'Aqua' / 'No Fear, No Hate, No Pain (No Broken Hearts)' / 'Paint A Rumour'

Touch Dance (May 1984)

(Vocal) 'The First Cut' / 'Cool Blue' / 'Paint A Rumour' / 'Regrets' / (Instrumental) 'The First Cut' / 'Cool Blue' / 'Paint A Rumour'

1984 (for the love of big brother) (November 1984)

'I Did It Just The Same' / 'Sexcrime (nineteen eighty-four)' / 'For The Love Of Big Brother' / 'Winston's Diary' / 'Greetings From A Dead Man' / 'Julia' / 'Doubleplusgood' / 'Ministry Of Love' / 'Room 101'

Be Yourself Tonight (April 1985)

'Would I Lie To You?' / 'There Must Be An Angel (Playing With My Heart)' / 'I Love You Like A Ball And Chain' / 'Sisters Are Doin' It For Themselves' / 'Conditioned Soul' / 'Adrian' / 'It's Alright' (Baby's Coming Back)' / 'Here Comes That Sinking Feeling' / 'Better To Have Lost In Love (Than Never To Have Loved At All)'

Revenge (June 1986)

'Missionary Man' / 'Thorn In My Side' / 'When Tomorrow Comes' / 'The Last Time' / 'The Miracle Of Love' / 'Let's Go' / 'Take Your Pain Away' / 'A Little Of You' / 'In This Town' / 'I Remember You'

Savage (November 1987)

'Beethoven (I Love To Listen To)' / 'I've Got A Lover (Back In Japan)' / 'Do You Want To Break Up?' / 'You Have Placed A Chill In My Heart' / 'Shame' / 'Savage' / 'I Need A Man' / 'Put The Blame On Me' / 'Heaven' / 'Wide Eyed Girl' / 'I Need You' / 'Brand New Day'

We Too Are One (September 1989)

'We Two Are One' / 'The King And Queen Of America' / '(My, My) Baby's Gonna Cry' / 'Don't Ask Me Why' / 'Angel' / 'Revival' / 'You Hurt Me (And I Hate You)' / 'Sylvia' / 'How Long?' / 'When The Day Goes Down'

212

Greatest Hits (April 1991)

'Love Is A Stranger' / 'Sweet Dreams' / 'Who's That Girl?' / 'Right By Your Side' / 'Here Comes The Rain Again' / 'There Must Be An Angel (Playing With My Heart)' / 'Sisters Are Doin' It For Themselves' / 'It's Alright (Baby's Coming Back)' / 'When Tomorrow Comes' / 'You Have Placed A Chill In My Heart' / 'Miracle Of Love' / 'Sex Crime (1984)' / 'Thorn In My Side' / 'Don't Ask Me Why' / 'Angel' / 'Would I Lie To You' / 'Missionary Man' / 'I Need A Man'

COLLABORATIONS

Track 'Everytime We Say Goodbye' on *Red Hot & Blue* compilation LP. (October 1990)

'Put A Little Love In Your Heart' Al Green & Annie Lennox.

A Very Special Christmas compilation LP, with Eurythmics doing 'Winter Wonderland.' (1988)

'Sweet Surprise' Chris N Cosey & Eurythmics.

Deep In The Heart of Nowhere, Bob Geldof LP, Annie on backing vocal. (1986)

'Night Full of Tension' Robert Gorl LP, Annie on backing vocal.

'Latin Lover' Gianna Nannini LP, Annie on backing vocal.

'Deep In Darkest Night' Maddy Prior 7", Annie on backing vocal.

VIDEO ALBUMS

Sweet Dreams (the video album) (1983)

'Prologue' / 'This Is The House' / 'Never Gonna Cry Again' / 'Take Me To Your Heart' / 'I've Got An Angel' / 'Satellite Of Love' / 'Love Is A Stranger' / 'Who's That Girl?' / 'This City Never Sleeps' / 'Jennifer' / 'Sweet Dreams' / 'I Could Give You (A Mirror)' / 'Somebody Told Me' / 'Wrap It Up' / 'Tous Les Garcons Et Les Filles' / 'Sweet Dreams'

Eurythmics Live (1987)

'Sexcrime 1984' / 'Let's Go' / 'The Last Time' / 'Here Comes The Rain Again' / 'It's Alright (Baby's Coming Back)' / 'When Tomorrow Comes' / 'There Must Be An Angel (Playing With My Heart)' / 'Who's That Girl?' / 'Right By Your Side' / 'Thorn In My Side' / 'Sweet Dreams (Are Made Of This)' / 'Would I Lie To You?' / 'Missionary Man' / 'Sisters Are Doin' It For Themselves' / 'The Miracle of Love'

Savage (1988)

'Beethoven (I Love To Listen To)' / 'I Need A Man' / 'Heaven' / 'Shame' / 'Wide Eyed Girl' / 'Do You Want To Break Up?' / 'I've Got A Lover (Back In Japan)' / 'Put The Blame On Me' / 'Savage' / 'You Have Placed A Chill In My Heart' / 'I Need You' / 'Brand New Day'

We Two Are One Too (1990)

'We 4 Are 3' / 'We Two Are One' (live and acoustic) / 'I Love You Like A Ball and Chain' (live) / 'Don't Ask Me Why' / 'How Long?' / 'You Hurt Me (I Hate You)' / '(My My) Baby's Gonna Cry' / 'We Two Are One' (live) / ' I Need You' (acoustic) / 'Rudolph The Red Nosed Reindeer' / 'The King And Queen Of America' / 'Love Is A Stranger' / 'Sylvia' / 'Revival' /

'*Farewell To Tawathie*' / '*Angel*' / '*Ballad Of Eurythmics Road Crew*' / '*When The Day Goes Down*' (*LP and Live version*)

Greatest Hits (1991)

'*Sweet Dreams*' / '*Love Is A Stranger*' / '*Who's That Girl?*' / '*Right By Your Side*' / '*Here Comes The Rain Again*' / '*Sex Crime (1984)*' / '*Julia*' / '*Would I Lie To You?*' / '*There Must Be An Angel (Playing With My Heart)*' / '*Sisters Are Doin' It For Themselves*' / '*It's Alright (Baby's Coming Back)*' / '*When Tomorrow Comes*' / '*Thorn In My Side*' / '*Miracle Of Love*' / '*Missionary Man*' / '*Beethoven (I Love To Listen To)*' / '*I Need A Man*' / '*You Have Placed A Chill In My Heart*' / '*Don't Ask Me Why*' / '*The King And Queen Of America*' / '*Angel*'

The Room (1987)

By Harold Pinter; directed by Robert Altman; starring Linda Hunt, Annie Lennox, Donald Pleasance, Julian Sands.

Columbia Volcano Appeal Video at Royal Albert Hall (1987) Annie solo/duet with Chrissie Hynd/ various.

For a list of international releases contact Denis Garese of the Eurythmics Record Catalogue, 2 rue Claude Debussy, 78370 Plaisir, France; or Claire Moisset, 74 quai de Jemmapes, 75010 Paris, France. Thanks also to Muriel Vieu.